MIDLIFE CREATIVITY AND IDENTITY

MIDLIFE CREATIVITY AND IDENTITY: LIFE INTO ART

BY

PHILIP MILES
University of Bedfordshire, UK

emerald
PUBLISHING

United Kingdom – North America – Japan – India – Malaysia – China

Emerald Publishing Limited
Howard House, Wagon Lane, Bingley BD16 1WA, UK

First edition 2019

Reprints and permissions service
Contact: permissions@emeraldinsight.com

British Library Cataloguing in Publication Data
A catalogue record for this book is available from the British Library

ISBN: 978-1-78754-334-8 (Print)
ISBN: 978-1-78754-333-1 (Online)
ISBN: 978-1-78754-335-5 (Epub)

ISBN: 978-1-78754-336-2 (Paperback)

INVESTOR IN PEOPLE

In memory of Claire Rosalind Miles 1974–2015

Contents

Acknowledgements

It is right and proper to begin acknowledgements with a shout out to those who took part in the research by giving me their time, energies and thoughts about the creative process. Therefore, big appreciation goes to Johnny Vincent, Duncan McIntyre, Ian Burton, CJ Bailey and Miles Simpkins of The Ruins and to Ian's wife, Sharon, for hosting us for group interviews and the weekly 'jam', rehearsals and recording sessions. It was a joy to be there. Thanks also to Peter Driver and Robin Wilson for their invites to join them at their studios in Reading and Oxford and for their detailed, fabulous thoughts on inspiration, action and value. They were awe-inspiring meetings where I learned so much about the artistic muse and the strength of the individual will to make things happen. Thanks also go to Katherine Webb for her insight on writing and authorial routines and for the most excellent cake and tea during numerous visits to her home. Appreciation is also due to those who have taken part in the research process but have chosen to remain anonymous for various reasons; it goes without saying that I respect and understand your ideas, thoughts and motives equally and would like to thank you for your time and hospitality.

Appreciation also goes to a variety of people who have assisted and encouraged me at various stages along the way, all equally inspiring: Graham Falgate; Chris Cheetham and Doris Crick; Nick Ellison, Steve Fuller and Chris Llewellyn; Ray Jobling, Rob Moore and Madeleine Arnot; Paul Willis and Phillip Brown; and to my Editor at Emerald, Philippa Grand, who gave this book a chance to exist, and to her colleagues Rachel Ward and Charlotte McSharry. Many thanks to my academic colleagues Andy Bennett (Griffith University) and Gary Manders (University of Bedfordshire) for their comments on earlier drafts of this book and for the encouraging early feedback of the anonymous referees. Respect and appreciation is also due to Paul Innes and John Hughes (University of Gloucestershire) and Rebecca Beasley (University of Oxford) for positively instilling the incentive to combine sociology with literary studies and to embrace the art of the possible. It is a work in progress, but the destination is now clear. A special mention is also due to Steve Hardy (scriptwriter, journalist, musician, raconteur) who has provided creative inspiration and the most exceptional friendship throughout my adult life while himself being a most dedicated contributor to, and supporter of, the creative arts in many forms.

Finally, the process of writing this book has been, in time-honoured fashion, suitably riddled with the most invigorating of stress, but to those who have experienced me daily as this oscillating level of anxiety has fired the process – Maria, Sebastian and Huw – the greatest debt to you must be acknowledged. I love you all. Indebtedness must also go to my wonderful parents, Ron and Yvonne Miles, who have given me the love and unconditional support to help me achieve goals in life. Finally, this book is dedicated to the memory of my sister, Claire Rosalind Miles, whose presence among us I miss every day.

Introduction: Life into Art

Where does art come from? What are the routines and inspirations that bring works of art into being and 'where' are these actions and inspirations acted out, made sense of and exploited? In the coming study, it is my intention to introduce, investigate and explain creative processes via the lives, work and subjectivities of 10 people engaged in the generation of musical, artistic and literary texts for public consumption, all entering or experiencing middle-age (or 'midlife' as it shall be referred to throughout) and living in England. These people are both distinctive and alike in many ways; they are male and female, working class and middle class, educated in different sectors and to differing levels and working in different ways, but they are also all engaged in what I call an 'authorial routine' based on transforming ideas into art forms via sound, visuals and the written word. The participants in this study are approaching their work in a variety of formats by utilising an assortment of skills to achieve tangible outcomes but are aiming, ostensibly, for the same *conclusions* both in terms of a sense of contribution and completion as well as obtaining a bolstered self-efficacy and satiation of artistic energies. Therefore, whether differentiated by gender, class or skill set, the participants are dedicated to the articulation of imagination and the realisation of novelty.

The narrative at the heart of this volume will involve a subtle mixture of foci that encompasses the dynamics of midlife, identity and creativity running throughout the text, never isolated entirely from one another but perceived as distinctive at times, prominent and energetic in their functions. It is the intention that the reader can consider the dynamics as interlinked and supra-determinant in the lives of the participants featured here and further within the analysis of their arts, routines and inspirations. While contemplating the format of presenting the research, I decided that I would offer an introductory chapter that set out the context, form and theoretical 'influences' of the process before introducing the data via the themes of 'music', 'art' and 'literature', organised into corresponding thematic 'sections'. These subdivisions will be expansive, handing over the focus of the narrative to the people who made the research come to life – namely those musicians, artists and writers whose daily core activity is to consider and create and make new and exciting things. These *things* are works of art that incorporate a process, or *routine*, that enables the inventive individual (or group) to step away from the humdrum of the 'everyday' and into a zone where the anxieties of what I shall refer to as 'late modernity' are quelled in a space of innovative zeal. The ethnography – driven by observation and interviews and the explanations proffered on meaning of art and craft — was designed only to seek and understand the culture of creativity that exists in some middle-aged people, the incentives to create, the sense cf worth that emerges from the process and the comparator of midlife routine in the 'real world'. What emerged was a series of fascinating portraits of artists as middle-aged men and women and some secrets about where it was that they 'went to' when they sought to summon the inventive muse. This was not a project that sought to prove or disprove a pre-existing idea or theory within the broader cultural study of creativity. Instead, I let the artists do the talking first, guided only by questions that I wished to ask on *why* they did what they did, *how* they did it, *where* they did it, how much regularity was involved in the processes that they harnessed and utilised and, importantly, what it *meant* to them at their stage in life to 'do' art and to share art with others. The theoretical framework evolved *after* the data in what is loosely framed as 'inductive' form with a surprising effect of capturing the creative process not as what one may think of as being a *serene retreat* but actually as an assertive and sought-after *resistance* to the tumultuous and insecure essence of the time in which we live, albeit that the 'tumultuous' and 'insecure' are viewed as 'normative' and predictable and art as 'chaotic' in practice, erratic in outcome and just simply *exciting* in comparison. Thus, if anything, it becomes clear that the insecurity of creativity is the *security* itself and that security of which I speak is a joyous *insecurity*; the biography and character of the individual is combined with a creative urge that provides a playful, expansive domain for riotous abandon that challenges the suggestion that art is merely vocation. Art is *life* to these people and their life is experienced *as* art and, quite frankly, life and art are perceived as possibly more unpredictable than the future simply because the future arguably has expected (or entrenched) cultural, political and social 'routes' whereas art, as I shall explain, is a continual engagement with the blissful unknown.

Throughout the work that follows is situated a recurrent, incremental argument (drawing on an interdisciplinary, eclectic, and occasionally esoteric literature) on the transformative essence of art — how things may *come to be* simply from the kernel of an idea, a sound, a smell or a random memory. Via ethnographic acuity and associative analysis, among other things, I will explain the often overlapping processes of rehearsal and composition in music, the maintenance of the communal and the sociality of creativity in midlife, the vagaries of the 'artistic routine' and the variations of process that leads to meaningful creation. I will gauge opinions on, and engagement with, commercialism; a sense of place; the perception of the penetration of individual identity *into* art and how art reflexively penetrates the identity. Overall, this book is dedicated to understanding a sense of value in the *decision to be* creative and, ultimately, where this creativity thrives best. In the final stages of the book I will explain my own theory of 'where the artists are' and where it is that they 'go' to be creative coupled with how late modern society, midlife and self-identity contribute to formulating this in-between state, or *'mezzanine'*, as a metaphysical (and occasionally physical) zone of detachment, bliss, excitement and productivity. Midlife creativity and identity, as I shall explain, are not a new lifestyle choice of the committed or languidly curious middle classes but are, instead, a state of *being* and a state of *equilibrium* that has been searched for, earned and exploited with equal verve, experienced individually and communally with equal value.

Therefore, in the following chapters I will begin — following the obligatory explanation in Chapter 1 of where the book is best situated in the wider canon of sociology and cultural studies — to explore core areas of artistic creativity by theme. In Chapters 2 and 3 I shall introduce The Ruins, an alternative rock band from Derby in the English Midlands who continue to write, record and perform exciting, innovative music into their fifties. They are fired by an acceptable mixture of self-belief, anxiety and sociality, emerging from a small studio in the suburbs to play occasional adrenaline-fuelled gigs before retreating to write and 'jam' and subliminally search for the moment of artistic 'aura' (Benjamin, [1923] 2008) where anything is possible and the structure of musical composition is joyously fluid. The study finds a band exploring the texture of their ideological and heuristic connective tissues — life, experience, expertise, skill and the personalities that arise from five decades of life — via music, discourse and the pooling of hope and the search for a 'satisfaction' to be found through the creation of new music, the permanent reinvention of existing sound and structure and a myriad of possibilities unencumbered by management-editorial interference or the assumed requirement to conform to an expected style. The band arguably provides a communal soul for each member in the 'phase' of life of families, jobs, diminishing youthfulness and other routine worries and joys of midlife. In Chapters 4, 5 and 6 I encounter Peter, Robin and Dominic, three artists engaged in what I shall refer to as 'fine art' — namely painting, printing, ceramics, occasional photography and sculpture/carving. The artists are disparate in background and personality as well as in practice, operating mainly as individuals in their routines of creation and connecting with different 'art worlds' (Becker, [1982] 2008) via domicile, teaching and project work — including Robin's fantastic Wytham Woods project in the Oxfordshire countryside. However, these artists do have some things in common, including having come to practice their skills driven by personal upheavals that has arguably seen art as squaring a particular — highly personal — circle in life. To these artists the practice of creativity is both a vocation and a *change*: completion, the potential for continuous renewal and embracing the limitless possibilities of life itself. Thus, art is about *transforming materials* as well as *transforming life*. In Chapters 7 and 8 I move on to speak with two published authors, one producing mainstream fiction and the other emerging into the children's literature market and both responsible for innovative, detailed and successful literary outputs. Both authors are women and both are encountering and continually developing their own authorial routines in different ways. For Katherine, creativity is experienced in isolation, is unpredictable, spontaneous and driven by deadlines and the *supervention of novelty* (Eliot, 1919; Kermode, 1975) inasmuch that it is her established back catalogue that drives her contemporary outputs. Annette is a new author — her identity anonymised here — who flourishes with the joy of liberation, the new opportunities that emerge during midlife via career change and the primacy of available time coupled with the possibilities of a new focus.

She has a new and exciting role to practice, protect and enjoy, but also a new opportunity to re-evaluate her identity as a middle-aged woman. Finally, in Chapter 9, I will combine the thoughts and observations of all of the respondents in a wider discussion on creativity, resistance and midlife and the comprehension of artistic routine as that 'in-between state' mentioned above, where the possibilities of creativity are celebrated as an opportunity to resist the banal, the ordinary and the expected. The notion of 'life into art' is understood as a series of chances, ambitions, freedoms and anxieties all presented as an exhilarating response to what may be considered as the banality and humdrum of 'midlife routine'. Creativity is seen to act as a stream of variable, simultaneous resistant consciousness and action to the increasing perceived meaninglessness of the midlife regimen and how this can be transformed into opportunities for advancement.

To begin, however, it is expedient to explore – in combination – the scholarly foundation and field for this book as well as discussing a number of theoretical ideas that assist in situating the work in the wider sociological oeuvre, along with the method for gathering data. I shall now turn to such matters mindful that the dominant narrative here belongs to the respondents as much as to sociological and cultural interpretations but also aware of the conventions of explaining from where a study like this is ostensibly sprung.

Chapter 1

Transformations

Art, it is argued, is about transformations (Berger, 2016: 100). It is about the transformation of things, time and of the self; such change can be affected by actions, thoughts and circumstances as well as by the structure and culture of society experienced via ideological frameworks (Thompson, 1990: 281–2), a *feeling* (Williams, 1961), a sensuousness (Willis, 2000) or via a form of interactive, individual instrumentalism (Bourdieu, 1993). Simple incremental human experiences of the 'everyday' understood, perhaps, by 'incorporeal, insentient' *familiarities* (Highmore, 2011: 82) can therefore be considered subliminal, subtle and affective and, of course, *transformational*. Art is therefore at once an esoteric and an 'everyday' thing (Read, 1956; [1931] 2017), empowering and active, deeply personal, illustrative of narratives and biographies, of space and time and age and experience. Art remains in continuous contact with the self via the media and the 'street' (usually via advertising, but also more subtly though architecture and colour as well as via graffiti and pavement art, etc.), as well as within the domicile (Racz, 2014) that also includes our interaction with fashioned spaces of our living (Bachelard, [1964] 2014). The individual may also, of course, have additional acquaintance with art via his or her *own creativity*. Art therefore is not exclusively a 'thing' that exists to behold, it can also emerge from within, realised through rehearsed routines, occasional chance and determination to make something new, to *make something appear* that did not previously exist. Therefore, creativity is a process of transformation (from idea to realisation) and such a *process* or 'change' can be considered manifest in a variety of tangible and abstract forms such as the physicality of objects (and the processes that bring such things *together*), the shifting 'meaning' of such objects to individuals and groups and their state of novelty or decay.

It is also possible to consider transformation as something that works in tangible harness with the process of *making art happen* such as a shift or sea change in an individuals' career, a notable change in *lifestyle*, or the arrival of new economic or cultural life chances. Transformations, consequently, can be physical and symbolic, and art, as a *practice*, can drive and represent such change for people as both the creators of art and as the consumers of it. The crux of this study is to understand the dynamics of this combination of artefact and inspiration, with focus on the *artist* rather than the art itself, the *process* of transformation rather than the *outcome* and, ultimately, the *value* of the process to those who make time to create.

Transformation of things and of the self is also potentially representative of the *nature of the times*. In its many forms, art (specifically considered here as works of music, fine art and writing/literature, but myriad in form in a wider context in society) is arguably symptomatic of micro- and macro-transformations in society, harnessing the dynamics of experience, action and intentionality (and the occasional tendency for serendipitous outcomes and their lasting effects) that combine to deliver what Raymond Williams might observe as something of a contrast of mechanism and emotion, a duality of capitalism and culture and a shifting pattern of *sense into sensibility* (Williams, [1958] 2017: 66). To be sure, art can be perceived variously as active orchestration of the enlightening thrust of music, literature or image/painting and it can be considered intensely personal, holding secrets of influence behind its façade or having new ideas inculcated upon its form by others separated from its 'author'. It can also be physical, considered 'complete' or 'perfect' or challenging us to merely consider its potential longevity in aesthetic terms (Wolff, 1983). However, art is considered here as a variety of intention and outcome, method and completeness, embodying the *personal and the private* and resultant of a combination of personally-held views of authenticity and self-value *in* the creator, manifestly benefitting *from* the identity – and assisting in *developing* the identity – *of* the creator. Ultimately, it can be synoptic of the myriad meanings that can be applied by both author and eventual beholder to the routine and methods of creation and impressions of outcome, thus continually transforming its own abstract narratives from day to day via time, setting and location as well as functioning, instrumentally, as a perceived resistant sense of vocation and self-worth to its creator. Thus, 'art' in this study is viewed mainly as a *pinnacle of process* that is situated in the turmoil of creation. What comes after the process of creation is aesthetic, malleable and given to be considered ostensibly powerless.

It has been posited over time that art is founded in the *social* (Read, 1956; Wolff, 1993) with a potential to transform sociality and individual thoughts, strategies and opportunities while acting potentially as something of an 'anchor' to the individual that creates it. This anchor may or may not be considered necessarily a *brake* on a personal or collective progress but, essentially, as a setting down of *permanence*, providing a sense of security and reassurance, self-efficacy and dynamism. Throughout this book, in what I will refer to as 'late modern' times (Giddens, 1991), *liquid*-like in economy, morals and sociality (Bauman, 2000; Bordoni, 2016; Davis, [2013] 2016) and beholden to accompanying risks connected to individualisation (Beck & Beck-Gernsheim, 2002) and the fragmentation of tradition and its associative 'biographical solutions' (Beck, 1992), the focus will be on the essence of security and reassurance sought by the creator rather than the effects of art on the audience. Thus, art will be considered in its various manifestations as having a subtle role to play in a personal resistance to the individualised anxiety and dislocation perceived within late modern times that is often understood (but not necessarily recognised) as manifest in transference of responsibility from state to individual and tacitly embodied as the way the biography must now assume primacy over experience via a process that has precedence for the way 'the story of life is told, rather than the way in which life is lived' (Bauman, 2002: 69). This inferred exhibition-ism and reliance of the centrism of the ego and flamboyance of virtue may not, necessarily, be a *bad thing* if such recourse to ego is understood as a form of *resistance* and, ultimately, personally transforming and instrumental. To be sure, the potentially eroding and unsettling effects of anxiety are possibly experienced via the fragmentation of social worlds and our relentless drift towards the attenuation of sensual collectivity, separated (and conversely 'connected') via computer screens (Miller, 2011; Turkle, 2017), mobile phones (*avec screens*), pri-vate transport, diversification of information (and modern problems of verifica-tion of reliability) and so on, but it can arguably be countered by the maintained assured solidity and familiarity of the ego, the biography and the creative self. While art (essentially communicative in nature) can be understood in creative terms as a *secluded* thing, arguably personally transformative but determined by thought patterns that are personal, personally *challenging* and developmentally *indefinite*, it is also inherently *social* (Becker, [1982] 2008; Wolff, 1993). I shall argue that the creative process is therefore *socially* as well as individually trans-formative, but that such sociality is itself potentially experienced in isolation (in this instance via the study of a rock group). The methods and value of creativity and the contrasting physical forms of art itself can accelerate a combined sense of artist and object 'identity' (and harness further connectivity between artist, artefact and audience) but also, as is the focus in this study, develop a powerful *sense of self* that drives the creative process forwards: not quite ego, not quite *biographical* in essence, but possibly a base instinct for *certainty*. There is a sense that, to the 'midlife artist', art is an omnipresent process of achieving meaning and I shall therefore seek to explain how such meaning can transform the every-day through the raw excitement of potential and the defence of the resistance to the banal. Thus, the 'audience' and 'reception' of art, while active, is peripheral when considering the simple value of creativity and its *routines*. Thus, to under-stand such transformational power it is necessary to talk to those who practice it. It is the task of this book to uncover what such power looks, sounds and feels like and how these dynamics can be sociologically conceptualised.

§

Let me continue by informally considering some insightful assertions by two profoundly influential individuals. Both Johnny Marr and Terry Eagleton have made considerable contributions to the world of the arts and literature over the years via the creation, performance and production of music and invaluable, entertaining and erudite literary criticism, respectively. An otherwise throwaway line in Marr's 2016 autobiography *Set the Boy Free* stated that, in the making of music, occasional moments occur when participants in the field of musical pro-duction are present, together and yet *apart*. Something bonds these people together, external to the sound waves that they are in command of; something exists in the moment that frames the milieu, however transiently. 'When a group of individuals are working instinctively and intricately, thinking within milliseconds of each other', he states, 'it's as close to real magic as you can get' (Marr, 2016: 180). Such atemporal synthesis can be considered the central bonding factor of any band; it is where art and life are fused via the combination of experience and skill and emotion to produce new things, new sound, new belief and where a sense of 'magic' is sought and occasionally achieved. Eagleton, writing in the context of the understanding of changing social mores, values and principles over time — and how it can affect the experience of *reading historical literature* — can add some important additional significance to this sense of *togetherness*. Writing, he argues, is a process and skill that involves developing how the *reader receives* the literature that he or she is encountering, thus creating an additional dynamic beyond the authorial routine and the skill of telling a story well. In making sense of what the author might have meant and how the reader may relate to such potential, Eagleton articulates the 'external' essence of the *experience* of art. Where Marr speaks of a closed intimacy, Eagleton recognises both such intimacy that people *feel* with the art and the relationship they sense with the *society* from which they are formed. In stating that 'my emotions are not my private property [...] On the contrary, there is a sense in which I learn my emotional behaviour by participating in a common culture' (Eagleton, 2013: 34), Eagleton nods (arguably) towards an established, generic narrative that life and art are *fused*; in many ways, it cannot be art unless it is observed and made sense of — an *a priori* 'language' of art is thus established, structurally. Art is merely a component of a language: social, symbolic, semiotic and lucid as well as personally emancipating, intra-theoretical (Kristeva, 1980) and functioning as both the manipulator and manipulated.

Within both statements lies a communal, communicative *thing*: Marr is speaking of a *group* engaged in unison, present in one place but yet detached, making sound as a language that all of the creative human components of such generated sound can recognise as a product of an elusive 'magic', whereas Eagleton is speaking of an inclusive, interpretative *culture*, described, *inter alia*, by Raymond Williams as consisting of something of a detectable *structure of feeling* that implies borderline conscious—subconscious awareness of the meaning of culture and how it is lived, how it is interpreted and how its transforming powers can be harnessed (Williams, 1961) or, alternatively, how culture can be perceived as something of an 'independent noun' of intellectual and *anthropological* use (Williams, [1976] 2014: 89). Such 'anthropology' is arguably in observing the interactive, cultural discourse of meanings (feeling) that are applied by individuals and, occasionally, recognised comparatively by groups, that are built upon the senses and — when enacted — in compliance with instinct resulting in a considered (but not necessarily articulated) change. Structure of feeling is important to this study because it partially characterises what I will later call the 'mezzanine' — an in-between conscious (and sometimes *subconscious*) state experienced by creative individuals and groups — explaining a form of metanarrative that can present something of a 'soft challenge' to the dominant ideology, hegemony or simply confront the expectancies of midlife as inculcated by tradition, values, norms and so on. I will return to Raymond Williams again below — and his arguable approximation with the multifarious work of

Pierre Bourdieu and the Birmingham Centre for Contemporary Cultural Studies – but, for now, it is fair to state that structure of feeling is possibly a nebulous *resistance*, a 'penetration' of the veneer of culture and capitalism (Willis, 1977) and a sense of *destiny* that comes from *within* the culture and is affected by such superstructural ideologies that, in this study, I will illustrate as deeply embedded, barely observable, but *there*.

Therefore, perhaps this latter elucidation is best understood as an occasionally diverse collective of behaviour, values, direction, conformity and history but also as a framework of educative uniformity that can have potential in creating a sub-missively powerless, though liberated, individual as part of its wider network of 'feeling'. Eagleton's inference of a democracy of emotions lends itself to an idea that the consonance of art and common culture is something of a method of 'structural' reproduction, resonating Williams's theme in cultural sociology. The moments where art is practiced and created may well be a *reflection* of the common culture of symbolic creativity and 'grounded aesthetics' of emotional and cognitive congruity in making art (Willis, 1990), repeating the language (however obscure at times), but also a moment of power, determination, deliberation and resistance. The artist-creator is 'in charge' of the interpretation of his or her own ideas, wherever the ideas may have been formed and influenced by whatever structure. The artist, therefore, is free to interpret and, in that moment of interpretation, is resisting the need to conform and this is seen, in the following book, as something to defend. Thus, I am seeking to illustrate how the creation of music, art and literature is experienced by creative people as a reassurance and a resistance in a 'society under siege' from a morphing, shape-shifting capitalism (Bauman, 2002) and, arguably, becoming increasingly post-traditional (Beck, Giddens, & Lash, 1994; Giddens, 1999), culturally nebulous via the nullification of 'auratic' cultural identities via media and economic globalisation (Waters, 2001: 172) and how the method of *intra-transmission* of such 'ideology' is witnessed and felt. The 'reassurance', I hasten to add, need not necessarily be considered as a *stationary* thing; the chapters that follow (that involve real people talking about real art that they are responsible for creating in middle age) suggest that art may be owned – and protected – as a technique of both *possessing* stability and *resisting* stability that middle age might unconsciously provide; there is a flourishing playfulness in the pleasure of creativity that is found here that both envelops the process and the value and, quite frankly, the *impact*. Thus, theoretically, I have seen the inductive focus of assembled data oscillate between what might be called the resistance of 'late modern anxiety' to the resistance of structural, cultural hegemony. This is a curious binary.

Art is an invaluable cultural, social and personal resource for subjective and objective stability, but what – as they say – *is* art in this instance? Is art a process or an outcome? Is it social or solitary work, or simply a social or solitary *pleasure*? Can art be considered as something that is initially owned and then disseminated, or as something that is *always shared*, considered as present in the domain of the many? Art can be an apparatus of resistance to changes in life and a record of such change, in a heartbeat transforming itself from a barrier into a sluice, allowing life to flood in and engulf an otherwise hermetically sealed

combination of thoughts, biography, interpretation and action that is intrinsically existing separated from the ebbing and flowing ordinary life (Highmore,
2011) that exists in the 'external' world. Art, as I will explain, is quite often seen
as something of an enigma by those who create it, considered a mixture of
praxis, pleasure and pride as well as a volatile blend of beauty, satisfaction and
considerable torment. It is action, philosophy and object all rolled into one,
embodying a vocation and a complex semantic of destiny while entering the
midlife phase. Life really does penetrate art, shaping how it is made and how we
may receive it. However, life is also linear, experiential, *lived*. This project is concerned with how art is chosen as an expressive, active thing during *midlife*. So,
how can 'midlife' be framed?

When considering what midlife might involve (or what it might look or feel
like), the analysis is pushed and pulled in various directions by both subjective
appraisals of our lives 'so far' and via the representation of what midlife might
be within the oeuvre of popular culture. This is often framed as the 'midlife crisis' that involves some extravagant purchase to symbolically illustrate the obstin-
ate grip on a perceived longevity of youth (Setiya, 2017), the participation in a
new, bespoke sporting pastime, leisure and recreation or reinvigorated and
reconsidered relationships and so on. All accentuate an impression of 'freedom'
and a new-fangled liberation from the routines and pressures of family, career
trajectories and a simple *lack of time* couched in the comical, sardonic take on
midlife resistance usually contained within a partially hidden personal directive
to somehow re-experience the rebellion of teenage life (see Ambrose, 2014).
Midlife is often popularly depicted as an historically recognised phase for self-
reflection and reaction (Bainbridge, 2012), existing through time as an observation of a stage that encourages a quasi-jocular resignation of life slipping
towards infirmity and death (Ramus, 1926) or as a *hiatus* in life best served by a
good dose of philosophy to calm the nerves (Hamilton, [2009] 2014). The question remains as to how we have retained this arguably outdated sense of *conformity*. In a more contemporary discourse, midlife is often seemingly excluded
from scholarly discussion on 'ageing', with the latter narratives being concerned
with the path towards *old* age and the challenges that it represents with, for
example, employment (Austen & Ong, 2010) and money (Hsieh, 2011) combined
with occasional forays into how older age can be negotiated and appreciated in
terms of fashion (Twigg, 2012), appreciation of the performing arts (Bernard,
Rickett, & Amigoni, 2015), music (Harrison & Ryan, 2010) and creativity
(Swinnen, 2018). Despite such scholarship being enlightening − and Swinnen
(ibid.) being particularly prevalent here especially relating to 'superordinate
themes' amongst writers such as sustainable routine, structure and continuity in
the literary field and writing as art/experience − most are concerned with something of a 'post-55' conformity, which effectively bypasses the age group of my
respondents (which was 40−57). Thus, for example, this project is concerned
with people who are *pre-negotiating* such searches for the stability that Swinnen
(2018) investigates. The respondents in this project are, in other words, hanging
onto comparative 'youth', celebrating freedom while mindful of the passage of
time; they are, metaphorically and literally, 'in the middle'.

The essence of midlife can therefore be considered here as 'in-between' but not compromised by what might be a naturally associative sense of 'indecision' or 'suspension'. This is not an interregnum, but a *stage* and, as I will illustrate through the words of the artists themselves, considered a *highly productive* stage. The study of identity, so often concomitant to the notion of age (i.e. 'youth' culture *and identity* and so on) can also be applied to an idea of midlife and, consequently, the dynamics of *response*. In the past, Mike Hepworth and Mike Featherstone conceptualised midlife as something to be 'survived' (Hepworth & Featherstone, 1982) but not trivialised. It was loaded with insecurities to be sure, but was also perceived as a phase where image, identity and vitality could be honed and transformed. All was not lost. Identity, therefore, can be considered a wide and complex discourse often inter-related to matters of class (Edgell, 1993; Savage, 2001, 2015; Skeggs, 2004), gender (Butler, 1990) and region/place (Rogaly & Taylor, 2009) and, occasionally, coalesced to great impact (Skeggs, 1997; Walkerdine, Lucey, & Melody, 2001). 'Identity' can be 'social', bounded in recognition of 'sameness' and further founded in the fundamental, intra-sensual requirement of 'knowing who we are and of who other people are' (Jenkins, 1996: 3−5), further elaborated by interaction and anticipations, 'normative expectations' and divided by 'category', empathy and prejudice (Goffman, 1963). Identity can also be partially defined by age (Bennett, 2013) and couched in ethnicity, race and sexuality (Mac an Ghaill, 1988, 1994), the way that society 'responds' to racially inflected moral panics (Hall, Critcher, & Jefferson, 1978) or the development of masculinity (Frosh, Phoenix, & Pattman, 2002). Identity, it can be argued, is perhaps also an 'action'-based 'unity' of heritage or language (Touraine, 2000; cf. Crespi, [1989] 1992: 25−30) formed in *time* but always malleable, reflexive and transformational *over* time should one weigh up anxiety, risk and expertise and act upon such calculations as an individual (Giddens, 1991), further reinforced by the diminishing of the traditional values of community, with 'identity' becoming 'a surrogate' for such values (Bauman, 2001: 15−16) and always somehow *incomplete* (ibid.: 64). Identity is further detectable in discourses of citizenship, respect and responsibility (Faulks, 2000: 124−31), or in the development and maintenance − a dialectic − of peer group and the hierarchy of value (Adams & Allen, 1998; Hey, 1997: 29; Pahl, 2000; Porter & Tomaselli, 1989), illustrating belonging and individualism simultaneously, detected strongly over the years in institutions of education via 'resistance' or 'belonging', sub-cultures (Brown, 1987; Corrigan, 1979; Jenkins, 1983; Silver & Silver, 1997; Willis, 1977) and in gangs and pseudo-criminal groups and entrepreneurial individuals witnessed by the intrepid social researcher as ethnographic participant and observer (Hobbs, 1988, 1995; Hobbs, Hadfield, Lister, & Winlow, 2003; Parker, 1974; Patrick, [1973] 2013). Such variables in discourse cause the (arguably non-destructive, reassuring) fragmentation of identity that permits individuals and groups to consider themselves as having a freedom to identify with a myriad of identity criteria in life. Thus, in this instance, it is important to certify identity as something that is connected to the practice of art (writing, painting, musicianship and so on) and not representative of *the* identity of an *individual*. Identity, therefore, is shaped in part by the artistic muse and the action of creativity and I will refer to identity as a mechanism that is found mainly 'in the background' as we explore the myriad dynamics of midlife creativity. In other words, I am interested in how art might help support the continually transforming midlife identity and how such an identity may come to inform the art as it is created.

Art may well be about transformations, but it is also couched in what I shall continually refer to as the everyday – namely the humdrum, routine and predictable foci of life as it is lived on a daily basis. There exists, in normal life, a consumer who utilises the written word, artwork or the construction of musical score as both an intellectual and leisure activity (Milner, 2005; Rojek, 1995) connected intrinsically to 'life as it is lived'. The study of everyday 'things' (Miller, 2008) and 'ordinary' lives (De Certeau, 1984; Highmore, 2011) are arguably representative of a sociological approach to the ostensibly *banal* aspects of daily routines, and the emerging sociology of 'personal life' (May, 2011) provides a scholarly commentary in a broader field that concentrates on the meanings that individuals attach to the segments of life that would otherwise be considered humdrum and invisible. In addition to this recognition of the function of the everyday, routine and the potentially banal is the energy invested into the researching of the *value* of the 'everyday' in its various practical, utilitarian forms (Pink, 2010), its *sensuous* nature (Pink, 2012; cf. Willis, 1978, 2000) and also the perceptions, 'life-politics' and values of the virtual community found on the internet (Horst & Miller, 2012; Pink, 2013; Pink, Horst, & Posthill, 2016), the latter of which being particularly prevalent (cf. Miller, 2011) in the modern age and useful for this research, especially on iconography, biography and lifestyle (Chaney, 1996) and potentially on the *considered effects* of what is known as 'fandom' (Duffett, 2013; Hills, 2002; Lewis, 1992) in relation to the 'afterlife' of works of art. Such production and consumption of art is reflective of its considered currency in everyday life, its recognition as a lubricant of social life and communication of values, culture and practicalities of existence.

Therefore, it is expedient to recognise that art is a process that does not end with the production of an object, but continues to evolve as a process of interpretation couched in the uniform and nebulous perception of what it is to simply exist (Ingold, 2013). Mike Featherstone wrote that lifestyle is fast becoming what he refers to as an 'aesthetic justification of life' where existence becomes formulated into some kind of strategy for experiencing a 'quasi-self' free from the burdens of expectancies that 'can be traced back to the Romantics' (Featherstone, 1991: 48) and has a post-ideological reverberation of Raymond Williams's suggestion that the arrival of automation and capitalism removed the freedom of art that had thrived in the age of the Romantics (Williams, [1958] 2017: 56; see below). Art, therefore, may well be reclaiming the broad autonomy of that pre-industrial era in an age of post-industrialism, couching it back in the everyday 'ordinary' existence that Williams spoke of (Williams, [1958] 1989) and potentially distancing the production of art from the ideological 'branding' of economic base, while subtly accepting that cultural product has a double hermeneutic rather than being a production of totality. Of course, the 'everyday' is also merely a stratum of living, but 'art' (in its various forms) arguably does have penetrative value in the wider study of biographical constructions of identity (Bauman, 2005; Jenkins, 1996; Lawler, 2015) in the social, economic and cultural age of what has been described – and termed – above as *late modernity* (Beck, 1992; Giddens, 1991). The construction of multi-framed identity and the dynamism of midlife remain a complex multitude of possibilities when considering how the creative self may *emerge*.

Such construction of 'self' – a 'socialized subjectivity' (Bourdieu & Wacquant, [1992] 2002: 126) – is often based on the narratives of things such as individual background and the domains of 'value' of (and the consequent struggle for) hierarchical dominance in life, sometimes theoretically articulated as 'habitus and field' (Bourdieu, [1984] 2010, 1990). This can play out in and amongst the capital value of one's education (Ahier, Beck, & Moore, 2003; Bourdieu & Passeron, [1970] 1977 *inter alios*; Burke, 2016), the individuals' nationality and language (Bernstein, [1971] 2009; Trudgill, 2000), one's social class (Hoggart, [1957] 2014; Skeggs, 1997) or other acquired or hard-wired fragments of the 'whole person' and cannot, arguably, be complete without an understanding of the intrinsic and discursive effects of the wider media, music, literature, film and associative 'external' stimulus available to us as we grow up, consume and (perhaps involuntarily) reproduce values and mores for emerging generations. Thus, 'sociology' is often attached to art (Dauvignaud, 1972; Hauser, [1974] 1982; Inglis & Hughson, 2005; Tanner, 2003; Wolff, 1993, 1983); the 'arts' (Alexander, 2003); 'art worlds' and musical networks (Becker, [1982] 2008; Crossley, 2015); youth (Frith, 1984), more broadly defined music (DeNora, 2003; Horsfall, Meij, & Probstfield, 2013); art and literature (Albrecht, Barnett, & Griff, 1970) and 'literature' (Barker, Coombes, & Hulme, 1978; Burns & Burns, 1973; Hall, 1979; Laurenson, 1978; Laurenson & Swingewood, 1971; Routh & Wolff, 1977), but arguably too little is researched on the enduring 'practical' penetration of literature, music, fine art, education and lifestyle *into* the biography of *those who create art themselves* despite the latest in a long line of scholarship, biography and popular works on interpretation and stimulations (*inter alia* Arnold, 2004; Cottington, 2005; Freeland, [2001] 2003; Gilot, 1990; Gompertz, [2012] 2016; Johnson, 2005; Stallabrass, [2004] 2006) augmenting classic works on the function and value of art in society (Berger, 2016, [1980] 2009, 1972). John Tusa (2003) brought together an enlightening collection of (self-) portraits of the creative self and Joe Fassler's (2017) recent collection of responses on influence in the creative community has been a valuable addition, but the dynamics of creativity in *middle age* is sparse whether it be understood via (lived) 'dramaturgical' or socially constructed context (cf. Berger & Luckmann, 1966; Goffman, 1959) or (philosophical/ideological) reversed 'penetrative' (cf. Willis, 1977), a way of understanding both the way that the artist penetrates the past (and the dominant ideology of capitalism) in tandem with approaches to understanding the flourishing of thinking that furnishes creative outputs or simply by the subconscious leanings toward inventiveness in the individual – in other words, a Janus-like 'look both ways' at influence, inventiveness and (dis-) empowerment. As well as a sense of 'position' there must also be a sense of *place* and while work, for example, has been undertaken on the *lifestyles* of artists who reside in urban areas, centring on the creation of a bohemian 'field' and associative enterprise cultures to be found there (Lloyd, 2010, 2016; Scholette, 2011), an alternative approach could well be to contrast this focus with the more 'ordinary', arguably less 'hip' bohemian artist who resides with family, in small towns or the countryside; art thus considered in a quasi-rural setting – the artist in isolation, to be sure, but additionally isolated in geography. Hence, there can be a mildly detectable effect of what Bourdieu called the 'double rupture' (Bourdieu, 1992), the 'simultaneous recoil from bourgeois culture and from popular culture' (Fowler, 1997: 53), landing the artist somewhere in-between. However, all of these perspectives are arguably built on the definition of a 'creative self' that draws from a multitude of 'capitals' (however potentially unequally bestowed) or a creative 'gaze' (namely, how the individual or group may perceive art or the process of creating art). There is not enough here on the process of creativity – so, how should this be defined?

In establishing something that resembles a 'definition' of creativity, it is expedient to seek to understand the word and the practice as it may be utilised as *demonstrative of action* before transmuting such expositions towards a translation into notions of 'culture' and 'value'. The word 'creative' carries, according to Raymond Williams, 'a consistently positive reference' (Williams, 1961: 19) and, although repetition is sometimes seen to deplete its impact, it is perhaps his assertion on the *origin* of the word that has the greatest resonance in understanding the focus on midlife here. He posits that creativity (or *creation*) to the Greeks was concerned with *repeating existing things*, or *imitation* (ibid.: 20) and, as such, *repetition* segues with a sense of routine and a sense of place that creativity holds with the socially and culturally reproduced essence of cultural materialism, but with reservations that are rooted in cultural and social variations. As such, the 'creative' being expressed by Monika Reuter as 'culture-bound [and] socially-constructed', thus meaning different things to different individuals, nationalities, occupations and existing as 'a function of fields and domains', is useful here (Reuter, 2015: 2). Reuter explains that there is little agreement on the definition of what it is to be creative, how it is defined within *art or music or writing*, and positing that 'it is the knowledgeable in the field who herald the new, the unexpected, the wonderful, the eclectic' (ibid.), thus situating the defining of creativity with those who *partake in it* and possess the power to be creative, thus shaping *the* creative praxis and self. This form of social closure is further elaborated upon by Sharon Koppman (2014) who asserts that the creative industry (in this instance, advertising) defined creativity and novelty from within, harnessing a tendency to reject novelty that is defined externally leading to an effective territoriality of definition (Koppman, 2014: 10). Defining creativity is therefore potentially framed in the structural, elitist, powerful and socially closed (bordered) domains and best understood as having origins in (and value associated with) the social *and* the *commercial* whilst having a sublime tension at the heart of its instrumental definition between individuals and teams. Reuter intimates that sociology has neglected focussing on the meaning of creativity (Reuter, 2015: 41), simultaneously suggesting that capitalism not only neglects its value, but is somehow fearful of its power. There is, she suggests, a tendency to want to snuff out creativity in the world of commerce because, possibly, it encourages thinking *beyond the routine* (ibid.: 74). However, despite the situating of the creative in the realms of the 'political' (power and control), commercial or the sociological, it is still possible to recover and reposition the essence of the zen-like aspect of creativity in the domain of the place and action of art and artist, suggesting that creativity is intuitive, subconscious and fitful. Artists, therefore, do not really know what is coming when they begin their creative arc and, as Tim Ingold says, they are flying 'in the face of the common belief among non-practitioners [...] that the essence of drawing lies in the projection onto the page of interior mental pictures' (Ingold, 2013: 127). Creativity, therefore, can be understood as indicative of *pure immediacy*, existing in the moment and transfigures art and artist and audience in a dualistic, oscillating form. It is communicative and unpremeditated, subjectively coded and potentially overtly decoded, telling us about our culture via words, drawings and sound as well as through action. Thus, drawing a line, says Ingold, is in itself a method of action and communication and has the potential impact of a cultural inculcation. It is

> descriptive of nothing but itself. It is, however, transformative. It transforms the draughtsman, in making the work, and it transforms those who follow, in looking with it. To correspond with the world through drawing, therefore, is to practise not ethnography but graphic anthropology or, to coin a term, anthropography. (ibid.: 129)

Such a slant on the meaning of what it is to be creative is fascinating and valuable: the inspiration and the creative act fuse to create an observation of the world through a practical, cultural responsiveness, correspondence and reflexivity via music, art and literariness. Thus, the focus of the research ahead is to consider 'creativity' as an amalgamation of power, skill, commercialism and cultural reproduction via ideology but also, crucially, as an act that sews together the identity, life politics and imagination of the creator in a moment in time. It is, as Ingold implies above, developmental and descriptive, comparative and fluid (a fusion of ethnography and the anthropological). Thus, to be creative is to *act* and to act in a moment of inspiration, developing a prototype of thought as a thing that has not only – by definition – not existed before, but is also an example of continued authenticity and validity in the midlife phase.

To 'dig out' the structure of such action – in effect, to 'visualise and comprehend' a myriad of meanings – it is necessary to return to the discussion of 'theory' to situate, prior to departure, the forthcoming research for the benefit of the reader. I will explain shortly that this project was analytically inductive (or as close to a theory- and value-free intervention as one can get at the outset), leaving the theory to affix, transfigure and flourish in the closing discussion. In adopting the outline developed by Raymond Williams (of more below), it is possible to frame the midlife creative routines, their nexus with identity maintenance

and resistance to cultural hegemony via penetrating the certitude of the dominant ideology (Willis, 1977) or, perhaps more likely these days, through the development of art as a post-industrial 'romantic vision' of ontological security
(Giddens, 1991) realised through, and bullishly enhancing, personal cultural capital (Bourdieu, 1984). Thus, the concepts of 'structure of feeling' and 'knowable
community' (Williams, 1961) are practical and evocative, shaping the thrust of
artistic creativity as situated in the everyday lives of creators, having essence via
a 'dialogue' with an established, sometimes 'folk', history of the oeuvre that is
achieved (arguably) via an informed hermeneutical process – in other words,
the artists are instinctively adding to the timeline of creative language, communication and aesthetics and challenging the 'selective tradition' (ibid.: 63–7) of
ideological filtering of meaning and value in art via their intrinsic ability to
situate themselves into an oeuvre either lived in the present or imagined. The
structure of feeling is an instinctive confluence of history and the immediate,
intimating something of a reproduction of values and ideology but also a weak-
ening of the base-superstructure concept enshrined in Marxist historical materialism via a re-evaluation of such determinism. Thus, culture (and art) exist as a
transformative influence on the individual and group, essentially separate to the
otherwise deterministic influence of economy. Williams's ideas segue with the
signification of the ethnographic data inasmuch that they situate art in place
rather than economy; art is a player in that structure of feeling, a dynamic in the
constructive, verstehen-like (Dilthey, 1996; Holton & Turner, [1989] 2011;
Parkin, 2002; Weber, [1968] 2013) interpretative domain of the knowable community and a two-way currency in the cultural, social and symbolic capital of
the individual and the group (Bourdieu, [1984] 2010; [1994] 1998). Such capital
can lead to 'cultural pedigree' (Bourdieu, 1984: 55) that itself is complex and
variable in form, but recognisable at times as illustrative of competence, skill
and a sense of an unintended 'elite' status that can run counter to 'dominant
taste' (ibid.: 280) or that 'selective tradition' noted by Williams, above
(Williams, 1961). I am therefore concerned here with Bourdieu's notion of field,
habitus and cultural production (Bourdieu, 1993) and how it augments
Williams's structure of feeling to the extent that the research is concerned with
age, space, action and personal value of creativity and the drawing on repeated
patterns of learning and articulation. Thus, '[t]he artistic field', says Bourdieu, 'is
a universe of belief' with cultural production creating

> not only the object in its materiality, but also the value [...] the
> recognition of artistic legitimacy. This is inseparable from the
> production of the artist or the writer as artist or writer, in other
> words, as a creator of value. A reflection on the meaning of the
> artist's signature would thus be in order. (Bourdieu, 1993: 164)

Williams and Bourdieu segue in that the research is concerned with how creative people do what they do and where they draw their creative power from. It
is this symbiosis of understanding and power that lends itself well to how midlife

creativity assists in the creation, revising and maintenance of identity via action. Thus, with this in mind, it is arguably not possible to conclude the discussion on 'theoretical structure' without recourse to the (at least potentially) influential work of the Birmingham Centre for Contemporary Cultural Studies (CCCS) (Hall, Hobson, Lowe, & Willis, 1980) insomuch that the Centre was responsible – ostensibly – for the furtherance of the debate that was arguably begun by Matthew Arnold ([1865/1888] 1964; [1869] 2006) continued 'through' F. R. Leavis ([1948] 2008; [1952] 2008; [1962] 2013; Leavis & Thompson, 1933; Moran, 2010: 24; Storer, 2009: 43–4) and exemplified by Raymond Williams ([1958] 2017; 1961; [1973] 2015; [1974] 2003). This debate on the roots, meaning and value of 'culture' was given more enhanced academic form by the CCCS following its formation by Richard Hoggart and colleagues in 1964 and given additional momentum under the Directorship of Stuart Hall post-1968. It is ostensibly built upon (and in tandem with) the 'cultural theorists' that link perceptions of culture to 'structure' such as Raymond Williams ([1958] 2017; 1961) and Terry Eagleton ([1976] 2002) and the various critical theorist, 'Frankfurt' scholars (see, in general, Adorno, 1991; Bottomore, [1984] 2002). However, the CCCS was not derivative, owing its trajectory to the foundational work of no others in particular. It was, instead, an innovative collective of scholars who based an understanding of society on the utilisation of interdisciplinary modes, essentially non-positivist, highly ethnographic and participant observatory in the mould of the Institute of Community Studies (and associative studies) urban sociology on class, socio-geography and culture (Coates & Silburn, 1962; Willmot, [1966] 1969; Young & Willmott, [1957] 1962) and celebrating a certain *locality* in its focus. Never had Van Maanen's observation that 'sociologists can commute to work in their Volkswagens, while anthropologists must arrive at and depart from their work sites on 747's' (Van Maanen, 2011: 22) arguably been so apt for application as it was with the CCCS. In addition to defining culture as 'the way social relations of a group are structured and shaped [...] experienced, understood and interpreted' (Hall & Jefferson, 1976: 11), thus giving the Centre an ideological bent towards the notion of culture as being social, lived and shaped by external 'things', the thrust was unabashedly concerned with working class cultures (Clarke et al., 1979) and the experience of, *inter alia*, history, education (Baron et al./Education Group CCCS, 1981), masculinity (Willis, 1977, 1978), gender and popular media (McRobbie, 2000; McRobbie & Garber, 1976) and race (Hall et al., 1978). Pervading these subjects and more was the essence of 'resistance', understood as (but prone, perhaps, to) what Hall (1980: 39–40) states is a lack of 'a rigidly imposed unitary theoretical position at the Centre' despite various theoretical foci centring on structuralism, feminism, hegemony and so on translated into 'concrete' research action. Resistance was couched in the formative notion that a dominant ideology – and the hegemony associated with such modes of control (Abercrombie, Hill, & Turner, 1980; Gramsci, 1971) – was somehow 'visible' in context and impact to those who were exploited by its grasp. Therefore, when applying such Marxist theory to a series of observations on individual (and closed-communal) creative routines and processes I will effectively argue that the *resistance* is aimed towards an ideological expectancy of *compliance* to a series of norms and values attached to what it is to 'be' in the midlife phase. This may be consequently (and conversely) considered 'security' as life and life-politics fragment into *in*securities all around us via processes of individualisation, globalisation and so on, reversing expectancies of secure routine by comprehending disintegrative and 'chaotic' creativity as a place of *refuge*. The 'hegemony' is therefore controlled by the individual actors and not by the 'system' – the 'penetration' described by Willis (1977) is therefore achieved but does not, in this instance, set the actors up to 'fail themselves' (it is quite the opposite). It follows that, in developing an inductive (reasoning) methodology, I may be inclined to analyse the 'role' of art, music and literature and seek explanations of 'value' via the understanding of, in aggregate terms, the reordering of value and connexion with symbolic totems of class (homology – see Willis, 1978), the 'affirmation of life' (Hoggart, [1957] 2009) and the resistance to mindless consumption and ideological affirmation of identity with full awareness of its value.

The CCCS, in combining Gramsci (1971), structuralism (Culler, 1975; Hawkes, 1977), French Structuralism (de Saussure, 2013; Genette, 1983; Levi-Strauss, 1966) and the ideas of Roland Barthes to understand stylistic resistance to the dominant culture, provide a rich, textured and meaningful foundation for a great deal of consequent British cultural studies but I intend to refer mainly to the broad outputs of the CCCS and Raymond Williams as primary guidance in understanding a modern resistance to banality and – it follows – compliance. There *is* a *homology of things* that are present in the case studies that follow; the organisation of sociality, experience, economic capital, the music and art itself, the 'requirements' of writing in addition to the sheer love of participation. This all combines to create a type of resistance that is connected to a broad sense of the 'subcultural' (Hetherington, 1998: 54–5) via the 'system of meaning' of the factors mentioned in that they are ordered to create the ultimate reward of self-legitimisation. In other words, people create to confirm that we are who we *think* we are. This, in itself, resists the dominant ideology and lends itself to a wider, more contemporary discourse that has superseded the CCCS over time via modes of thinking that suggest a post-subcultural essence to (youth) cultures, enveloping the ideas of late modernity and recognising the fluidity of time and the retention of what might be called an ideology of resistance (see Bennett, 2013; Bennett & Hodkinson, 2012; Bennett & Kahn-Harris, 2004; Muggleton, 2000). The post-subcultural is particularly useful in the coming analysis because it throws open the opportunity to understand artistic creativity as a 'role' in identity construction at whatever point of life it may embrace, shifting the focus gently from base-superstructure and towards what is called a 'cultural sociology' (Back, Bennett, & Edles, 2012). Everyday life has also been enveloped as a topic of focus within wider cultural studies over the last 20 years with arguably a good starting point being David Chaney's *The Cultural Turn* (1994), which took as its central thrust the essence of a refocussing of culture as a *framing* dynamic of experience as well as the more traditionally considered *translator* of such experience. This has since been augmented by work by Andy Bennett (2005) who declared that while much has been done by cultural studies 'to enrich the

theoretical and empirical understanding of mass culture [...] as a site of hegemonic struggle in late modern everyday life' (Bennett, 2005: 26–7) it remains
open to criticism (after Bennett, 1986; Harris, 1992) for failing to unlock the
polarising tendencies of (cultural) hegemony itself which is discernible via individualisation of technology and media choices; their confluence is at once disempowering and withheld in consequence from those who participate in the theatre
of consumerism and – in this case – sub-cultural 'resistance'. Thus, resistance is
disempowering when aligned to consumption – it is a clever sleight of hand
determined by the system. This book will hopefully shed greater light on how
empowerment can be achieved via resistance to the conformity of midlife; it can
be seen, if you like, as a sub-cultural thing, but it is arguably about setting one's
own conditions for the hegemony that is in practice. Nowadays it might just be
about 'self-improvement' and the utilisation of individualised powers rather than
being in opposition to structures, powers, systems or things. The fact that,
according to Terry Eagleton, we '*can* improve ourselves suggests that there are
creative powers within the self; that we *need* to do so tells a less sanguine tale.
Culture thus becomes a secular version of divine grace' to make us human, but
unequally so (Eagleton, 2016: 28–9). Art *is* about transformations and, in this
instance, it is almost exclusively about transformation of the self *from within
the self*.

§

To bridge the scholarly embedding of this project, the theoretical considerations
and the explanation of the method of undertaking the research, let me turn
briefly to Roland Barthes who once noted that art and literature had different
dimensions – or depths – of language and meaning. Classical art, he said, was
'transparent' and 'left no deposit' being 'a language 'closed' by social and not
natural bounds' (Barthes, [1953] 2010b: 9) and literature was separated from art
and thus objectified by this process. There is, it follows, a complex mystery in literature that art – arguably as a pure form of communication – lacks. I believe
that this distinction is worth investigating by understanding the conscious (and
subconscious) layers of creativity that pre-load a work of art, literature or music
with subjectivity and objective negotiations. However, Barthes' (arguably most
famous) assertion that there has been a 'death of the author' (Barthes, 1977) tips
this narrative into a symposium of symbolic *post-partum* for the art created here.
This book is not a study of reception theory (Willis, 2018) despite the fact that
reception is in the mind – occasionally – of the artist after the point of creative
pique. What I come to call the creative 'mezzanine' is not an exclusive place for
reception at all and neither, arguably, is midlife itself; both 'places' are in-
between states of mind and place suspended from the future, while having historical thrust. Foucault (1980) perhaps reaches into the narrative with more precision via his suggestion that the author is an historical player in the *personality
and form* of art, but this is still suggestive of the more social, longitudinal, intellectual and practical context of the *art world* (Becker, [1982] 2008; Wolff, 1993)

that I shall observe — but not fully enter into — here. So, if there is no focus on 'art worlds' or the 'afterlife' and value of art in the public domain, what (briefly) is this *mezzanine*?

As is now established, this book has at its heart analysis of some ethnographic work that was delivered via an analytic inductive approach to collecting data, thus signalling that there was no setting out with a theory to prove or disprove and no presuppositions made of the participants and their creative drive or inferred in conversations or interviews with the participants. However, despite all research (arguably) having an element of inquisitor-subjectivity present in the deed and outcome of interaction, and therefore values and ideology firmly (however unintentionally) at play in the generation of data, the data — in this case — produced themes that were given a freedom to organise themselves into various clusters after the research was done. One such cluster articulated the very strong sense that the 'place' where art was created was a location of unpredictability that resulted in a certain 'chaos' being constructively harnessed to bring about novelty. Thus, following Deleuze (1990; Colebrook, 2002), there emerged evidence that a tension existed in the subjective interpretation *of* the zone by the artist *within* the zone between 'simulacrum' (or, copying, facsimile, no 'original' to speak of, but newness nevertheless in the canon of creative art) and a belief in the objective authenticity of the process itself coupled with the outcome. As a result, the zone framed itself as something of an 'in-between state' of creativeness, positioning between the structural 'everyday' and the boundless possibilities of the imagination. However, as I will later elaborate (both within the text of the ethnographies as well as in a concluding chapter that considers the embodiment and effect of the mezzanine) the 'zone' or 'state' of creativity theorised here is open to various interpretations, utilises many variations of routine and is, ostensibly, subject to what I will call 'positive' and 'negative fantasy' in relation to the artist, the ego and the 'afterlife' of the art itself where the artist engages with a naked ontological playfulness, a positive application of *doing* and the discarding of the spectre of *regret*.

The project itself, instigated in 2014 and completed in 2017, utilised interviews, observations, written responses from participants and online communications. The main data was drawn from interview transcriptions, themselves a product of 'sit-down', semi-structured sessions (Mann, 2016) and a lot of reflexive, unscheduled, 'stand up', unstructured 'chatter' with participants (King & Horrocks, 2010: Ch. 8). This latter approach, always undertaken within the agreed parameters of the field research (i.e. on the move, overt and on-subject) would take place in cars, walking between locations, in bars and in other *ad hoc* venues associated with the participants (i.e. recording and rehearsal studios, gigs, standing with a cup of tea and admiring the view across the countryside from the window adjacent to a writer's desk and so on). The research was undertaken using what can be described here as a 'traditional' ethnographic incentive — namely to undertake initial fieldwork and write it up, representative of the culture (in this case, a *creative* culture) and as a *narrative* of such culture (Van Maanen, 2011: 4). It draws on the qualitative data to formulate a vision of a *culture of* musical creativity, of artistic *expression* and of literary authorial *routines* and influence and associative senses of ownership, resistance and self-identity. I therefore undertook planned and extemporaneous interviews and hosted group discussions (some of the 'interviews' were essentially 'focus groups' where it was applicable and practical) and included fleeting elements of time-honoured 'intimate' participant observation technique and circumstance akin to those undertaken, *inter alia*, by Paul Willis in *Profane Culture* (1978) or Howard Williamson in *The Milltown Boys Revisited* (2004). These 'backstage', private spaces are joined by the more mundane, run-of-the-mill public 'being there and watching' approaches usually associated with safety and arranged, pragmatic data collection (see Gilbert, 1993; Hammersley & Atkinson, 1990; May, 1997). In collating the data and writing the ethnography I adopted a pen portrait, or (at a stretch) 'vignette' style in notes to gain extra 'feel', and developed such vignettes into a form and style echoing that so expertly delivered by Dick Hobbs in his *Bad Business* (1998), a book that explains the *people* as well as the *lives of* the people and their meanings, while adding my own quasi-realist presence into the narratives of my own case studies here.

There is always, to be sure, the 'trap' of, as Ruth Finnegan states, reducing the understanding of music to 'an epiphenomenon of social structure' or, as she goes on, being 'swept away by the facile romanticising' of music and 'art' (Finnegan, [1989] 2007: 10–11). Therefore, with these warnings clearly understood, there was a consideration of an 'ethnographic self' that existed as a crucial distinctive factor in my appreciation of, essentially, 'art' that I was *very close to* (Coffey, 1999; Spradley, 1979) often in what might be called a 'sensory' manner of hearing and vision (Pink, [2009] 2015). Such reflexivity in the field was important because I was aware of two factors that might affect the generation of neutral data: firstly, I was familiar to some – but not all – of the respondents, albeit mostly in a 'distant' context (i.e. initial contact many years ago and so on and not maintained over intervening time) and, secondly, I was entering the field of artistic creativity as a creative artist (of sorts) myself, having written fiction manuscripts and music lyrics, written and recorded music and played live with various bands I had formed and joined, and harnessed a significant appreciation (and collection) of recorded music, printed literature and visual art over the years that provides ample opportunity for regular discussion. Consequently, the ethnographic self was a potentially *compromising* self when it came to entering the functioning creative worlds of those involved here; there was nothing resembling value-freedom here, but purposive sampling and the role of analytic induction went some way towards letting those creative people 'do the talking' and, thus, setting up a task for me at the end of the process in 'making sense' and creating a semblance of order from their responses. There is, it follows, an understanding that ethnography can essentially seek to find out what people do not know, by studying them with the express intention of finding out things about people and their routines that they themselves 'don't know' or *don't know they know* (see High, Kelly, & Mair, 2012). It is through delving into the psychosocial aspects of art and music and writing via questions, exploratory discourse and analysis that we may gain a small peek at the mechanisms of the creative self, the very same 'self' that many creative people cannot see themselves. The participants in this project were, in addition, all aged within the 40–56 bracket that I decided, arbitrarily, would define 'midlife' for the purposes of this study and I am also in this age bracket, further enhancing awareness of the ethnographic self. While there is arguably no existing universally recognised definition of what 'midlife' *is* resulting in a nebulous available discourse exploring – unsurprisingly with an ageing population both in the UK and internationally (Andrews & Phillips, 2005; Komp & Johansson, 2015) – ageing and the *consequences of* ageing or, indeed, a consensus on what it *might* be or what it should, or should not, entail (and I sense that it would be vigorously challenged if it did exist), it fell to me to define what I wanted from the dialogues on midlife, while explaining to respondents that their midlife status was a core focus of the research. Therefore, on this and other matters I went with the 'sense of self' as it is reflected in others. In other words, if I consider myself to be at this stage of life, then those around me who share the same age consequently share similar traits of objective biography and are, thus, situated in midlife too. I reflect myself back into the sample; it is not ideal, but it gives the project a set of parameters. Future research will seek to address wider demographics but, for now, it is best to focus on history, biography and routines, life-course and perceptions of the 'now' and the future.

Despite my own identity and characteristics helping shape the trajectory and context of the project, all participants in this study self-identified as experiencing this stage of life – comfortably and without dispute or recourse to debate – and, thus, all participants fitted this purposive (non-probability) requirement for taking part (Arber, 1993) while also facilitating the development of a theoretical sample as part of the inductive method employed (Glaser & Strauss, [1967] 1999; Manning, 1982). Following the participants' self-definition of their midlife 'status' (following my own explanation of definition as a guide), the research progressed to explore those aforementioned 'hidden selves'; this was a project designed to let the artists expose their identity themselves, I had no intention of telling anyone what it might mean to be creative and how identity criteria might have consistency similar to a Jungian personality survey. Instead, the inductive approach allowed me to explore the creative individual's personality, history, and so on while mindful of the fact that this was ostensibly a 'public' discussion held in private settings; in other words, the respondent was giving me 'their version' of things and I was mindful of the pitfalls of interpreting their words as 'truth' while seeking to understand their thoughts and ideas 'sequentially' (Becker, 1971), developing 'an idea' of the value and meaning of midlife creativity as I went along. To augment this methodological process, there is always the vigilance of depth. Paul Atkinson states that he does 'not believe that interviews can give us access to unmediated private experience' (Atkinson, 2006: 161) going on to suggest that all data generated is something of a 'performed identit[y]' that is 'mediated and framed by culturally shared forms and genres' (ibid.: 161–62). This is astute thinking; he suggests that we are always 'enacting' our pasts in our present and this should be considered a very active dynamic in the understanding of, in this instance, how art is made and valued by an individual or group. I always refer, informally, to the 'dark matter' that researchers must consider when critiquing a data set ready for writing-up. This verstehen-like (Truzzi, 1974), hermeneutic process − where one knows that information and meaning exists but one cannot actually *see* it − is present in this project. I was meeting the creative people briefly, asking questions in our transient windows of face-to-face contact about things that exist permanently in their thoughts and active lives. There was bound to be a bit of sociological assumption along the way, dancing along the edge of grand and grounded theory while having greater faith in the latter to allow the data to speak for itself.

That aside, I needed a 'way in' and gained it via both my own contacts and my personal knowledge of the art and artists that I sought to speak with. While Andy Bennett, in his ethnographic work with various musicians in the north of England,[1] stated that he was able to productively network in the field due to his existing status as a locally active musician (Bennett, 2000: 6), in Derby I was able to identify a little as a musician in terms of (very) limited live performance, composition and recording history[2] and more prominently as a lifelong fan, collector and amateur historian of popular music and thus gain access to the network in the city. Having spent some of my teens in Derby also aided this historical musical and local knowledge, further facilitated trust and mutual respect with the musicians and helped to create immediate depth in the consequent individual and group-based discussions. The knowledge of the area bypassed the requirement to engage in a more 'community-based' format for gathering material on a 'scene' (i.e. seeking a wider sample to give context to 'Derby' and the musical heritage and so on) such as that undertaken by Sara Cohen in Liverpool (Cohen, 1991), or necessitating the wider subject 'reach' of Stith Bennett (1983) despite having a similar essence on occasions to these studies relating to the (arguably) more universal mechanisms and conditions of creativity. Contact with further respondents was facilitated by my initial 'gatekeeper' in Derby and by direct contact with the artists and writers involved, secured via random suggestions, research into active creative people and a little knowledge of the histories and trajectories of some of those who took part. Therefore, I am aware that the sample detected and utilised is not ultimately 'representative' of artists or 'creative people' as a whole and I recognise that the data generated was situated in time that is susceptible to mood, curiosity, time of day, situation on the creative cycle (i.e. stress caused by having deadlines or the delight of a recent completion) and, as a result, all data is compromised by such deficiencies. I am mindful of the fact that I was dipping in and getting out

---

[1] Bennett also undertook field research in Germany as part of this project but mentions his access in this instance specifically to his work in the north-east of England.
[2] I played bass in bands at University, writing songs and playing gigs as colleges, May Balls and in pubs. However, I also 'shifted' equipment for bands on the road, did occasional lighting and a little bit of what might be called 'stage management', recorded in professional recording studios and, more recently, on fabulous home-recording equipment in 'home studios' much like the studio owned by Ian from The Ruins.

of otherwise busy routines, that the data generated was dependent on consent, and that such content may have been determined by a desire on the respondent's part to 'say something' about themselves. However, I am satisfied that every word spoken to me was about their routines and their perception of their art (and skills) as ultimately a possession that empowered them to be what they want to be in life. There was no detectable ego, just simply the pleasure of talking about what they do and how and why they do it.

Thus, despite the interviews being based on the catalysts of career, art creation and the subjective and objective meanings attached to their works, the contact was based largely on 'educative' terms: I had a lot of listening to do. The same approach applied to the penetration of the field of literary production, seeing data generated in public cafés and private lounges and writing rooms seeking to expose the routines that lead to what Callahan and Stack called the 'focused flux', or moment of sublime creativity, in the creation of new literary form (Callahan & Stack, 2007: 269). The data I gathered, in essence, differed from location to location and subject to subject, influenced by my own prior knowledge (or lack of it) and was affected, in all probability, by gender and professional status and the time we had together to talk and so on. However, all of the data generated was detailed, authoritative and adequately and purposively explained what it *means* to be creative to those who gave me their time, and I could not ask for more than that.

PART I: MUSIC, MIDLIFE AND AUTHENTICITY

Part I: The New 'Hidden' Musicians

To this point I have sought to introduce 'art' as something that is personally transformative, occasionally affective, intrinsically performative and something that initiates action in the individual. In addition to this active context, art is also framed as a segment of the creative self, an actor in the diverse and transitive theatre of midlife and situated firmly as an historical dynamic of social and cultural reproduction, a vehicle of ideology and an emblem of subculture. The routine with which art enters and frames life can be potentially understood as continual, confrontational, flamboyant and dramaturgical and having transmuting properties for individuals and groups in the middle phase of life. I posit that art is potentially a language, a feeling, an 'ontological now' and the theories of late modernism provide adequate interdisciplinary frameworks for seeking to understand art's role in the mechanism of self-regulation, exhibitionism and contentment and self-efficacy. The structure of such action, however, is open for investigation. I stipulate that creativity and art matter, but what routines and practices *make* it matter?

Rock music is often theorised as counter-cultural, expressive and urban (Chambers, 1985; Grossberg, 1992) and *public* via performance (DeNora, 2000). This perception is a partially accurate appraisal of how popular music plays out in the public consciousness largely because it arguably focusses on its intrinsic 'public' narrative – the flamboyancy of style and the occasionally provocative stance of music and bands (and their associative, fashion-driven subcultural groupings of such counter-culture towards the 'establishment') are primarily detectable. However, as stated, this tends to be a public dialogue that exists largely via the media and the 'street' (Hebdige, 1979) effectively placing into its shadows the omnipresent *private* sphere and its generation of artistic form (sometimes simply for art's sake) where 'rock culture' is ostensibly *privatised* with no notable effect to behold beyond the influence on the creative self or collective. Creativity can therefore also be understood as a process that exists informally and in private but with no discernible 'output' apart from the participation in a *routine leisure*, albeit a routine leisure that is aimed at making the art *better*. For example, there is a seeming dearth of research into the meaning and practicality of *rehearsal*, despite it being a crucial element of performative arts creativity (i.e. music, dance, theatre and so on). Scholarship often conceptualises rehearsal in its literal form – to practice, to run through and to rote-learn and so on. Occasional forays into rehearsal spaces are juxtaposed with music education (Karlsen, 2010), development (Westerlund, 2006) and focus upon educative practice and peer research centred upon development of 'soft' and 'hard' skills realised through the creative process of children (Blom & Encarnacao, 2012). The expansive *sociology of rock* oeuvre tends to focus on rehearsal and creativity as part of a wider process of labour that also envelops performance and the focus upon individual and shared ambition (Cohen, 1991) or the lengthier, organic process of *being* a musician (Bennett, [1980] 2017) and as something of a banal necessity in the pursuit of honed excellence (Finnegan, [1989] 2007). The associative *sociology of youth culture* occasionally analyses the meaning of performance, communication between actors and articulation of narratives of resistance and cultural authenticity (Bennett, 2000). Rehearsal has been additionally described as a loosely organised, ramshackle, amateurish gathering with a central purpose to play and plot (Fornäs, Lindberg, & Sernhede, 1995: 85–86), mainly tedious in practice with occasional sparks of excitement thrown in (ibid.: 129–130). These studies are mainly observations of youth at play with their instruments, involving associative dramas, creative sensibilities and the articulation of ambitions; rehearsal can *also* be understood as these processes in tandem with a *rehearsal of creativity* – remembering *how* to write, to contribute, to delegate and to lead, to *make* music as well as remember it and make what already exists somehow better (Finnegan, [1989] 2007). To be sure, this fusion of such aforementioned functions in the rehearsal room is not unusual, but in *creative* arts it can differ from the generic function of rehearsal in, for example, a classical orchestra setting where rehearsal is arguably about reciting the work of *others* (see Small, 1987:6–7 for an analysis of classical *performance* as 'ritual' and 'celebration' and a 're-enactment of a shared mythology of a culture') or as a power-structural, 'directed' routine (Glynn, 2002; Khodyakov, 2014). Thus, a gap exists where a conceptual fusion between art as *creation* and art as *reproduction* (Benjamin, [1923] 2008) can be applied to the study of rehearsal, incorporating John Dewey's (2009) philosophical interpretation of art *form* with emphasis on the patterns and structures of meaning *heard* subjectively.

However, music is – of course – something that is communicative and is further promulgated in band rehearsals (and what are known as 'jam sessions') involving musicians often playing with ideas, writing and rewriting song structures and ostensibly 'warming up' for such tasks via a 'run through' and 'sound checking'. More widely, music is additionally (and more conventionally) externally communicated via product and public performance, a veritable 'triad of responsibility' being formed that summarises the responsibilities of 'being in a band' involving the said writing, recording and gigging, emerging from those 'shadows' and into the lights of both 'day' and the 'stage'. It is often considered, in modern times, that simply 'playing' is not enough for serious bands; they need to be additionally creating music video (Frith, Goodwin, & Grossberg, 1993), compact discs and associative ephemera, developing social media presence and using the 'gig' to attempt to 'sell' their product in an aggressive age of downloads and online piracy (Cummings, 2013). Augmenting this point, as is so often anecdotally detected these days, the gig can often be considered a money-generator in itself, bypassing the need to 'shift units' in shops and online (Byun, 2016), but most 'amateur' bands use the manifestation of the regular stage show as an opportunity to illustrate skill and command of their repertoire (Kingsbury, 1988) and as an opportunity to practice the combination of art, organisation and communication in synchronised form (Stebbins, 1989). It is, ultimately, an opportunity to undertake a process that leads to the enhancing of simple human self-awareness in musical terms (Evans, 2014). Ruth Finnegan contributed profoundly to this thesis in *The Hidden Musicians* ([1989] 2007) where she penetrated amateur music-making fields to elucidate the dynamics of creativity via sociality, song writing, performance and the mechanisms of participation in balance with everyday duties in work and the home. She stated that music making is an 'intensely human' activity (Finnegan, [1989] 2007: xv), a central consideration when basing her study on locality, different genres of musics (ibid.: 10, *original emphasis*) from 'country and western' to 'rock' to 'classical' and so on. While recognising that she lacked the space to penetrate deeply into any one given 'society', scene or world (ibid.: 11, 17), Finnegan was able to calibrate essential routine and practice across the whole variety that she encountered. In this instance, while practice/rehearsal had an 'appeal', performance was viewed as an 'essential' and 'active' event (ibid.: 158–159) and, in the creation of novelty within the oeuvre of *rock music*, originality was desired and achieved through the repetitions of deliberative song writing and perfected in performance – a performance that ultimately functioned as the platform for the elaboration and transmission of the partially hidden lyrical message held in the songs (ibid.: 170). This is suggestive of a holistic view held of the musical-performative routine and one that is challenged below, but it is fair to note that Finnegan is also reporting evidence of resistance of passivity in the face of a delivered mass culture (Bennett, 2001: 142), the appropriation and application of 'professional' status to musical labour despite endeavours remaining largely unrewarded financially (Shuker, 2008: 49) and the empowering 'active' consumption of music via imitation (Negus, 1996: 29) that segues with Bourdieu's subconscious mimesis theorem of habitus (Bourdieu, 1993) where (mostly) voluntary consumption leads to a subconscious reproduction of influence via performed routine, habit, skill and perceived incentive.

Like the subterranean desires, skills, actions and inducements that Ruth Finnegan detected and analysed in Milton Keynes, the musicians that I am to introduce are also arguably *hidden* from view, but not assimilated into a wider mass as Finnegan observed. Instead, they are revealed occasionally, but predominantly concealed as a unit via their own volition, in an in-between state in their rehearsals and in their acts of recording in their studio, phantasms in their chosen art world, creating at all times together and benefitting from their acquired power bestowed via their midlife status in work and leisure and habitus. Let's meet them.

Chapter 2

Lost in Space: Music and Aura

I first travelled north to see Johnny, pitching up at his family home in south Derby, on a wet autumn day. He is not working at the hospital this particular Saturday; instead he wants to introduce me to his philosophy of music and life. He greets me outside his house, smiling, smoking a cigarette, his body protected against a chill wind by something resembling a battered sheepskin coat. He is 49 years old at this particular juncture, but is turning 50 in a few weeks' time and his band are to play a live slot to mark the occasion at a punk bash at Derby's Victoria Inn, a pub venue with a big converted 'back room' complete with the obligatory matt black walls, low stage and functional light rig that is suspended seemingly inches above the performers' head. This afternoon, under grey skies, Johnny's face emanates a weathered intensity (he reminds me, in physique and looks, a little of the late Rob Gretton, erstwhile manager of Joy Division and New Order), and his voice is notable for its gravelly Derby lilt. It's good to see him and he speaks a lot from the moment we shake hands; I sense that he has an interesting story to tell.

Back in 2008 Johnny wrote a self-published history of the Derby 'alternative' rock scene (Vincent, 2008) and he says, by way of beginning our conversation, that this was the catalyst for re-entering the music scene that he had hitherto walked away from years ago. 'You don't do an awful lot because you've got your family', he says, 'and when you're bringing up your kids you can't spend a lot of time [making music]'. Things changed when his book was finished and his thirst for performance returned. He states that he had always wanted to 'do music' and with teenage bravura he threw himself into singing and fronting bands. 'I couldn't play anything – still can't', he says with a smile before alluding to the necessity of possessing brawn when setting out with raw enthusiasm and little else. 'When you're 15 and in a band, it takes guts', he states with assurance. It is about gaining a confidence in yourself very quickly indeed, and this determination and courage to *get involved* transmogrified into playing, performing and promoting various bands. He got close to a commercial breakthrough as a member of The Stance in the early 1990s, before taking time off to concentrate on family commitments, re-emerging onto the Derby stage once more in 2010 as part of a one-off reunion show with The Stance before turning his attention to new projects, playing live regularly again, and recording, with Exit the Network. After the sudden death of the bands' lead guitarist, Johnny's musical odyssey looked to be over again, before The Ruins emerged to assist him in rediscovering his creative muse. Music, to Johnny, is about the creation of 'memories', project to project, song to song, and it is all about pitching the art in a moment in time and allowing it the space to grow there.

> **Johnny:** When you're doing your music, nothing else matters. You forget about everything [...] work doesn't matter, all the other shit you're going through in the week doesn't matter [...] it's quite therapeutic but quite knackering, you come out drained [...] it's about the *moment* (original spoken emphasis)

This sense of 'being in the moment' is a strong and consistent theme when talking to The Ruins. Johnny began our interviews with the assertion that music can be used to leverage additional meaning in life for the individual while also lifting the *band* up and out of their ordinary lives (cf. Highmore, 2011; Moran, 2005), placing them in an extraordinary – *earned* – setting. 'Ninety-five percent of the time [in life] we're doing normal things [...] driving your car, having a cup of tea, going to work and then you do your five percent as music', says Johnny. The people who eventually *consume* The Ruins' music, he believes, are getting music that is isolated from the full identity of the creator, effectively representing that 'five percent' that acts as a small – but significant – window 'into' the creator, but nevertheless is isolated from the 'rest' of the creator, essentially being a disembodied fragment. The listeners 'are looking at this work and not the person, [...] they just see it as *songs*', he adds. The deeper meaning is lost in *transmission*, neutralised in the space in-between inception and listening forcing a relinquishing of autonomy via the sharing of his creative self. His 'five percent moment' can only *be* experienced and enjoyed *in the moment* as a result – the end result (of a Ruins output) is a synthesis of all of the 'five percent moments'.

Sharing the remaining 'five percent' with the listening public is not without reward, compensation or satisfaction. To get to the point where someone actually says that the music is good, where it is introduced on an American radio station by someone with an American accent, makes things very worthwhile indeed to Johnny and his band (Barnes, 1988). Such recognition acts as the considered fine distinction between success and failure, it *makes things happen* and can be experienced in the slightest of doses (sometimes via just a single email, webpage comment or a verbal aside at a gig), but always confirms that the effort is worthwhile. In Johnny's life, that five percent of creative time is itself diluted down to provide a smaller detection of excitement, but 'recognition' in whatever form can confirm creative legitimacy.

> **Johnny:** *being in a band* is 95 percent shit and hard work and five percent of excitement [...] you have to go through so much for so little – I mean, there must be easier things to do, to go through all that rubbish to get that one comment that makes you think 'OK, that was worth doing'.

At our first meeting, a couple of months away from turning 50, he was adamant that creativity was a continual, natural process where 'you have to do it; it's something to look back upon, something to enjoy'. Thus, anchoring the music in the present and 'casting' its value *into the future* is a strong working philosophy that he repeats. John Berger echoes this idea, stating that songs hope 'to reach a listening ear in some future somewhere', the song effectively casting from the past, with fleeting liminality in the present, and into an imagined future where '[s]ongs [...] lean forward' (Berger, 2016: 95). Success, to Johnny, is about leaning into a future and 'trying to find those people' who like your music; it is a quest to communicate, and this requires a committed and talented band that performs like a *team*.

Pausing our conversation, he announced that he had organised a 'surprise' for me and proceeded to drive us up to a preliminary round FA Cup tie in a suburb of Derby. After chatting in the Club bar while sipping soft drinks we took our seats in the functional grandstand and continued our conversation about matters of music and life and death and teamwork (while intermittently watching the match). Johnny turned to me, as the home team struggled against higher league opponents, and made one last profound comment before we parted. Bands are like football teams, he inferred. Bands reflect real life scenario's too. 'If one part of that team doesn't function, you're fucked', he stated as the away team simultaneously crowned the moment by scoring yet another goal. Less than half an hour later, after the daylight faded faster than the quality of the football, while standing in the dark in the car park waiting for the traffic to disperse Johnny lit up a cigarette and leaned on the roof of the car. 'A lot of stuff over the years has just *happened*; it wasn't planned; you just sort of end up *living* it', he said. It seemed a perfect coda to the day and a statement that articulated how art can be experienced as a soaring sub-narrative of life, sometimes a little more audible or visible to some people, but always there, valued and celebrated. We agreed that I would return soon to watch the band in action, in an evening rehearsal for the 50th birthday gig, interpreting the inventory of songs at their disposal and firmly on their own natural territory.

2.1.   The Function of Creativity: Writing Repertoire

This was a very private space; it was a sanctum where anything was possible and where a culture of creativity harnessed a deeper, personal state of awareness. Less than a week after Johnny and I had departed the football match I was sitting in a suburban house in north Derby with a notepad in my hand and a pair of headphones on my head watching four men (soon to be five) running through a musical repertoire. This was a rehearsal of a middle-aged band in the *home* of the drummer, taking place in an extension built solely to provide a space to write and record music, complete with an array of expensive sound recording consoles, computers, acoustic and electric instruments and electronic drum kit. In the corner of the small room sat a corner sofa too; it was a compact, welcoming, comfortable space for a band to experiment and hone their songs. On first impressions, watching The Ruins in rehearsal, the sound quality is exemplary and the musicianship is tight, occasionally virtuoso and redolent of a curious mixture of styles that combine well. It is difficult to pigeonhole: vocals, bass and guitar all adding layers of stylistically influenced sound (punk, funk, 1980s 'alternative' distorted, occasionally shimmering guitars etc.) set to a background of solid, conventional rock drumming. What is 'different' about this primary experience of a Ruins rehearsal is the affected sense of *studio-style isolation*. Gone are the draughty rehearsal rooms in semi-derelict urban warehouses of previous eras, carpets nailed to damp walls for soundproofing and the incessant hum of amplifier speakers and rattling, hissing snare drum wires. Age and responsibility has transported us to suburbia where musicians stand closely together, wear headphones, plug their respective instruments (including electronic drum kit) and microphones into a mixer, close their eyes and *contribute* to a produced sound (rather than *compete* in a slightly uncontrollable, largely unmanaged cacophony of energy). To be sure, the musicians are *present*, sharing space, communicating with each other through microphones that is heard in the headphones, but my initial curiosity in the uniqueness of the situation soon transmogrifies into a perception of sterility, safeness and *comfort*; this is a creative studio space and a convivial venue for middle-aged musicians to play, create, record and discuss their art free from the bedevilment of the clock, the cold and the hassle of regular commuting to and from rented rooms *avec equipment*.

Despite the wearing of headphones often being perceived as a privatising or 'personalisation' of musical experience (Blake, 2007), there is an immediate sense that the band understands effective 'separating' in rehearsal as contributing to a sense of *coming closer together*; they are sympathetic to each other's contribution and no-one is fighting to be heard above the others. Duncan, The Ruins' guitarist, (short, red-haired, slim and full of friendly, erudite intensity) explains that '[in conventional rehearsal] you can't hear each other; it's just not a conducive way of working at all'. The contemporary method is cherished as *productive*, facilitating something better musically and socially. The comparator of the 'home studio' and the conventional 'rehearsal room' is a clinching factor in the band's decision to use technology rather than an *open musical space* of a rehearsal room. For instance, CJ (the band's bassist), spent half an hour talking me through his equipment as he unpacked, describing the 'biographies' of his guitars, the connection of the instruments with people and places and times. It is not lost on him (or Duncan) that, in a traditional rehearsal space, this kind of relaxed attitude to time would be verboten by convention.

> **CJ:** [...] you don't have to pay for two hours [...] one eye on the clock all the time
>
> **Duncan:** You've got another band knocking on the door at eight o'clock or whatever because they're due to go in and you've got to get out; three flights of stairs!

Time now belongs to the band and they can do as they please. Should they wish, 'rehearsal' functions as a weekly social gathering where music and daily life can be discussed. Johnny says that they now have the luxury of spending 'the first half hour discussing everyone's problems!' This creates a togetherness that is valued. 'When you're in a band, you've got to like the people that you're with [...]', Duncan says, adding that 'the music's the core, but if we didn't enjoy being here we couldn't create'. Thus, it is clear that rehearsal in the studio, with headphones, is a social and creative experience.

> **Duncan:** We are making a racket; it's just confined to headphones [...] you've still got the visual connection [...] it's still as intimate as the old rehearsal room; it's intimacy with some comfort.
>
> **Johnny:** You're not having to shout at each other! [...] in an old rehearsal room, if you're trying to talk you can't hear what you're saying. Here, you just take the headphones off and people know exactly what you're saying.
>
> **Duncan:** You've got two worlds — the normal world and the headphone world.

Thus, there is a distinction between the 'world' of sound and the 'world' of verbal communication and sociality. The headphones are taken off and 'you're back in the room'. What happens *in* the room is important, but it is also not necessarily seen as the dynamic of creativity. Johnny clarifies this by stating that 'you're not necessarily taking what's in the surroundings of your practice room as making you creative, it's what you're seeing in the week that makes you creative'.

> **Duncan:** [t]he environment is important [...] It doesn't create the creativity but when you are being creative it's far easier to channel it, to bring it to a focus quicker and to record it quicker. So, just because it's a nice, comfortable area doesn't make it more creative per se, but when you are on a roll you're not going to lose it because you've got the recordings, [...] everyone's listening to each other, it just compresses the time between that initial spark that you can get anywhere and bringing it to a fruition.

Rehearsal is considered a *place* that houses spontaneity, and the home studio — and its comforts — assists in achieving this. Draughty, 'acoustic' rehearsal rooms, where music is performed 'live' are considered simply 'gigs with no audience' and not the place for creation and innovation. Duncan, recalling such places, stated that the band would 'practice gigs' at such external rehearsal spaces. 'We would set up and face away from the [drum] kit, as if facing an audience', he says, 'but we didn't like it; it had no connectivity'. The difference, these days, is that they can gather at *the space that is rehearsal* and do whatever comes spontaneously, recording their ideas and mixing their sound to understand nuances and exploit strengths. Writing repertoire requires less intensity than in the past, but has greater yield with the home facility. Ian, tall, slim and with gregarious mannerisms, explains how his home studio delivers this balance.

> **Ian:** We're less ambitious, but it's easier to obtain the finished article […] in the past […] you'd put them onto cassette […] that's as good as you get […] but now, you can do it all from home, and cheaply […] you can record it at home, you can bang it onto CD at home, it's so much easier to achieve that.

There is a sense that the original essence of organic creativity has at once become both sterilised by the abundance of modern, affordable machinery and technology, found 'in the home' – in this case, Ian's home – as well as become democratised by age, affluence and venue. In the past, a belief in something rough, raw, was also a belief in something *ready* for listening – a statement, however imperfect. This, in effect, is revisited and realised once more through the bustle and arguable disorganisation of creative rehearsal. The 'run through', complete with headphones, *is* just recital, but held in more comfortable surroundings and with the facility of technology to record for posterity and revision but not, crucially, considered a final, listenable artefact.

It begins with the acceptance of the studio as a facility that translates an abundant time capital into an abundance of *possibilities*; it moves through the acceptance of the facility as something that could not have existed in earlier years, as musicians using the pay-per-hour facilities of the city, shared with other bands and into a space and time that is unintentionally – but productively – harnessed for the *creative* muse as well as the pursuit of *perfections*. There is also a third factor that appears: production. Where recital and creativity might be considered 'soft' yield, production must be considered hard yield; this is where the 'soft inventiveness' meets something of a statement of bold resistance to the cultural hegemony of 'middle age routine'. Music is not just about creation but also *affirmation*. The transitory, situational output is one such affirmation.

Thus, Ian's studio, as Duncan says, 'is not just about rehearsal and creativity, it's also about the production of material'. The studio is an industrious and social facility – made possible via the fruits of labour, age, experience and the pooled income of Ian and his wife – and facilitates the very existence of The Ruins. Middle age hands a conciliatory prize to those who have missed out on the euphoria of commercial stardom in the manifestation of a cosy, modern studio within which to write, play, socialise and *plan* – but not, necessarily, *dream*. Middle age, therefore, does impact upon – or *shape* – the structure of creative worlds via such enhanced individual financial capital, incremental wisdom and the mellowing of cold ambition. It also arguably *fragments* the sociality of a band and dulls collective aspiration. The studio – the *space* of rehearsal – is therefore a stage for the *process* of *rehearsing self-efficacy*; 'rehearsal' is an opportunity to resist that cultural and economic hegemony of 'middle age' and is an example of a 'creative mezzanine', *an in-between state* that occupies the central point of symmetry between individual self-realisation and the mundane liminality of 'middlescence' (Blaikie, 1999: 184). This feature of the mezzanine is the point where the artists synchronously desire to maintain their sanguine and contented status of middle-aged life while experiencing the abandon and freedom of youth once again. This is not nostalgia; this is simply being in a band to chase the lost love of 'genuineness' in the moment where the creative muse delivers, before such genuineness is lost to simple *musical accord*.

The rehearsal studio is the venue of experience, where art may or may not *come*. Rehearsal is an *action*, viewed as necessary but, in effect, disputed as a function. A few decades ago, in Liverpool, Sara Cohen spent most of her time observing bands in rehearsal (Cohen, 1991: 47), understanding the dynamics of the bands she followed and the social spheres that they both attracted and – sometimes – developed and encouraged. She recognised the distinction and combination of rehearsal and creativity and observed the hardship of cost, the genuine dangers of equipment theft (ibid.: 48), the crucial centrality of making synergy between creative activity and performance and the time-consuming effort of advertising such events (ibid.: 67) as well as additional strains on finance, time and self-efficacy. The Ruins are different; their rehearsal is not geared to such strategy or latent anxieties.

2.2. Rehearsal and Supervention of Novelty: Value, Aesthetics and Feeling the Moment

'Art is a social product' declared Janet Wolff, the product 'of real, historical factors' (Wolff 1993: 1); it is 'a creation of individual members [of society], who, in their turn, are in many ways formed *by* society' (Wolff, 1975: 7, *original emphasis*). Art can also be described as being a discursive, phenomenological process (Berger & Luckmann, 1966) seeing appraisal of creative self clearly geared towards the way that individuals articulate a worldview (opinion, knowledge and expertise) and – in the instance of The Ruins – share desire to make original, legitimate output. Arnold Hauser (1982 [1974]) also connected the notion of the social production of art, quasi-phenomenology and the central idea that culture creates art – broadly echoed by Paul Willis, who also suggests that culture as a way of life naturally produces art that is ostensibly *aesthetic* (Willis, 2005: 74) – but also that there is a *dialectic* at work understood via reasoning, negotiation and consensus, stating that

> Just as social totality comes about not through the summation of individual attitudes but by the functions individuals perform only after they have come into contact with one another, so the unity and totality of works of art do not arise merely as the sum of words, notes, lines and colors. They are the dialectical result of the tension which is renewed, heightened and sharpened from word to word, note to note, and brush-stroke to brush-stroke, whereby the structure of the whole arises *pari passu* with the differentiation of the details. (Hauser, 1982 [1974]:70 *original emphasis*)

The Ruins have a similar dialectic, but where does the process start? It is an individual dynamic, drawn from the biography, harnessed and utilised through influence and resistance to a perceived peripheral authoritative determinism, linking the creation of sound to labour and the sociality of such creation?

> **Duncan:** I don't have music in my family, but I do have art [...] I started picking up on music when I was eleven or twelve; I was interested in *listening* to it before then, but [...] it was watching a Beatles film — *Let It Be* — that was the first thing that kind of thought 'well, I've heard their music and I can see them playing it now so, do you know what, I can make that link between hearing it and seeing people playing it'. [*original emphasis*]

The Ruins see rehearsal as something of an action that can achieve unspecified ends, ostensibly linking *playing* music with the sense of creative resistance; there are no plans, no agenda and (occasionally) no music, but just a sense of togetherness. This is camaraderie, but also reflexivity and a corroboration of shared value and values. When something *does* emerge the band is alert to its potential; an automatic shared aesthetic bonds the band together. Raymond Williams suggested that aesthetics can be considered a 'sense activity as the basis of art and beauty as distinct [...] from *social* or *cultural* interpretations' (Williams, [1976] 2014: 30, *original emphasis*) and aesthetic value — in this instance, subjective beauty in sound — could be seen to exist *beyond* the influences of biography, peers or media and come from within and, ostensibly, *how you feel*. Art should also not be shrouded in clandestine mystique, interpreted as the product of otherworldliness via the imaginative realisation of elevated individuals — untouchable, distant and beyond reproach. Inside the sealed mutuality of rehearsal there is a sense that the music that is created and amended has — fleetingly — similar essence to the lingering emotional impression left by the initial impact of important tunes that cling to our consciousness and our biographies (Green, 2016). The aesthetic, therefore, is experienced in the moment of purest creation — where genuineness is briefly experienced. Consequently, Simon Frith (1987: 101–102) explains that access to songs is usually through their words, but the words are *felt* through the music. Words, he suggests, are the lubricant of social use; the song does not 'reflect' the emotion of the listener, but instead empowers the listener to articulate their innermost emotion. This is true of The Ruins in the moment of genuineness, of creation, of realisation of legitimacy as a middle-aged amateur musician. There is a sense that everyone has input, which creates an organic technique for what Ian calls 'stirring emotions'. The songs start with the music, with some 'lyrical rhythms' considered in the creative stew of sound before *sense* is applied to lyrics. This latter method is understood via lyrics reflecting the music being generated, seeing life itself, and the experiences of the band, reflected into such music and further generated by proximity.

> **Duncan:** You are finding where the words fit rhythmically — it's
> an old jazz style, so there's a rhythm and a beat to the song and
> you come up with any old random words that fit the beat [...]
> that first time that we'll do a song, the lyrics are not necessarily
> meaningful [...]

As Christian (1987: 231) states, 'musical composition is taking place continu-
ously in a jazz performance both individually and collectively' and, on balance,
this is also true for The Ruins in their rehearsal place. However, as meaning
begins to develop there is a belief that the musicians are drawing from each
other's well of cultural/creative 'capital', leaning on years of learning through
experience in both instrumental musicianship as well as through the lessons of
growing up and growing older. In other words, they *trust each other more* and,
as Duncan states, they somehow want each other to succeed in their collectivity
and their mutual task of making something happen.

> **Duncan:** You don't listen to each other as musicians [when you're
> younger], you're very much focused on yourself [...] the drummer
> will be looking at the drums and the guitarist will be looking at
> the guitar because you're still learning and also still trying to be
> louder than anybody else [...] we don't have that with this band
> [...] partly because we have the massive benefit of coming here
> [to the rehearsal/recording studio] and we're all facing each other
> [...] and we're *forgiving* of each other. [*emphasis added*]

Everyone has a role and each member trusts that the person *in* the role will
succeed. They recognise each individual contribution as a collective, supporting
each other and encouraging development. In private, in the studio, the band
members mutually lose the *organic* originality, concentrating instead on mental
and musical *segmentation*; they effectively disembed the music from a state of
organic completeness, looking for reciprocal originality, genuineness and attack
the prevailing musical idea as a task that must be instantaneously perfected.

It follows that they keep a permanent record of all their creative rehearsal
(something that was not possible years ago when younger and with less financial
capital), which they will occasionally use to refresh the creative process — existing, primarily, as a 'reference' to build on next time. They have 'hundreds' of
such 'started songs' that sit in unfinished, partially recorded, states. Duncan
explains that 'the art is capturing what it was about that [rehearsal] that was
unique and the hard graft [...] is to bolt something onto that'. A song will then
emerge from this process and will be altered and 'perfected' in rehearsed states
until ready to record as a final 'version'. The genuine 'work of art' that is effectively altered and reproduced emerges from this phase of creation, built upon collective will, trust and faith and camaraderie that exist in this private sphere. On
stage they are performers; in private — once a week — they are *artists*.

Duncan: we all do jobs during the day that are relatively mundane and relatively routine [...] when you come along to [rehearsal] the gloves are off, we don't know what we're going to achieve that night but, on so many levels, it's new, we will *achieve something new* [...] it's stimulating your senses that, at our age with all the other stuff that's going on, are not being stimulated in other ways. [*emphasis added*]

They have seen it all before, they are, as Duncan continues, 'anaesthetised against all the triggers emotionally − after a band rehearsal, you know that you've been through an experience that's *unique*' [*emphasis added*]. There is always improvement to be had from running through things but, as Ian states, 'when you come out with something that gets you going you're like "we're onto something here you know!" You get a buzz from it'. This is indicative of the *buzz of not knowing*; the band is high on anticipation, of confirmation of continued musical legitimacy as individuals, realised through their mutual reliance of collectivity. The moment the composition is committed to tape it is 'gone'. Thus, rehearsal is a *stage* where the sacred is discovered, toyed with and ultimately exploited; it is where genuineness is practiced before it is wilfully abandoned by *recording* and the process is begun again. Such initial joyous abandon is ultimately reduced to perfunctory chronicling before novelty is once more sought, as Ian explains:

Ian: I record my drums [...] in patterns, [...] I'll set it up and break it down into bars or eighths and then I'll play eight bars on the drums and that'll be that, and then I'll go onto the next piece [...] it's mechanical really.

We bear witness, in this ethnography of artistic creativity, to the conception of art in the moment by a sequestered reflexive culture of musicianship before the audible, hitherto invisible, aesthetic is recognised, momentarily cherished and destroyed in the committal for posterity. Accordingly, there is an effect on the producers who are also the *listeners* − a process that reveals an *intra-poetics* of creation, consequently drifting beyond hermeneutic interpretation and centring, simply, on the emotion of the moment. It does not matter what the song is *about*; it matters so much what the song *feels like* to those who have 'found it'. It arises from a pre-existing 'knowledge'; there is a sense of 'what good sounds like' and what 'good *should* sound like'.

Art, to T. S. Eliot (Eliot, 1919; Kermode, 1975) is a synchronic creation always affecting the wider diachronic narrative of the specific oeuvre − developing a sense that the new art form will affect our views of what already exists while being a product *of* the art that has come before via established genres and preceding work in the field. This relationship, what Eliot calls 'supervention of novelty', is present in the rehearsal and creativity of The Ruins, with the synchronic genuineness arguably disembedding from the narrative in its genuine purity with an assured *liminality* of which the musicians are partially aware. However, as Eliot (Eliot, 1919; Kermode, 1975) suggests, this artistic essence can never be *completely pure* because of the influence of encompassing tradition. However, while the sound may have traditional, quasi-structural influence, the creative fusion is found by chance; the band drift back and forth between their own musical indulgences within a rhythm and tacit agreement of genre and the collective unanimity of sound being created by four musicians seeking correlation. They drift from unification to individual isolation; there is an innate awareness of structure but not of production. Leadership of innovation varies between members; they pull and push each other creatively within the agreed boundaries of songs, developing ideas, genuineness in the moment. The rehearsal is also physical habitation of space; it is communicative in emotion, expertise and physicality.

> **Ian:** You're suddenly creating something that is making you buzz [...] it's probably more about wavelengths that we actually understand you know?
>
> **Duncan:** It flows [...] you are unified, you then drift apart — it's not a linear thing, it's a wave, up and down.
>
> **Ian:** I'm not 100 percent aware of where everything [is, or] of what everyone else is doing.
>
> **Duncan:** As an individual you have your responsibility to do your bit [...] Ian can't decide to go too far off-piste because he has to drag us with him [...] the lead changes like a relay race really, the baton passes from one person to another [...] and you've always got to be with them or, at least, within sight of them [but] if you can get yourself into that plane of not actually thinking but being purely intuitive that's a rare space to be [...] there comes a point [...] where you simply have to run through and you almost disengage from what the song originally was, you are almost by rote, you are playing it because you know you've got to and it doesn't have the same impact [...] it becomes a process.

Replication, therefore, is simply another way of articulating disengagement. There is, to all intents and purposes, a sense of *forgery* in the replication found in music and art and, in some cases, *literature*. Jonathan Bate suggests that a 'paradox of literature' is 'the simultaneous presence and absence of the author' (Bate, 2010: 38–39); the 'written voice' is that of the creator and, consequently, the reader then becomes the 'author' via interpretation. Science, continues Bate, is a *predictable* thing; literature is not. Literature is communicated, but is it also created uniquely. Science is predictable insofar as someone would eventually end up doing 'it' whereas, with artistic creation (in the case of Bate's argument, *literary*) it is chance and uniqueness that ends up creating the work of art in question. The art is sprung from imagination and toil but is somehow given to others to process. It is *shared*; this 'death of the author' parallel (Barthes, 1977) can also be applied to the creation and committal of music to tape. Thus, art does not need *evidence* to be legitimate per se, and while art must be mechanically reproduced to survive (cf. Benjamin, [1923] 2008), it cannot be *replicated*. It is through their written voice that The Ruins communicate to the outside world, not necessarily or uniquely via performance. Gigs are organisational, functional but their *works of art* are 'found' in rehearsal; art is also rehearsed in rehearsal; the art is mechanically reproduced *once* in recording and the moment of creation and the embodiment of the reproduced art cannot ever be reproduced accurately, creating one original (genuine), a second faithful reproduction and a third phase of *legitimate forgery*. Rehearsal is therefore, if no genuineness is forthcoming, merely *forging the repertoire*.

Supervention of novelty is a process where art is created, disrupts and reorders the existing oeuvre, where art is influenced by art but somehow 'damages' the perfection of the art that came before. This is a blueprint for The Ruins in rehearsal: they practice destruction and re-invention and fleeting glimpses of genuineness. The value of this process to the middle-aged musician is aesthetic and functional, a defiance of formality and a utilisation of power where cultural, social and economic capitals of musicians in middle age are most faithfully exploited. To 'make' the song and then play it again and again and again is simply a process of seeking to obtain a new, original aura (Benjamin, [1923] 2008: 9) each time without recourse to an 'original product' (recording). Rehearsal is a cyclical routine time that locates 'newness' in 'old' and offering the perpetual *promise* of creating genuineness from nothing. It is at the same time both *profane variation* and *legitimate originality*. Once the song is completed as a recording it exists as a *unique piece of art* but one that can only be *improvised* within the public field or imitated in a cover version (forgery). Rehearsal offers the chance to practice the creative muse and experience the nexus between imagination and creative legitimacy without committal.

Several of the works cited above, notably Finnegan ([1989] 2007) and Cohen (1991), suggest that rehearsal is a location of creativity, but it is ostensibly prioritised as a preparation for performance, a recital of existing composition as well as an occasional setting of creation; song writing tends to take place elsewhere, honed in-session at rehearsal. The Ruins do not conform to this accepted norm; they use rehearsal differently, because they have the studio facility to do so and less time in everyday life to commit to song writing individually. Middle age means less time to think, dream, consider and write − there is more to it than, as earlier discussed, 'trying to look ten years younger' (Hepworth & Featherstone, 1982: x); the rehearsal offers convenient time-out from everyday commitments to create and is mostly *done together*. Therefore, the band is not 'public' at all − its *image, product* and *performances* are public, but the band itself is *private*, offstage. Membership is closed, closely guarded and such negotiated familiarity produces finished music. Rehearsal is territorial, intimate, dramaturgically *offstage* (Goffman, 1959); a band naked *with* their art, *in transitory communion with their creativity* and their biographical, experientially informed standpoints, malleable opinion, honed expertise and expansive, sophisticated imaginations. Rehearsal is therefore not only the recitation, considered repetition of existing music and the honing of originality, it also represents a palpable tension between artistic purity and compromise, bearing witness to the created art and the subsequent touching up and subtle alteration of such art; rehearsal is a negotiated compromise between the pure moment of creation and its *accepted violation*. This is a private sphere embodiment of originality contrasting with the public *performance of facsimilia* that are merely 'versions' with fluid properties via interpretative dynamics of emotion and a susceptibility to error, wilful amendment and abandonment. Performance is both the *artists and audience* bearing witness to disembedded and transitory *performers* rather than offering a peek at the *artist at the place of work*. It can be argued that The Ruins exist as an entity *of* rehearsal, *in* rehearsal, in *private*; live performance is merely art taken out of its genuine setting and delivered for subjective interpretation by the witnesses in the crowd and *on the stage*.

The Ruins in rehearsal is creative, artistic and pragmatic (Dewey, 2009), illustrating simultaneous innovative musical creativity and reproduction, synchronic function and repeated application of the values of learned creativity for the purposes of finding something new, original and exciting while *owning the moment* in a way that Walter Benjamin – speaking in this instance of the historical development of techniques of reproduction of art – would suggest was 'the here and now of the work of art – its unique existence in the place where it is at this moment' (Benjamin, [1923] 2008: 5). Rehearsal is a theatre of the *immediate*, art *in the moment*, always *situated* in its purest original form. Performance, formal recording and perfecting, photography, media presence and so on is simply extraneous after-product and justification, where the art is *reproduced*. Rehearsal is the purest 'capture' of the essence of what it is to be creative, *in a band*, expressing individuality and collectivity simultaneously and *experiencing* art rather than producing it as a *commodity*. Benjamin argues that 'genuineness is not reproducible' (ibid.: 38*n*), thus situating rehearsal as an ephemeral, fluid collectivity of instantaneous properties (notes, ideas, mistakes and praxis), every one thing in imperfect union, original, artistic and somehow never to be efficaciously captured but always chased, perfected, *replicated*: this is the hidden joy of rehearsal and what *genuineness* is. Julie Sanders states that Benjamin may have considered the post-creative 'deconstruction' of aura as being an act of liberation for the original art itself (Sanders, 2016: 192). The rehearsal may just be the liberation *before* the replication (recording); art is consequently never an *original* physical or audible *product* for The Ruins (or, arguably, other bands who record versions of their repertoire), but is *experienced* intimately, in transient form, uncaptured but eventually *recalled* via recording. The inspiration and incentive for, in this instance, middle-aged *men* to continue to make music is therefore nothing to do with chasing the fruits of economic capital and power (or adulation and respect) but is simply explained as *authorship* and the moment of subjective legitimacy obtained in the momentary fusion of creation and rehearsal. Rehearsal is, at once, the *process of creation and the process of destruction* of a work of art, the theatre of industrious fraternisation and individualisation, spontaneous invention, consolidated creation and artistic forgery. Often overlooked for its function, it is perhaps the point where musicianship and liberty, self-imposed marginalisation and self-efficacy combine to create, for The Ruins, a perfect, hermetically-sealed space to retreat into to forget the shifting, pressured time-narratives of 'middlescence' and the imposed cultural hegemony of the delineations of success.

§

In this chapter I have introduced The Ruins and explained how they consider their creative process as a series of stages, happenings and random chances and as well as a dream-like unity achieved, as Johnny Marr stated earlier, as a moment of unified 'magic' where music, as The Ruins have explained, happens 'instinctively and intricately' (Marr, 2016). This instinct is priceless and fickle, difficult to summon at will but best found, if not omnipresent, in the *in-between place* that is rehearsal. However, following on from the experience of writing music in the moment, what of the experience of actually being in a band?

Chapter 3

Music, Sociality and Identity

The creative process brings on a sense of being lost in a moment of aura, of originality and of *legitimacy* but there is also a colder, more quantifiable aspect of *being in a band*. This functional essence goes beyond the moment of creation and attaches itself to an idea of individual and collective *identity* — of who you are and how you respond to the function of the band and its transference into the public domain. Thus, there is an additional theme of sociality and exhibition that prevents the band being permanently 'hidden', forcing it out into the gaze of an audience. In this chapter I will explore the idea of what it means to contribute to a collective, the anticipations and expectations of live performance and the juxtaposition of music, creativity, exhibition and midlife. In other words, we know how they do it, but *why* do they do it and what *value* does it have?

3.1.   Motives and the Forces of Progression

A band is, of course, a sum of the parts, an instrumental unit that — in this instance — meets once a week and dissolves at the end of the evening. *Transience* is paramount within this creative social 'contract', itself a largely subliminal concept and something that peaks in unison and ebbs away into the hours and days that they are apart. Understanding the dynamics of the motives of creativity is hard to pin down.

> **Duncan:** It's quite a big challenge for us to analyse motives, because as a musician, by and large, you don't; the creativity is almost a separate thing that exists on its own and sometimes it meets other creativity and it creates a product but you don't *analyse* it.

Creativity thus — to paraphrase Williams (1981) — becomes a noun as well as a verb. It is about *doing*, but is also a *thing* and that *thing* is difficult to understand *before* the event, only notable *after* it and is also a process that requires other inputs in this instance — it can only be perceived as something creative by being *socio-generative*. It is as if the kernel of an idea is just that — an *idea* — before it is certified as valid, as creative and as *useful* in a group dynamic. Prior to the socio-generative moment, the creativity is simply *potential*. The Ruins' members have creative moments external to their group dynamic, but in all cases detected and spoken of the creativity is pre-channelling a Ruins song or a song that is, ostensibly, to be used in conjunction with significant others (Ian, for example, writes and records 'solo' work that often involves other members of the band as supporting inputs as well as Duncan's additional work with previous colleagues in Derby band, The One-Eyed Jacks). This organic connectivity with other musicians is simply a manifestation of the 'scene' (Bennett, 2006; Bennett & Peterson, 2004; Cohen, 1991) or the 'art world' (Becker, [1982] 2008; Crossley & Bottero, 2015) in which the musicians partake (currently and in the past). As previously mentioned, The Ruins were formed on the shock wave that split up Johnny's previous band (the sudden death of a member) and that band – Exit the Network – had been formed on the back of a reunion and consequent split of Johnny's previous band, The Stance. This 'musical community' is not unique to Derby – far from it – and the natural genealogy of bands is almost a *de rigueur* involvement factor in local musical 'family tree' histories by way of the epistemic defending of acquired genuineness and strength (there is, if anything, always the essence of a local 'super-group' lingering in the air of any moderately successful band). Johnny has written about the 'scenes' of Derby himself (Vincent, 2008) and continues to be an advocate of the creative muse, the spirit of recording and performance and the value of knowing your own patch's history. The Ruins are just the latest in a long line of bands; what makes them special is that they are the combination of people who *still want to do it*.

Being in a band during midlife may therefore have a multiplicity of value and a myriad meaning but it is clearly something that the members of The Ruins intend to continue to practice. There is also a 'philosophy' of the group, where creativity meets logistics and the *modus operandi*. Thus, as the research continued, the band were joined by a second guitarist/keyboardist called Miles. Hailing from Ian's home town of Burton-on-Trent, Miles is a qualified teacher and experienced musician, well-read with a large presence and welcoming attitude to reasoning on the value of participation in the creative arts. 'I used to sit, fascinated, watching my dad play things at the piano; I always sat there and thought 'I wish I could do that',' he says as we sit in a coffee shop inside a supermarket on a cold November evening. Like many, his love for popular music comes from an 'inherited' appreciation of music as sound and as physical artefact via elder sibling's record collections. He goes a long way back with Ian – through school and teenage years – and was invited to join the band prior to CJ's unexpected departure, expanding The Ruins to a five-piece band and consequently developing their sound. Miles was a good fit, having similar musical tastes and similar musical 'ideology' to the others; he was, in short, cut from the same cloth, the same age group and had similar art world battle scars. 'I fucking hate *routine* […]', he says with a mixture of mild resentment, emotion and humour, his square face (that sits under a mass of vertically sticking-up hair) emitting a big, broad smile, 'I hate the idea that something is organised to the point where you can't do anything *spontaneously*'. Experiencing unemployment, he says that his days presently have little routine or structure but that his intermittent insomnia causes late-night creativity; he considers himself a somewhat involuntary night owl and thinks that the intervention of what can be thought of as conventional 'working life' affects his creativity. This is interesting, as Miles is clear that normative sleep patterns can zap the creative muse. To him, being *close to sleep* is a creative 'inter-zone', the *verge* of sleep is where the *mind is wandering*. Occasionally, he wakes up in the night with tunes in his head, necessitating a requirement to get up and write down the melodies before they dissolve into blackness. He says that he battles with concentration but that music helps him forget his problems and he can relax, concentrate and lose himself in the creative process, adding that he releases angst and imagery through the writing of poetry; it is an intensely personal thing he says, looking into my eyes and adding that *the passion and the will* 'sits here' while gently thumping his chest, 'it allowed me to express feelings and thoughts'. Alongside poetry there is a personal set of values that condense parity and fraternity. 'I hate seeing injustice and that's why a group dynamic works for me – it's all equal parts', he states, taking a massive gulp of cappuccino. Miles sees himself as a different person when at home with the family and with the band or friends, an interesting separation but with no favourable distinction between the binary – family is separate from the band, but both have function and give him joy and meaning. 'Music gave me the opportunity to express one of those facets of my personality that wouldn't ordinarily be out there [...] as a child I always felt that I hadn't got a voice', he says. The Ruins give him that voice as part of a unit, their togetherness makes Miles feel together as a person.

As I inferred above, there is a sense that The Ruins' *togetherness* expands beyond the initial functioning unit of five people. Sometimes the muse can be experienced in fragmented form, amongst constituent parts of the band, but shared nevertheless and making frequent the sense of novelty and excitement. Ian and Miles, for example, have a splinter project that utilises Ian's studio when The Ruins are absent and Duncan has been involved in reunions of previous bands that he has played in as well as the continued role of family. Ian – as I will expand below – is the only band member with young children (he also has a grown-up child too) – but he, along with the rest, is mindful of family and the role that they play in permitting the band to exist and function. I asked Duncan if the band are 'in debt' to anyone or anything, the debt being less literal than metaphorical in context. It is, he says, 'owed to the people who support what we do [...] It's owed more to our families', who deal with the loss of time, occasional invasion of privacy, disruption of routines that exist predominantly as a result of recording, playing live, rehearsing and so on. Throughout the research I met the band's partners and wives but I did not interview them, engaging instead in idle chatter and appreciating the sense of participation, support and forgiveness in their partners' preoccupations with creativity. The band members themselves were, it must be stressed, vocally appreciative for such space to create, perform and socialise. The 'forces of progression' may therefore be summarised as the *inclination* to continue, the *support* that a band receives from significant others and competitors and the sense of togetherness experienced both as a unit and as participants within the broader art world of the gigging rock community. As Duncan sums up, there is a clear incentive to continue to produce, play and write new repertoire when significant others across the board, from family to competitor to colleague, show significant empathy for suffering for the cause of art – especially when channeled through the exhilaration and apprehension of performance.

> **Duncan:** There's a lot of *schadenfreude* [amongst musicians] occa-
> sionally after a gig [...] you do get people who come up and say,
> 'that was really good', and that is a massive boost really. It kind
> of justifies partly why you do stuff and then you remember that
> as to why you want to carry on doing it.

The 'outside' (biography, family, variations in working practices) clearly influences and shapes the 'inside', penetrating the creative core of the band and affecting their self-concept and their incentives to continue invention. Progression is perhaps best measured through a combination of original recorded outputs and the bands' visibility to the public. Performance, as opposed to recording, is a situation within the wider set of creative routines where *doing* is the necessity that is particularly notable *after* it has been accomplished.

3.2. Performance and Identity

While The Ruins are a unit of five individuals who see the world in different ways and have differing careers, domestic arrangements and influences, they also value the *collaborative* essence of performance. The band insist that they were initially formed as an almost exclusively 'studio-based project' and that the gigs they undertake are merely a routine that effectively 'announces' their music to the public. The gig is a stage on which to authenticate their recorded output, 'making real' their exploits in the studio and proving to an audience (and to themselves) that they can still 'carry it off up there' in front of an expectant and critical crowd.

The authenticating thrust of 'gigging' is arguably crucial to any band; there must be a moment of 'making public' the work, illustrating the skill used to create and 'own' the songs. Roger Scruton wrote that there is a need for the performing musician to look to be identified accurately as the author of the work and, thus, gain *legitimacy and authenticity* from an audience for doing so (a suitable, accurate and virtuous rendition of a song, etc.) but also to recognise what Scruton calls the 'living tradition' in music via a perception that people hear things differently across time and space, thus making the live performance a little more challenging (Scruton, 1997: 444). Recital (as I mentioned earlier) is anathema, but it is necessary and, consequently, adds – curiously – to the challenge of the gig. While The Ruins do perform 'live' in front of an audience, this 'liveness' (Sanden, 2013) is a different form of live performance to their *studio rehearsals*. Sanden (ibid.) asserts the difficulties in creating a typology of the 'live'; the transmogrification of recording, sampling, performative duty and so on merge with the sense of what he calls a 'traditional liveness' (ibid.: 3) that may, for example, differ from watching a 'live' performance on TV, beamed from Glastonbury *sans* smells and wind gusts across the PA. Despite this 'ontological inappropriateness', Sandon compels us to consider 'the concept of liveness' as 'active in the creation of music's meaning, especially (though not exclusively) at an aesthetic level' (ibid.). It can be perceived as authentic as *performed*, spatial, temporal, spontaneous and corporeal and interactive (ibid.: 11). If anything, The Ruins are playing a gig every time they meet at Ian's house; in person, expressive and assertive (see Merleau-Ponty, 1964). In other words, the studio offers space for the creative muse whereas the stage offers little space to diversify, but both are 'live' by definition. The challenge is arguably to make the live recital crisp, clean, lifelike, exciting, reflexive and somehow consequently entirely *unique* to the time and place. If anything, it is disembedding the song from the recorded entity, re-embedding it with liminal impact in a public space (with a 'mood' and an atmosphere and acoustics and tensions and so on) and disembedding it once more on conclusion from the present without losing its initial emotional impact on the listener experienced elsewhere. Of course, gigs can also be where people *hear things first* – adding to the aura of the living tradition but also adding a requirement to recite the song accurately, with little deviation, as a platform for potential sales. However, as Bennett ([1980] 2017) suggested, the relative disparity between live sound and recorded sound – while, arguably 'part of the understanding' between producer and audience in live performance contexts – was narrowed by the rise in electronic/digital devices and processes that could arguably enable both more organic sounding recording and more accurate reproductions of complexities on-stage. Playing live, in short, is about balance, compromise and the drive to create accuracy in combination with exhilaration. It is also a combination of sound, theatrics and the assertion of a soft power over an expectant audience.

Such mutuality of music, performance and power is summarised by Henry Kingsbury who, in attaching the central tenets of Giddens's structuration theory (Giddens, 1976, 1984) to the performative aspect of music, states that 'musical performance (including [...] relations of power), musical meaning, and musical structure are linked in a nexus in which each aspect is both product and producer of the others' (Kingsbury, 1988: 110). As such, bands and, arguably all artists, are engaged in a process where performativity begets meaning begets a holistic command of the artefact (song, painting, novel and so on) that exists separately to the beholder and rests exclusively with the producer in an almost unbreakable grasp despite its ubiquitous *shared exhibition*. In short, The Ruins are playing live simply to add layers of meaning to music that is essentially heard in private while simultaneously asserting their ownership of the music itself via their performance of *their own songs*. 'You take your results out to a wider audience', says Duncan. They trail the gig with some new recording, usually released via their social media outlets and, while not considering live performance as a hiatus – or even a *derailing* – of the creative process, the band contemplate the gig as a moment where 'the door is now open, briefly, to the public'. Performance, to the band, is therefore simply an accompanying activity to the process of music making. 'It just goes with it', says Duncan plainly, while the other members chip in by insisting that The Ruins were never planning to play live at the outset, stating further that the gig does not *add to the music*, they just 'play stuff on stage'; playing live does not make a song anything better or more special, it just isolates it as theirs, delivered straight, with passion and feeling, but straight all the same. There is clearly something of the temporal and spatial in this attitude towards the value of public performance; as The Ruins and I have already elaborated (but is worth revisiting fleetingly), reproduced music (recorded) lacks aura, but there is an argument to suggest that it is 'authenticated' (Auslander, 2008) in live performance, in such a time we also 'hear the record'. In rehearsal, it is arguable that The Ruins 'hear' the final recording ahead of the recording (Sanden, 2013: 34); the band *also* hear different things − beginning with *themselves* and then the band as a *unit*. The group also hear other songs, other tones and riffs and chord structures that are floating around, ready for harvesting into a new version of a developing song that itself is beginning to achieve aura that will be lost in the final version. In many ways, we hear a live version of a song that does not yet exist; the aura is withheld while four identities grapple for dominance as part of the creative process. To this effect, they jam in the studio but not on stage, insisting that being creative does not extend to performance. They feel they do not have the courage to 'freeform' live, contending that they see themselves as accomplished free formers, but that it simply is not part of their live essence. However, their understanding of live work and the form of the song *is* developed; there is an understanding that gigging offers the chance to be special, original and innovative. This emergence into an art world (they resist the external art world, or *community*, of musicians as influences when they are in their aura-drenched jams as much as is possible in order to develop The Ruins' sound) gives them a rare opportunity to *view* the art world and to take stock of its 'condition'. The art world appears initially chaotic, unstructured, not conscientiously put together − but 'with hindsight there might be a structure' considers Duncan. However, it is not necessarily the art world and its structure that dominates the self-perception of the band as a live unit; they are aware that their collective is creative and special. Such specialness comes from their awareness that they are fully in control of their own creative delivery − from beginning to end, they have control of the product. It is best understood in the following exchange:

> **Duncan:** Your 'art world' then; are you saying that that's an overarching term for any kind of creative art?
>
> **PM:** Yes.
>
> **Duncan:** You know, music is so different [...] an artist, like a painter or something, is very solitary thing [...] then a theatre group is a collective of actors and technicians, there is an element of creativity in terms of who's going to write the play but they may be just interpreting a work that is already out there, so that is the equivalent of a covers band [...] what we do is team-based which sets it aside from other art streams.

The status of originality in the music world therefore sets it arguably 'above' the dramatic arts, because, in many ways, the author of a stage play will not, by and large, be responsible for its performance. To be sure, stage direction is an integral part of play writing as far back as Shakespeare (Crystal, 2007; see also Brook, [1968] 2008; Williams, [1954] 1991) – and may include the writer in the cast too – but music, when performed *sans cover versions*, becomes the creators interpreting the art, their own art, over and over again in different settings, to different people, at different times of the day or night, in different seasons and in different moods. Music *creativity* is super-interactive, establishing an inter-activity in creation, in *performance* and in *interpretation*. In many ways, it out-plays all other art forms in its *completeness*. The Ruins recognise that they deliver music live this way; they are pure and complete, inclusive and socio-generative. The author 'dies' (Barthes, 1977) and is then revived each time the song is played, comprising a *ghost* author, a phantasm that *interprets* the ori-ginal while *remaining original* to the end. 'That makes us serial killers!' says Miles. '*Live*, [a song] can take on a will of its own [...] you let go that little bit more [...] we re-write it every time we play it so, in a sense, it's never finished'. Pierre Macherey ([1978] 2006) suggested that literature (and, consequently 'texts' or art) exists to skewer, 'deform' or alter our perception of reality. Thus, this idea can be applied to the instance where every time The Ruins play a song, whether it is in a 'jam' or on a stage, the song is a deliberate distortion of the 'real thing', a way, therefore, of making new art from existing art, remaining suitably close to the original so that the mutation is witnessed rather than lost and the refraction is acknowledged also.

That said, performance art seems to intrigue them – the possibilities are exciting and tempting. The Ruins, says Duncan, are 'a song-based band by and large and, while you can extend *bits* of a song [...] the song is the song is the song'. Johnny chips in that the enjoyment of recently playing their song *Chemical Rush* while improvising on stage gave them an unscheduled 'sense of freedom, going with the music, really banging out, this is ace (!); at other times you don't get that'. Live work, all said, is not their self-confessed speciality; they *are* experienced performers, but the band itself is considered fresh, slightly new, more studio-based and there is a belief that this status should be maintained, continually pursued and celebrated. As a result, there is less will to develop a language of performance but, instead to see performance as a necessity with function.

> **Johnny:** We haven't got to that stage where we can just look at each other and go 'do this'.
>
> **Duncan:** Each time we do a gig it's almost like our first gig, because it's been weeks or months since the previous one [...].
>
> **PM:** So, for The Ruins, the gig is almost like an *event* [...] an event that stands on its own?
>
> **Duncan:** Absolutely stand on their own, every single one is entirely different [...] each one we can pretty much recall.

PM: The dynamic of the band is not gig-based, is there a value in gigs, or do they have to be done to keep a dynamic going?

Johnny: You get your stuff out to people!

In 'getting their stuff out' there is an evident sanguine acceptance of gigging as part of the process of being a creative unit, but getting to the point where they are able to get the stuff out is not without logistical difficulty. They have a 'gig strategy' that sees them forced to occasionally turn down gigs due to members of the band being on holiday, having family matters to deal with and the continual tactics of organising adults who have a variety of responsibilities connected to midlife. Johnny bemoans the fact that they lose so much time to these matters of 'everyday life', the challenge becomes about coordination and hoping that vacancies in venue schedules line up with the bands' own availability. This is something that was not experienced as younger men. 'If a gig came up', says Duncan, 'you probably pretty much dropped anything, probably because you hadn't got anything to drop, whereas now we've got holidays, commitments, work and all these other things that do potentially get in the way'. However, the wider value of the gig is in the immediate feedback that they receive (something that is not possible, in their view, via the releasing of CDs) and 'are a chance to increase your profile', says Ian. They are, he continues, 'a bit of a buzz on the whole [...] quite nerve wracking' but ultimately rewarding both on a collective and individual platform. Regular gigs suppress the nerves he feels, but there is a sense that this anxiety is something the band find productive, invigorating and inspiring despite increasing the omnipresent sense of self-doubt that plagues the members in the run up to the performance. Routine, they suggest, helps them prepare for the big night; getting the balance between confidence and desire is central, of knowing that you can play, you can perform and, crucially, *wanting to do it* as part of the combined output of being in a band.

There is a clear sense that gigs prove something to themselves and to their audience, announcing the band as 'real' via the volume and the virtuosity of their playing. Ian says that the cabinet speakers power out the music, giving the sound 'authority' and communicating both their presence and their intentions. It gives the band a sense of belonging to a community of people as well as a network of music, an art world of musicians, promoters, fans and peripheral onlookers who may dip in and out of the art world based only on chance and circumstance. 'When we supported The Chameleons',[1] says Duncan, 'we got to stand back and say we were on the same stage as The Chameleons, same sound system, same engineer, same back-line; in that sense, it's a validation because we

---

[1]The Chameleons were a band that existed c. 1981−87 and c. 2000−2005. At the point that The Ruins were performing on the bill with the band they were called Chameleons Vox, consisting of bassist-singer/songwriter Mark Burgess and some new/old supporting musician colleagues, playing a set that consisted of Chameleons' originals.

all came from a background of admiring The Chameleons' work'. The gig, in that case, adds another special layer of authenticity to a performers repertoire of identity – namely, the moment where one can say, ostensibly, 'I was there and I stood *with* those who do this professionally'. As a result, the merging of two worlds on a stage creates equality, camaraderie and the continued option to dream and aspire.

This sense of achievement is a very separate thing to the process of being creative. The gig is, as intimated, self- and collective-affirmation rather than a location of genuine novelty. The 'buzz' is temporal, satiating but startlingly transient. There is a pervading sense that the gig offers the midlife male the chance to effectively *take away from it mainly what you want it to be*. I ask if it is the moment where they feel like 'rock stars'. This is met with a reaction of incredulity. Sometimes Johnny wishes he could be at home 'watching *Match of the Day!*' In being the sole focus up on the stage, there is a sense of exposure, a nakedness where the art and the man is revealed to a necessary, but chilling, scrutiny. Nerves are a major part of things, they say, but with the sound check over, the mood improves – having stood on the stage the sense of territoriality emerges; this is *their space* and they ultimately seek to *own* it. The gig itself gives them nowhere to hide; in their own words this is something that is ultimately advantageous because the art itself must be merged with expertise, driven by intent, skill and ego. It is hard work: hot, nervy, stressful and they hold out for, as Johnny states, 'the moment it's brilliant [...] where you know, at the end of this song, the audience are getting it as well'. The reaction from the audience is the final validation, a confirmation of quality and a loud, energetic response that offers support.

However, there still appears to be a division between the band and the outside world, between the environments of stage and audience. The gig, if anything, is something that *is* 'everyday'; it is a commonplace segment of being in a band, workmanlike and transactional, occasionally rewarded with sales. The Ruins, like most bands nowadays, tend to stream their music via social media as a taster for the CD album that is to follow. A turn to physical copy, away from the download, represents a combined desire to make a little money from the sale along with the satisfaction of seeing a real product displayed in the record shop. Duncan made an important point about the depth of meaning of the physical artefact when he said that 'we still aim at a recorded output [...] because that [...] legitimises it, which is why I personally like to put CDs out because it *legitimises* it [...] I can see it on a rack next to my favourite bands'. In an age otherwise arguably dominated by 'Bowie Theory' (Byun, 2016: 39) that embodies a 'play for pay' inevitability in an age of downloads and piracy (see Cummings, 2013: Ch. 7 for a discussion on responses to this), The Ruins circumvent such requirements. While they do not make anything significant from sales they, at least, get the satisfaction of *not being ripped off*. Playing live is just an opportunity to meet their fans and potentially *gain some more*. In the bubble on stage, where the band are separated by equipment both between themselves and between the band and the audience, the in-between essence of creativity is once more, symbolically and emblematically, practiced. The 'togetherness' is palpable, together as a band gaining primacy over being at one with the audience, but the event of the gig is also a curious melange of *barriers*, borders between the creation and reception of sound, band and audience and togetherness and physical venue.

To combat the loneliness on stage, there is the benefit of *trust* sensed between the performing artists at their age when playing live; an unspoken security is *felt*, a sense of camaraderie that reassures when playing live, but old habits die hard. They worry that they may let each other down in both commitment and in technical terms. It comes from years of being in bands who were, perhaps, focusing more on themselves as individuals rather than how they might pull together. Naomi Cumming states that a musician's *character* 'will be heard in the choices that he or she makes [...] a performance style' and the musician is listening firstly to their own sound, feeling privileged that they know they control what comes next and are willing participants with their own objectives (Cumming, 2000: 9). This segues with the way that The Ruins merge together as a unit on stage – namely via the individualised insecurities, built over time, and the honing of styles, habits and idiosyncrasies. It is very human and builds confidence together in the field of musical reproduction.

The gig is an omnipresent factor in a serious amateur band; if anything, the gig begins as an ambition and then becomes an *instrumental necessity* before becoming, eventually, a routine. I ask the band whether the feeling of a gig has changed for them over the years to which they respond that it *feels* the same as it ever has done, that each gig is *different*, but The Ruins also have a self-perceived 'problem' in that they have a tendency to be primarily support band. This, they concede, is built upon a choice rather than a haphazard chance, but accept this as something of an Achilles heel; people are not necessarily there in the venue to see *them*. The gaps in-between gigs are therefore seen as regressive; they understand that gigs are valuable but not as imperative as making music, but they also recognise that they do not pay enough attention to the shows, understanding the inconvenient truth that sporadic performances do not build reputations. Therefore, prioritisation is required to keep the momentum in the value of the band alive and impactful and the *recorded sound* is therefore given precedence and arguably, for these musicians, always has been.

> **Ian:** Now it's the expectation of doing a gig, getting through it, enjoying it, hopefully its sounding good and some people liking it; that's my expectation of a gig now whereas before it was always an expectation to get out and win fans, to try and make an impact, to move on and build up [a following].

> **Johnny:** I think the thing is, when you're doing gigs you're going out and meeting people [...] it's not just about the playing, is it? You're meeting people who might want to know about your music, you're meeting people you've not seen for a while, you're making new friends, you're seeing other bands and seeing what they're up to, it's a social side as much as anything else and you don't get that when you record, you see?

PM: The social thing is important?

Duncan: Talking to people afterwards is the most enjoyable bit about doing a gig because, invariably, somebody liked it even if you didn't think it went very well.

The social side of gigging therefore appears to be separating the sound and performance from the social – a binary effect that balances the apprehension of performance with the pleasure of camaraderie. The fans actually appear to care about The Ruins, with their personalities and their music seemingly equally sought and appreciated at the gig. The band mingle separately with friends and strangers alike, sharing cigarettes, drinks and idle (often animated) chatter and this encourages and pacifies the band, making them feel like part of a wider network; people ask them if they are ok, ready to perform, wishing them well, requesting songs, joshing and observing strengths and weaknesses. 'There's a sense of people actually caring about what you do and hoping you get through it', says Johnny and this is clearly valued by the band as an opportunity to learn and as a confirmation of quality and approach. I ask if the gig is really an opportunity to celebrate their collective spirit, their *bond?* The response is quite surprising as they claim that they do not see themselves as a unit *at* the gig or before or after the event. They commune at the venue but do not hang out together, travelling to and from the gig separately, coming together 'almost only when we're on the stage and that's probably less than when we come together in a rehearsal scenario', says Duncan and this, says Johnny, is 'probably for the best' due to bespoke ways of preparing for, and coming down from, the high. The gig is discussed at rehearsals, the two functions of the band isolated from each other, very binary and illustrative of how midlife can invisibly cleave what might have been considered at one time the *raison* d'être of a band – namely a single objective achieved by single-mindedness achieved itself with a unified, collective defined vision of what that ambition *looked like*. Thus, midlife responsibility is never far from the otherwise unified illusion of being in a band in midlife. It looks like and feels like a band, but it operates instrumentally as a vehicle for satisfaction, achieved individually first and collectively second. Life is affecting the dynamic, but it is not always immediately detectable.

One thing that does remain as a commonality is the image on stage that the band wish to convey; this, of course, is no new thing in the world of performative arts, especially rock music. I asked Duncan if clothing had an effect on how confident he feels on stage. The idea of some kind of coordinated clothing amongst the band – an invention of an *image* in all but name – 'doesn't work' for him; mentally, he feels that wearing clothes that are too formal would make him feel *less confident* on stage. Clothes can assist him, he says, in feeling better about playing, though 'aesthetically you are donning a camouflage [...] but I'd say that *my* camouflage is my *business suit*, actually [...] as opposed to what I wear on stage'. This distinction – and reversal – of the conformity of clothing is interesting, alluding to the sense that his midlife, formal professional persona is something of a mask that hides the real person or, alternatively, assisting in supressing his real desires. 'Everybody dresses for the occasion […] what the measure of appropriateness is [can be] radically different from one person to the next', he states. Some people deliberately dress inappropriately in bands because they see that as appropriate but Duncan dresses to simply illustrate that he *plays* in a band. They agreed to have a simple rule on stage that they must wear something black. I ask whether black is seen as 'alternative'? It can be, he says, but it is a colour that 'tends to work', it has a slimming effect on the body and this 'is particularly important for us at our age!' The Ruins do work through these ideas about image, but it is done with sensitivity. Duncan and Johnny tend to be the drivers of image management but, ultimately, they prefer to let the sound dominate the experience of both creating and delivering the music and in the ears of those who are present.

The Ruins have stated many times that the majority of value experienced by being in a band tends to invariably return to the *sound* and the *value of the sound* in the eyes − and ears − of those who make it. Duncan is quick to state the eclectic and transformative − though essentially powerless − aspect of such sound when he states that an 'aural aesthetic' comes 'by accident; you sound like you sound'. It is a *happy* accident, he says. A *collision* occurs. The visual aesthetics come with work; this is a planned and considered commercial-style thrust, but the music is 'free'. He adds that there is uniqueness in every band, whoever they are, whatever they look like and sound like, but there is a belief that exists inside The Ruins that they should stay on a particular *theme*. The limitations of the band and the styles in which they play their instruments creates a *sonic aesthetic*, but they do not consciously *decide* the sound. Augmenting this, Ian states that playing live does not allow for the lack of boundaries that are felt in the studio. The recording of music is a permanent revolution, that allows for 'freedom to roam in the song […] I'm not trying to recreate note for note […] gives it a little bit more *life*, you know?' People, he says, will always like different versions of songs, differing tastes allow for differing takes − the rise of the 12" single gave us this facility, he says, introducing us to a slightly more bespoke pitch at a prospective audience and offering the audience choice. Bootlegs, he says, also provide this facility, albeit with traditional differing quality. 'People like hearing songs *differently*', he says of bootlegs. This is all very interesting simply because instead of destroying the art, it revives, strengthens, gives more life to a song, as if each note is a new heartbeat that can be celebrated, rather than replacing something that exists in the past. This is a very 'forwards motion', the songs *lean forwards* once more, celebrating the continued vitality of the song, sensed here as something of an affirmation of life. This is life as resistance; a midlife aside to the perceived fading of the light. There is life in the old thing yet − whether the thing be the 'song' or the 'creator', the spirit to renew and revitalise exists. The band, it seems, will always return to the creative in-between state that encompasses that zone between 'real life' an uncertain future in its various guises, in this instance relating to life and art, and the uncertain, unpredictable essence of gigs (a vibrant *now*) is a method to achieve this.

Thus, on the whole, there is a pervading sense that performance is a dutiful requirement while recording and writing is the essential, contested space of all creative musical people. Ian recognises that playing and recording is still about being 'within boundaries', but that recording gives the breadth to approach some songs differently – slower, faster and so on, as well as in the effects and mixing associated with recording. This is the nexus of creativity – the brush strokes of skill. Playing live is the *forum* and Ian conscientiously avoids recreating the sound of recordings live, but live things do, it must be said, *sound better* to Ian. It is drilled into the tradition of gigging (and entrenched in the Musicians Union 'Keep Music Live' logo, found on stickers adorning instrument flight cases just about everywhere) that somehow 'live' is best. Drum sound that is gained in the studio is hard to achieve on stage; equipment can be manipulated in the studio to make drums sound good, and this is possible on stage but mostly this ends in a failure in his view. On achieving the right sound – especially for his drums – he illustrates his point by engaging me in a detailed explanation of his cornucopia of recording equipment that is set out before us – but he returns always to his workhorse machine, a Tascam DP32 that he calls his 'deck'. Literally waving this chunky piece of kit in the air he concedes that recording track by track can occasionally 'lose the creativity, lose the passion', but a deck, he says, is something that 'let's you *make* the music'. A computer, he says, 'distracts you' and he is adamant that a recording console upstages the computer every time. Waving his hands across the top of the Tascam deck he illustrates that it is all about buttons and faders, it is about the *nakedness* of the machine; with computers, there are too many things going on that create a falseness of the sound. This approach and set of beliefs is nothing, he says, to do with 'being 49', being more to do with purity, familiarity and security. Being in a band and playing live is all very well, but chasing the perfect sound is something that is best found, ultimately, in the workshop of the studio.

3.3.   Creative Midlife: Music and Being

Playing gigs is part and parcel of the holistic experience of being in a band and, for the record, The Ruins find this experience self-affirming. However, what of the alternative? What value and attraction does 'sitting in the studio' have over the ego, the performance, the public exhibition of their art? Does the 'status' of musician set them aside from everyday folk and give them a sense of exclusivity? Does social and economic background channel into the self-affirmations of their status, or does it play with their sense of self? I suggested (with a mixture of jocularity and curiosity) to Duncan that he is an artist, sitting at his easel in the conservatory – why bother getting gobbed at on stage?

> **Duncan:** Your artist sits in their garret somewhere and produces a picture [...] he's focussed on the end result; he doesn't then have to go and sit in front of an audience and paint [...] he's done his piece of art, there it is, you either love it or you don't [...] critically the artist paints that picture, he doesn't expect you to watch him painting that picture over and over again, whereas

with music, you go on tour and […] essentially the show is the same week in, week out […] that hamster wheel you find yourself on when you've decided to be a professional musician, the compromises […] there are *elements* of creativity in that experience, but arguably it is a facsimile.

The further up the scale of fame you go, artistic integrity is compromised more and more because of the expectancies of the audience – they *expect* stuff, you *need* to do that stuff. Duncan mentions that The Who were *required* to smash up their gear, and so the routine of performance unfolds. It is yet another routine and one the that The Ruins are keen to swerve in favour of composition. Duncan defines music as a creative process that is forced out of the in-between state of what I will call the 'mezzanine' – fine art, defined within the 'artist as genius' oeuvre here, is at liberty to remain almost fixed in a state of private contemplation and action. Fine art is only public when it is divorced from the author and, even then, it is a perfect facsimile or an original that one beholds, rather than facsimilia of the processes that got the work of art to the 'completed' state. The viewer makes an aesthetic – and ideological – call on the quality based on permanence. Music, on the other hand, is never really 'completed' when performed live; while retaining the aesthetic and ideological call on quality from the audience, it is fluid and impermanent when performed – the version is never the same twice, but this *is* routine. The audience, says Ian, are 'hearing you *new* for the first time'. There is a sense that The Ruins experience live performance as something that is a 'first time, every time' and are clear that the lack of *routineness* in the *rehearsal*, where creativity abounds, is what determines this band. 'We can be truly sensitive to the muse', says Duncan. *Nobody* tells them what to do, when to do it, where to do it, how and so on. This is 'the purest form of art because we are in *total control*', he states. It is a crucial distinction and appears to be a product of experience, desire, empowerment and chance and all of this, arguably, is reward of age.

There is a clear sense that the dynamic of 'age' is not something that diminishes the desire to make music but, instead, is something that is *scheduled*, cherished and enjoyed. Music is something that temporarily relegates other responsibilities, shutting out the noisy outside world for a moment of freedom, energy, acknowledged confidence, activated self-efficacy and edgy uncertainty that, in effect, *enhances* the experience of making the music.

> **Duncan:** At this age, sometimes music is an activity that gets fitted in around the responsibility of being part of the "sandwich" generation – kids and parents to look after […] as a younger musician the thrill of going to new places with the "gang" was an imperative. Being older, the gang mentality is not the same. Back then it was us against the world but now it's more like get in […] and get home for the Horlicks!
>
> **PM:** Do you think that having those responsibilities increases the legitimacy of the music the band writes and performs?

Duncan: I think it contributes to the mix, for sure. I think we all got together for some fun initially, having broadly retired from public performances. But, we realised that we were able to create the best music of our collective lives together and what started out as studio project became one that we could take on the road [...] the few gigs we get to play — we have turned down so many due to lack of all being in the same place at the same time — are all the more important as each one could turn out to be the last.

The band taste the exultation of performance as a continued exhibition of their resilience and guile, acting also as a demonstration of the transmutation of the banal into the legitimate fomenting of experience, knowledge and dexterity in front of supportive, empathetic and informed audiences; performing is a thrill, a challenge, an *opportunity*, but the ultimate reward of such accumulated, incremental artistic adroitness seems to be measured in freedom, resistance to the traditional art world structures of capitalistic 'peer review' measured by image, sales and loss of integrity.

PM: Do you think the music gives your 'life' a greater sense of thrust? Does it make you feel like you still have something left to give?

Duncan: Having suffered perceived failure at the hands of record company scouts turning me down in the past — in the old world where success was mainly judged by the ability to sign a [record] deal — what's different now is that we are our own judges of success as we have no desire to sign a deal, even if such things exist anymore! [...] we can make music that we like, and that, in terms of lyrical content, can make observations on life in 2016. It's music on our own terms at last!

It seems like The Ruins have it all: the space, the commitment, the talents and the combined experiences of men who have existed on the 'scene' for a long time, consuming life and making sense of experience and, having reached a stage in their lives where music is only a partial dynamic in the everyday, they are at last free to practice their art, their *creativity*, in instrumental terms for the greatest effect — namely, to tap into a creative sociality and do what they want to do *sans* interference. They seem to grasp this opportunity with an intensity, humour and verve that is infectious. However, what is it that *allows* them to grasp this chance? I suggest that art is a middle class 'thing', something that is toyed with, considered, set down and taken up at will. The band are less sure; in fact, they are not even sure whether they are 'middle class' men at all. A common informal response to class labelling is bafflement or resentment (Pakulski & Waters, 1996), as if the mantle of authenticity comes from struggle rather than privilege. It is a question worth asking though.

There is a traditional invested essence to an idea of working for a living; thus, the mantle of working-class authenticity is passed on, situated in an idea of toil, work, relationship to labour in a most traditional sense. To Miles being 'working-class' is 'about how you live your life and how you view others' as well as having a rudimentary influence on the way that people communicate with one-another, how they *relate* to people. Duncan, for example, sees himself as working class even now 'because I work for a living, *still*'. He does not have any reliance on the state, 'this is the new working class to me'. He ranks himself within the self-defining scale of whether the world owes him a living or vice versa. 'You have to produce something', he says. This is fundamental, but also symbolic of the creative soul − the striving to produce something is reflected in his desire to create on two levels − a dichotomy emerges, or even a *border is erected*, between the formal and the informal, the financial-work and the creative-work. It is questionable which of the two has the greater personal, emotional value. Considering themselves in-between being rich and poor, 'mentally' working class but with accepted middle-class advantages at this stage in their lives, the value that they attach to their creativity is founded in a sense that they have *earned the right* to indulge and they place a large value on this freedom. Art, however, is not perceived as exclusively a 'middle-class thing'; being creative transcends class barriers. Ian is certain that class plays a role in access to the spirit of artistic participation and the barriers that can − sometimes unintentionally − be placed in the way.

> **Ian:** It's possibly a mind-set [...] many working class people are into art [...] and *participate* [...] but then many working class people − more so than middle class − would be drawn away by other things that don't allow them to get into art and the rest of it; their parents aren't into art or their parents are just hard working, factory, on the dole, drinking, smoking, just *not into* that sort of thing [...] so they're not introduced to [art].

Middle-class kids, he suggests, might get 'taken out' to cinema's, theatres and other locations where art and creativity thrive, investing the value of reception, interpretations and respect for the various art forms. Cyber cultures, he argues, are beginning to create barriers to this exposure for youngsters; people spend hours watching the television or on their smartphones and this distraction simply conditions kids to receive, consume and not contribute. To Duncan, art is occasionally pretentious (both in viewing and in creating) but '[i]t's the emperor's new clothes really, isn't it?' You could grade art, in his view, as something resembling a hierarchical gradient of exclusiveness, much in the broad, arguably 'élite' approach associated with the oeuvre of Matthew Arnold ([1869] 2006) or F. R. Leavis ([1948] 2008), thus, he sees poetry as being 'right up there', but there are other forms and genres − roughly equating to a common taxonomy − that are depicted in the regular dialogues and discourses of artistic value that relegate rock music to a lower art form than he believes it should be.

> **Duncan:** You've got your classical music and opera and ballet, you've got stuff that traditionally associated with different classes

of people, but I think if you come down to music − and call it 'rock music' to take all types of popular music in − that's class-less to me. [...] People can debate high literature and paintings [...] have opinions about it [...] but that doesn't tend to incorpor-ate music.

There is a clear inference to a perceived 'classlessness' of rock music here, in contrast to the positioning of other art forms as hierarchical, but this standpoint also is open to an alternative interpretation that popular music, by its definition as 'popular' and democratised is somehow monocultural, or 'working class' in its essence as a 'job', 'vocation', or via its breadth of penetration into ordinary lives − culture, after all, is 'ordinary' (Williams, 1958). This is not an uncommon view of popular music; years after its initial impact (though still relatively in its infancy) 'the pop arts' were viewed as working class and transitory in nature (Melly, 1970). The longevity of popular music is proof enough that it is fighting hard for its place in the hierarchy of music, the performing arts and the wider arts and that the place itself should be elevated higher than been seen as indica-tive of mere commonality. I ask Duncan if art *defines* him as a person to which he shoots back that it is not defining, but key to his identity. 'I would eliminate some of the more traditionally highbrow elements of art', he says, 'I'm not so broadly minded that I can appreciate every type of artistic endeavour [...] it's an interest more than a definition'. Not one thing defines him he says, 'like most people I am a mixture of elements'. However, according to *Miles* art *is* classless because it is communicative and '*the* universal language', but the power of com-munication and the interpretation of the 'language' of music lies initially with the creator, defined by Miles as redolent of 'when you can move somebody with a piece of music [...] it's a special kind of talent to do that'. The transmission is, of course, a result of a process, an authorial routine undertaken in private, designed to be received but with the receiver not in situ when the design and implementation is achieved. While de Saussure (2013) and Barthes ([1957/1972] 2000) might argue, signifiers and signified are conceivably universal in form but not, feasibly, in reception (they can be manipulated by structural ideologies), the latter is not essentially possible without the former, placing the power to con-struct and manipulate emotion firmly with the producer and, consequently, raise the value and longevity of the musical art form in time.

So, does this 'power' equate to an 'élite' essence of musicianship? It is a ques-tion that, when introduced into our discussions, caused perhaps the greatest depth of thought − largely because no-one engaged had conscientiously reflected on music as an élite productive force. To be sure, well-rehearsed beliefs and opi-nions on music elitism were present (as Duncan earlier confirmed), but the con-sideration of their own élite status was confounding. It began with Miles inadvertently stating that a border has sprung up between inter-generational routes into musical validity and inter- and intra-musician respect. 'As an artist you want as many people as possible to hear your music', he stated, using the example of Sheffield quartet The Arctic Monkeys as being 'the last band to earn their spurs' that he could cite. Bands like this, he suggested, 'have slept in vans, played the toilets' while younger bands of the contemporary era have a tendency to believe 'that all you've got to do to get a record contract is stand in a fucking queue'. I mentioned, at this juncture, that he is suggesting that there is an elite vibe amongst proper bands, but this elitism is created by *earning the spurs* rather than selling records and appearing on TV. In other words, these are elite bands in the Raymond Williams sense – borne *of* the culture, special, elite, thorough-bred, egalitarian and genuine, reflecting a 'structure of feeling' that can only exist amongst such bands while refuting an 'elite' tag. It is an interesting tension and it has the effect of *reversing* the idea of elitism while not making it a *negative*, instead having the feel of an 'elite culture of the people', bringing expertise back into the common ownership rather than 'setting it aside', with the 'people' in this case being the community of musicians from the earliest, youngest amateurs to the highest-paid professionals worldwide. Hard work equates to earning what you get and those bands – successful bands over time – are therefore actually elite, but *not elite*. They are highly talented, have earned their right to be considered authentic and skilled, excellent at what they do but possibly remain *not* 'up there' necessarily in sales, but up there in *authenticity*. To Duncan, such elitism can be detected in performance; the musician needs to know how to play. He has a democratic belief that anyone can enjoy music, but the capital of expertise is always subjective. 'You don't realise it […] you don't consciously tell people you have an elite talent', he says. You simply do not brag, there is just a desire that exists deep down that people will *enjoy* it. 'You just produce it […] and you hope people will like it', he says. He does not like pretention. To Ian, alternatively, it is about choice – and, just maybe, this is where the distinction between creative and non-creative people may lie. 'You need to rehearse, practice, put in the hours […] to get to that standard to do what you want to do', he says. There exists an 'inner ability' in all people, but such inner ability is *defined, honed*, rather than just existing naturally in all contexts. Thus, he says, you have 'to work on it to achieve it'. This is how you personally establish if the creative thrust is strong; the pre-existing *context* is robust, but, as Miles says, it takes time to build up the strength to articulate the knowledge, to flex the creative muscle and to recognise the creative bent. However, being 'value free' has its advantages, even if it might be considered unnatural.

> **Miles:** I'd be jealous of someone who *didn't* have that pre-existing knowledge, because they would be able to create something original and different to somebody who's got decades of musical knowledge behind them, not necessarily being tainted by it but the influence that that music has created over the years can have an effect, and in some cases dictate, what kind of music you end up playing.

In the end, as Ian sardonically concludes, art is a 'malfunction of the brain!' Art and the forces of creativity required to articulate its form is a naturally existing 'thing' in many people, *people who often come together* to realise their 'visions' of art as a collective, but it takes something beyond the ordinary, something plausibly 'elite' to realise the form and understand why it is that you have created it. This equation is ostensibly classless but also responsible for applying such classlessness into an idea of being elite: art and creativity are, therefore, simultaneously exclusive and democratic, existing between the lines of separation from the mainstream and compressed and subsumed into the fabric of the everyday. It is a curious place to be.

3.4. Midlife and In-between States

There can be little doubt that midlife is, by definition, a sense of being in-between phases in life between the vitality of youth and the routine of the later years. It is also evident that this phase does have an effect on the creative soul. Ian was thinking hard about this effect; he spoke about family, daily routine, the sense of engagement with significant others and the incompatibility of creative composition and children, mealtimes and school runs. This, of course, is not unusual and is – or has been – experienced by others in the band over time, but Ian is unique in that his children are young, requiring attention and time. This has a knock-on effect for him with regards to his outputs. An avid songwriter, he sees himself as less creative these days (but there is no sense of regret; he is a happy family man). His inspiration comes at unexpected times, the individual in-between state where he can compose tapping him on his shoulder as he gets tired. 'Now[adays], it's always bloody bedtime' when he gets inspiration for songs he says, 'melodies keep coming into my head late on'. He spends his evenings, after putting the children to bed, talking to his wife rather than watching TV and, after his wife has gone to bed he has a few minutes to think, contemplate and 'that's when it's probably the quietness of everything, that's when my mind is free to receive the incoming melodies. In the day, there's not a great deal of time, but you fill that time with doing things'. These 'incoming melodies' are profound, captured on his recording equipment before they dissipate and eventually vanish. Like Miles – one of his best friends – Ian senses this creative time (which he likens to the process of knitting a jumper) late at night is a time 'to empty' the tank of inspiration.

> **Ian:** [you can] let your feelings out [...] It overtakes you and you are thinking about in constantly and you are using the power of your mind to construct that song because that's where a lot of it happens, you're *thinking* [...], you're disconnected from the world [...] so you're cutting off worry or stress, you're free from that [...]. Music is something that is meant for humans [...], everybody responds to it, emotionally, physically and whatever [...], when we're jamming we are creating that [...] sound that's going to give pleasure in whatever sense that is.

Ian clearly believes that music is something that is reflexive: we *respond* to it and we *make* it, gaining pleasure from it in *both* the making and the

emotional returns we get. He mentions that it is hard for him to get the finished sound he craves in these late-night, transformational moments because
he lacks the capacity to do everything, especially vocals. In his view, it is nice
to be in a band for these reasons alone; this is a strength of the collective. He
is, he says sanguinely, *disappointed in his own limitations*. These midlife in-
between states are therefore collective (as illustrated in Chapter 2, above) as
well as individualised; the individuality, in many ways, is an in-between state
itself, separating the humdrum routines of the day and the thrust and bustle
of family life with the restfulness of sleep as well as separating the creativeness
of the collective band with the ideology of self and the infirmity and uncertainty of mere ideas. Given that the muse is regularly experienced in those
moments   before   sleep,   expected   though   unexpected,   uncertain,
unpredictable and oscillating in quality and impact, I became interested in
whether the creative *urge* diminishes in midlife – essentially framed, in this
instance, not by responsibilities but by *energies*. Does the urge dissipate in
favour of this unpredictable emergence? Miles is adamant that creativity
increases as you get older, potentially bucking the popular belief in a decline
and dilution of inventive powers. 'No, if anything it's more intense [...]', he
says and, when the membership of various bands 'dried up' in his own past,
he turned his efforts towards writing poetry (a passion he has nurtured over
his life and retains). During these musically fallow periods he states that '[e]
ven though I wasn't playing music, I was still listening to it', and, when The
Ruins came looking for him he was ready, still able to 'reconnect with musical
roots'. These roots, perhaps, are more deep, defined and stubborn as age progresses and are aligned to an idea of companionship, encouragement and rap-
port. True friendship, to Miles, is best understood through the relationship he
has with old friends in the band – the years in-between simply melt away
when one is playing music with old acquaintances. The urge, therefore, may
simply be a *desire* for *involvement*. The creative juices are simply piqued at
unusual times and, as I will go on to explain, this is not something that exists
in an 'anytime' daily timeframe of a musician, it happens for artists and writers too.

   With the inventive piques, comes a belief that tolerance is considered more of
a virtue when older; there is an understanding that life *intervenes*, that things
happen these days. There is no 'masterplan' as to where they want to get to with
the music, instead it is viewed as an incremental process of 'milestone to milestone' creating laughter in the studio on this particular evening, on this particular point. The band appear to be saying that it is best not to get a *glimpse* of
anything, because glimpses of success only make things worse! Instead of finishing gigs with a rendition of the MC5's *Kick Out the Jams* and then returning to
smash up their hotels, they just long to *sleep at* hotels and have a good breakfast
in the morning. It remains the subject of much mirth. Times change; attitudes
change; humour still pervades the band, but it is wry humour that is based predominantly on an *acceptance* rather than an ambition. There is, if anything, a
belief that everything is 'middling'.

Duncan: Everybody who ages, there is a certain novelty about life
that tends to fade away; maybe we become a little more immune
to the highs and lows of life – you don't get quite so euphoric
about the highs, but you don't get so down about the lows
because you look back with a perspective [...] there's less excitement in the purest sense.

However, is it a paradox that they have more time now to do things than
when they were 'young and free'? There is, says Johnny, 'more time when young
to be creative'. 'You work harder with the time you've got', counters Duncan.
Time was potentially wasted when younger; rehearsals were slower, deliberative
and time consuming, whereas these days it is about using the time better, more
mature and somehow *urgent*, taking 'five minutes to set up and you're away'
says Johnny. There is no time to argue, no time to let ego's get in the way of the
sound. Ian notes, as he did earlier, that family and responsibility compresses the
availability of time. If anything, he thinks, the lack of time improves the creative
output.

Ian: now, you don't have the time because you've got kids,
you've got your work, less time to focus on your music [...]
churning along over the years, you are still developing maybe
even if you are not doing it physically, but you're still listening to
music, still influenced by it [...] but less time, the quality gets
better.

There is articulated here a *hiatus* in *writing*; alternatively, *creating* is never
really a hiatus, just a process of obtaining and analysing a back-log of thoughts
about what to do, to play, to sing and how to make it sound good and this is
consequently suggestive of a biographical art world, a personal library of ideas
that are never discarded totally. This is a process of internalisation of art forms
as triggers for perfection. The band now have the space and time to unpack
those ideas conceived in the 'hiatus' and the studio offers them another symbolic
location of production, free of the ideologies of everyday life. The in-between
place is most certainly the studio. The *band*, to Duncan, is 'an outlet'; jobs and
responsibilities along with age play a part in their overall lives, but the pressures
also stimulate creativity and the best place to realise the almost *physical* manifestation of such urges and thrusts is in the studio. Duncan says that they
'cocoon [them]selves in Ian's room', lauding it as a 'sanctuary for playing and
talking' and 'no-one can get us there'. Miles adds that the value in shutting
themselves away to simply *be* musicians is viewed through the lens of recognising that 'the band is a weekly constant; if anything, *that* is my one routine'.
Always on a Thursday, this routine never changes and there is no desire to
change it; *uniqueness* is a strong driver, a sense of *revitalisation* is in existence
here, a mission to deliver something to *themselves*; there is a sense that their creativity sets them aside from simple musicianship, that something is special.

Midlife is simply a bystander, albeit an influential one, in the studio. Excitement is functional, recreational, invigorating and, above all, challenging the creative fustiness that they perceive as potentially pervading midlife.

> **Miles:** because I'm the age that I am, it's no longer excitement in the way that you would be as a teenager or a younger bloke, it's more the [...] *anticipation* maybe? It's something you enjoy and want to get back to each week.

> **Duncan:** If all that mattered for us was coming together as a group of people to play music, like we might say we want to play five-a-side football on a Wednesday night, then that would be a whole different thing – but this band has always been about producing new products, material, song, whatever [...] otherwise we'd go down the different route of simply coming together as musicians [...] but you're not creating something new and unique.

> **Johnny:** we would have never had that [uniqueness, vibrancy, creation], if we hadn't gone to try and do that.

Thursday night is the night that you get to play your instruments and forget about things. It is like a 'club night' where you have responsibility to actually do something rather than phase in and out in a leisure haze. Duncan is adamant that the 'band night' is still a routine that requires commitment and desire. 'You need a certain amount of habit to make you do it at our age', he says before adding that 'whereas when you're younger, maybe different things drive you towards each other'.

> **PM:** Is your band a 'habit'? It's an interesting word!

> **Duncan:** It's about momentum, I think. I mean habit is probably right, but as a band you need a level of momentum, you have to subliminally acknowledge that Thursday night is band night.

> **Johnny:** It comes in peaks and troughs. At the minute we're in a bit of a quiet time [...] some practices, do we *have* to go?

> **PM:** An involuntary vibe to it?

> **Duncan:** You get a bit more satisfied by being at home; that's the big difference between me at twenty and me at fifty, definitely.

> **Ian:** When you're younger, you just want to practice, get on your drums [...] whereas now I'm finding myself, more and more [...] the longer you leave it between practicing your sort of ability starts to go down [...] less comfortable doing what you're going to do.

There appears a *promise* that *they will be heard* that keeps them going. The drive on a winter's night to do stuff can be hard to raise oneself for. However, in the end, it is all about making the music, the resistance to the quagmire of banality. Is midlife all about being straight and conventional? 'If you let it, yeah', says Duncan, sipping his coffee and affecting an air of someone halfway between regret and jocularity. If the 'happy coincidence' of getting reconnected to Johnny on Facebook had not happened, he says he is not sure he would still be connected to music and performance. He would still be playing at home, noodling on his guitars and − perhaps − writing the odd song here and there but, he says, 'I might have tried one of these *band dating [web]sites* as you do now!' This is an interesting metaphor, comparing (coupling?) musical relationships to middle-age searches for love. This is like a virtual 'post office window notice' for needed musicians he says, just like in the old days where an advert in the NME or a shop window or noticeboard in a Post Office would draw in the hidden musicians of the town. After the hiatus of getting his career firmly on track after the demise of his previous band in the 1990s he was actually involved in a lot of musical action concurrently − two reformations and one new band (The Ruins). It went from nothing much to a great deal very quickly. 'It got me back in the game', he says. So, I ask, *is* music a resistance to humdrum middle age? 'Undoubtedly, and increasingly so', he says, smiling.

> **Duncan:** for all of us [...] your day job is dumbing down all the time with automation [...] we all need a contradiction to that, we all need to do something different [...] because it's a creative thing [...] the additional resistance to the humdrum is that you are creating something new every time you go out.

He finishes his drink and puts the large mug on the table and looks at me and says, 'In a world that is increasingly homogenous, if you can produce something different every now and again it proves you've still got a part to play'.

§

I began to explain The Ruins by exploring creativity as a private matter via understanding rehearsal as a functional space to practice creativity. This infers that the creative process is solitary and couched in the pursuit of perfections, excellence and novelty. The Ruins, in their own words, have intimated that the creative 'whole' can be experienced as a series of recognitions of the transformative power of music and music making. Thus, music has a primacy, being extraordinary in otherwise ordinary lives. Music making is instinctive, creates a record of life as it is lived and is gifted to midlife men via the availability of time and the prevalence of technology. The creative self effectively funnels into the rehearsal, with rehearsal itself seen as a *space* rather than a *place* of action, creating rough sound in preference to the 'perfection of recital' and creating self-affirmational effects, *rehearsing self-concept*. Art, to these men, is dialectical and social and ideological, resting in the senses, creating *feeling* that is itself

democratic, collective and situated in the oeuvre of history and biography realised together. Rehearsal is anticipation, emotionally fulfilling via the discovery
of novelty, a glimpse of genuineness and a revival of the stale. Creativity, while
private, is understood publically and *experienced* rather than *produced*. In addition, the band are bridging the private and the public spheres, resting initially
on an unwritten and unsigned social contract to be creative, harnessing desire to
build new experience, to be expressive through the elusive, prized 'voice' of
ingenuity and to bring their sound to the open market of the public via performance that involves the band in an historical tradition. Such tradition facilitates
the assertion of the rights to their music; the gig is rare, special, bonding them
together while reminding them of their midlife 'sobriety' brought about by
work, family and other commitments but allowing them to experience another
domain of super-interaction that augments their studio work, furnishing the
music with additional dynamics of sociality, camaraderie and public feedback
via applause, discussions, sales and visuals. This art of music making is democratic and instinctive, fluid and exciting, providing the levers of control that can
be grasped in midlife on their own terms, pertaining to a labour that identifies
them as working, *working class*, having earned the right to experience creativity
as legitimate, meaningful labour where talent defines a power, creativity is
framed as an elitism of the people, a structure of feeling conveyed through the
folk cultures of popular music, social, involved, urgent and honed and as art
with such history, conversely defining in its wake a desire for such elitism that
can in itself chain the musician with its values. The Ruins represent a midlife creativity that is about reward on their own terms but shared with a partially visible
oeuvre, a detectable structure of meaning delivered via the pantheon of popular
music and culture, a *visual* history and an anxiety of (paradigmatic) influence
that shapes their understanding of the creative via a rear-view mirror, but from
within which identities can be shaped and maintained in the present.

The Ruins are a band who wish to continue what they have always loved
but, in midlife, they are arguably free from the overpowering pressure of
advancement towards a defined goal that exists beyond the simple satisfaction of
making good music, celebrating their own expertise and dedication of time to
new ideas that need not make it beyond the rehearsal room unless explicitly
desired. To David Hesmondhalgh (Hesmondhalgh, 2013) music can heighten
the sense of 'continuity and development' in life; it can make us reflective and
self-aware via action such as dance and via less expressive movements (combining thinking and feeling); it creates empathy and sympathy via synchronic and
diachronic processes than span timeframes and eras as well as bridging cultural
and linguistic apertures. In practical terms, music also does *reward* those who
perform it; rehearsal leading to virtuosity and recognition (ibid.: 55). Thus,
music is of value to both those who consume it and to those who write and perform it; there is, arguably, no loser and no sense of partiality towards producer
or consumer. The Ruins recognise the value of reward; they are survivors and
they are dynamic. They are not finished, instead seeing themselves as vibrant,
active and inventive whatever their ages. They value rehearsal as a private space,
music creation as self-affirmational, being in a band as a negotiation between

creating and reciting, the private and the public and between the ordinary and the less-ordinary in everyday life. Being in a band, therefore, is best summarised by Duncan who says that the essence of creativity is 'a melting pot on ingredients that you throw in and the whole is greater than the sum of the parts [...] suddenly you'll click into something that is the *interaction* [...] the lift off is when musicians come together [...] you *listen*'. It is all about rhythm and collaboration and, most of all, about action, *making* and togetherness. The band are also firmly aware of the limitations and freedoms of midlife in equal measure, sensing that they had 'earned' the right to be hidden, to have control and to choose the magnitude of their participation in their broader art world. The band are in-between writers and performers, they exist as people of elite skill sets with a common habitus and field. They are ordinary men doing extraordinary things in ordinary contexts; they utilise the structure of feeling (Williams, 1961) in a way that both affirms their validity as real musicians (despite being *sans* record contract and so on) as well as exploiting such validity to achieve personal ends in recording, releasing and (occasionally) performing their original art. I will return to a closer analysis of the impact of such ontological and epistemological instrumentalism in Chapter 9 but, for now, it is enough to conclude that The Ruins are an example of a midlife resistance to the ordinary, losing themselves in their spaces of creation and exhibitionism in the studio and the stages on which they perform and, all the while, affirming their right to be there with an outstanding verve and earned self-efficacy.

PART II: ART AND IDENTITY

A dilemma exists when seeking to define 'art'. Is it the stuff we 'look at' on the walls of galleries, people's homes, urban underpasses or the covers of CDs or is it a wider, penetrative and omnipresent 'thing' that consists of a cornucopia of forms such as music, literature, fine art, film, sculpture, graffiti and the perception of a *job well done*? Throughout this book, 'art' is defined as creativity via music, 'fine art' and writing and an 'artist' is the creative force in bringing these things to fruition, but art − in the instance of the following three chapters − is best defined as what Read would call 'plastic' or 'visual' art (Read, [1931] 2017; 17), namely a desire to 'create pleasing forms', appealing to a sense of beauty and harmony (ibid.: 18). It is the use of the word 'sense' that best frames Read's analogy of the function of the artist and the art they create, a symbiosis of action and sensuality, created and transmitted but not necessarily pertaining to an agreed idea of *beauty* (ibid.: 19−20). Art, as is initiated below, is a process, a routine that utilises the senses, skills, intuition and experience and does not extend to a definition of the 'end product' as art at all, but merely a production, a thing that has a multitude of meaning in both its creation and its afterlife.

It is not the place of this book to be entering into detailed discussion on the definition of art, or the apparent neglect of the appreciation of visual arts as a subject of research (Bennett, Savage, & Silva, 2009), instead I am concerned with how 'art' is *done*; the focus is on the biography, the routine and the meaning of the artistic process to three men engaged in midlife creative activities. All three exist as creative *individuals* that are invariably, somewhere, connected to an 'art world' (Becker, [1982] 2008; Thornton, 2008) that influences their actions (whether it be via communications with others, financial and social input, supply, exhibition and so on) but are also engaged in a deep, contemplative and explosive haptic process, generating, *inter alia*, woodcuts, linocuts, painting, sketches, charcoal drawings, pastel still-life's and pottery coupled with exhibition, performative exhibition and events associated with intellectual appraisal of their art and the art of others. There has been, over recent years, work that has focussed predominantly on the definition of an 'artist' itself, with definition difficult, oscillating between the placing of an individual as an artist by external designation or via self-definition (Lena & Lindemann, 2014). Both are problematic, perhaps obviously.

Introducing the artists − Peter, Robin and Dominic − is best left to the ethnographic accounts detailed below, but it is expedient to trail such conversations with a foundation of how the art is done and considered here. For instance, Edward Laning, writing in the early 1970s, stated that '[d]rawing is a language, and our lines, marks, and smudges are, to our language, what letters are to a writer's. But words are not things; the name of a thing is not the thing itself' (Laning, 1971: 16). In echoing Barthes' linguistic theory (Barthes, [1964] 2010: 30−31), but this time on connotations or *inferences*, the notion that art is perhaps a 'second-order system' (ibid.: 30) or *language* of formations, arrangements and colour and dimension is strong, but it arguably needs the polysemy of language and the sociability of people to make it somehow come alive *as* art. This additional 'plane' of meaning is important, arguably, in all art, denoting the penetrative effect of emotion as a felt reaction to the manifestation of art itself in the individual (Gompertz, 2017).

The 'sociology of art' developed over the duration of the 20th century, oscillating between (arguably) early attempts to sequester the role of 'art' into a discourse on taste and the spirit of the age via literature (Schücking, [1944] 1966; later contested by Leavis, [1952] 2008) and, around the same time, being couched in a discourse on value and interpretation that excludes the social application to art and the socio-cultural variables between advanced and primitive societies and the anthropological challenges in bridging this gap (Tomars, 1940: 17–20). Tomars continues that early pontifications on the subject grapple with the lack of attention to the subject area, himself couching art in the communal and the civic, discussing trends, class-based social closure and 'ownership' of art and the growing influence of the state upon art at the turn of the 1940s (ibid.: 308; Ch. 11), all of which point clearly to a future opening of the subject into key areas of further discussion relating to affect and the shaping of art via the establishment and the role of capitalism. This was later taken up by Alexander and Rueschemeyer (2005), arguing that the state's role in the defining of, support for and policing of, art was delivered via the law, markets, training of artists, educating the receivers of art and so on. They continue that, in the 1980s, there was a move 'towards a more market-oriented funding of the arts' (2005: 16; Ch. 3) that developed an enterprise culture and an air of corporate sponsorship that started under Margaret Thatcher and continued under Tony Blair and has arguably changed the way the public are exposed to arts via power, control and regionalism. In many ways, despite the 60 years that divides them, this approach conjoins the prospective approach of Tomars (1940) and the modern era of state sponsorship (and the development of an ideology of commercialism that surrounds art as an industry). Art can be alienated from its deeper, aesthetic meaning by the coming of money, where art becomes investment, where paintings and things become like bonds or stocks but there is always a counter force that can be detected, creating equilibrium between the venture and the value, the capital and the aesthetic effect. Raymond Betts and Liz Bly articulated this balance of speculation and *people* by stating that

> Art has been seen by many corporations [...] as a form of sound investment, and Progressive Insurance boasts [one of the] largest corporate contemporary art collections in the world [which is] not viewed as a capital investment, but rather as a spring board to inspire creativity and as a cultural asset among employees and visitors. (Betts & Bly, 2013: 67)

To be sure, art speaks here as both investment and the sensual response of the human intellect, but this is not the only sociological focus that is applicable to art as both an action and as a career or industry. It is also possible to make sense of art as a done thing – that is, being separated from the aesthetic afterlife of the artefact that is essentially finished by the creator. In other words, I return to the idea of art as a process that does not require validation externally to the artist's routine. However, as I will illustrate, sectioning off the two dynamics is virtually impossible when art is considered – as it is – a career, a career change, a commercial prospect that emerges from the learning and application of skills. Thus, while the focus tends to be on the routine and the process of creation (routine being practical and process being intrinsically unplanned), there must be an awareness of the perceived value of the art. In effect, the crux is whether the artist values the value of the art or not.

As already noted, in Chapter 1, the 'sociology of art' is often a variety of discourse based on the *arts* (Alexander, 2003), the intellectual appraisal of politics of art, gender dynamics in creativity and production of art and meaning (Pollock, [1988] 2003), aesthetics, cultural interjection and reflection and the application of case studies to sociologically interpret art with (arguably) a likeness to the methods of literary criticism (Ingis & Hughson, 2005; Wolff, 1983) or to a combination of philosophical, aesthetic *embodiment* that considers the indivisibility of 'content' and medium' leading to a 'discovery' experienced by the artist in 'carrying out a plan' (Reid, 1969: 76–77). Essentially, in aesthetics we have communication (Marcuse, [1978] 1979) or 'structural' poetics (Swingewood, 1986) or hermeneutics (Wolff, 1975) channelled, of course, through the dialogic semantics of creator and appraiser but rarely, effectually in *conjunction*. Over time, dialogues of affect have arisen that place the semantic emphasis on reception in art (Berger, 1972) and text (Willis, 2018), but this study — while acknowledging reception and affect as crucial, often substantive, after-effects of the process of creativity — is not concerned with *what happens next* per se. This kind of approach was covered in a recent special edition of *Poetics* (Alexander & Bowler, 2014), focussing on 'sociology' as applied to art via commercialisation, markets, financial valuations, funding streams for the arts and the ubiquitous tension between ordinary lives and elitism in the arts and the arts industries. Instead, in the following chapters, it is my intention to ask the artists themselves to explain their *approach* to both art as 'pastime' and art as satiation of desire. I am interested in how they *do* it, *why* they do it, what they do and what it means *to them* as well as the inevitable swerve towards understanding more about how they feel when their art is released, passing power from the artist on to the 'viewer'. Thus, it is about that semiotic language spoken of above, the pressure to create anew, the anxiety of competitiveness and of validity of 'meaning' and the omnipresent influence of personal trajectory. Life and its oscillating fortunes penetrate art. It is a fascinating juxtaposition: life into art into life; life, to be sure, but perhaps just not as we may intuitively know it.

Chapter 4

The Subterranean River

The first thing that I noted about the stairwell that rose towards the artistic studio of Peter Driver was the white, glossy brick walls, the stone steps, the echoing of voices and the faint whiff of the 'institutional'. Despite appearing like an old prison both inside and outside, this was – at one time – the army barracks on Oxford Road in Reading, these days it is far from the conventional or the conforming. It is, instead, the setting for ideas and expression and pursued originality: art is practiced here by painters, sculptors and additional varieties of creative, exuberant and imaginative people and the place struck me as having the most liberated of airs, clean and exciting, open and welcoming and, above all, encouraging of the harnessing of potential. It was a cathartic experience to visit, time and time again, to talk to Peter about his work in his *place* of work, *look* at his work and wonder.

Inside Peter's studio there is a melange of canvas, wood, iron presses, paint brushes, pots of liquids, paints and aprons, easels and towering, steel shelving units that support a web of strings that inadvertently exhibit pegged works in progress next to finished works of art in frames of wood and glass. At the centre of all of this ephemera is the magnificent press, sourced and paid for by a 'Kickstarter' crowdfunding exercise for which Peter expresses profound appreciation; its centrality is both emblematic and functional. It is 'through' this equipment that Peter produces his colourful, detailed and inventive prints, the juxtaposition of the press and the prints that decorate the studio symbolically expressive of a mode of work that progresses through many phases from conception via realisation in the press and completion in the frames. The organisational presentation of the studio and its contents are characteristic of the synchronic routines, skilled processes and patterns of thinking that go into the production of art, both in sociological and 'social' contexts (Wolff, 1993) and via a proprioceptive and exteroceptive arrangement – what Witkin (2005: 65–67) describes aesthetically as a *haptic system* of *perception* and *manipulation* can be applied here as a theory of tactility, of presence, of sensing the materials and their usefulness and their physical malleability, to hand at all times. Thus, despite the seeming *dis*order (this is a *working* room, a place of creation and a highly individualised and *personal* space) there is an orderly, contrasted atmosphere of artistic *physicality* complete with a perceptible human, contemplative calmness in league with the curious, *audible* juxtaposition of the traffic thundering past on the busy road outside. The windows let in sound, but also the all-important light that makes or breaks a good studio and, paying a peppercorn rent to the local authority for this fabulous space, Peter is able to concentrate on his passion. This is the culmination of brave choices made at difficult times, of shelved ambitions being taken down and dusted off under fluctuating levels of duress and the eventual realisation of destiny through art and teaching and the simple joy of creation. Peter Driver is a man with a mission to achieve recognition and satisfaction in his work, but he is also a man who shares his passion, teaches and encourages and, above all, finds peace in his work as a creative man.

Within these thick walls, spaces converted for creative minds to consider their muse and to bring into life new things, artists wander and converse like paint-spattered ships in the night over a brief coffee or tea and biscuit on a battered sofa in a common room. It is a 'not for profit' enterprise, with a bit of outreach into the local community, and Peter has been in residence for three years, initially taking over his studio from a German who had moved back to Berlin. They have an 'associate scheme' in place here where people outside the walls go on a waiting list of sorts, taking part in exhibitions to stay connected to the scheme and invariably getting a studio when one comes up at £70 a month. Peter spends about one day a week there at the moment; he has just finished a Master's degree in Art and so felt compelled 'to get a full time job' and a return to previously abandoned routine.

> **Peter:** it was back to the coalface [...], so that meant my time in the studio was really limited, I was coming in really early in the morning before work still trying to [create] because I had exhibitions and stuff and then checking in after work and doing a bit more before I went home

Nowadays he teaches part-time at his old art school, a place where (on starting out as a conventional painter of oils onto canvas) he 'kind of fell in love with print making' while soaking up the educational experience in midlife, merging the often-contested perspective of *adult citizen* and free spirit into what Randy Martin (2006) calls *artistic citizenship* where art and civil society are commuted via art schools, art worlds and exhibitions and where 'the artist epitomizes unsullied individualism, an inner-directed free spirit who answers to the muse' eschewing the conventional citizenship dualism of privilege and obligation (Martin, 2006: 1–2). To Martin, the 'keys to artistic citizenship lie in understanding how art and artists are brought into the world' with the art school being the connective glue between art, artist and conventional forms of citizenship. The artist, he says, has suffered in the intermediate zone of 'aesthetic creativity and the public realm of exhibit' and the art school offers some respite from this despite not being a refuge from the professional world itself (ibid.: 1–2). It might not be surprising then, in view of such tensions between individualism and obligation, that Peter still finds it hard – in his late fifties – to *define* himself. Enlightenment may come through mixing routine with personally held ideology and the natural world around him. 'I guess it's about how you practice, how you do something', he explains, stroking his thick, grey beard, smiling and

looking into the middle distance. 'What I do is a mixture of printmaking, drawing, walking and trying to integrate my interests in landscape [and] bird watching into the artwork as well as my interests in social concerns, politics, the way
society works', and, he is keen to state, he creates art out of his *walking*; artistic
documentation of his walks has built up into a considerable physical portfolio
and a metaphysical contentment. 'I make work out of the experiences of those
walks', he states. Walking and drawing is 'ritualistic' and communicative — and
he likes to *share* such ideas, art work and thoughts with those who follow him
on social media. Ritual, according to Shepherd and Wallis (2004), is indicative
of 'deep commitment and empty formality', a combination between deep
invested meaning and rote reproductions (ibid.: 118) and, it is fair to suggest,
Peter is aware of both applications of meaning. Thus, an exposure to
significant — and less significant — others crystallises the meaning of such ritual
as creative commitment leading to communication and this seems to propel him
along in his quest for inspirations. Peter came to practice art late and, with the
Kickstarter, seems eager to involve those around him in his practice — the ritual
becomes the communicative, the delegated, the inclusive muses.

The upheaval of redundancy facilitated the fulfilment of ambition, an ambition that had its genesis when growing up on a council estate in the
Cambridgeshire fens. Considering an economic poverty as linked to a poverty of
opportunity as he grew up, he 'scraped out' of school having failed 'O' Level
Art, finding eventual inspiration in Sixth Form where, he says, he gained 'a new
lease of life, it was where I unleashed all my creativity [...] a band, did A Level
Art and History of Art, drank a lot of tea'. He blossomed into the person he
wanted to be at this point. 'I failed to get into art school the first time [...] where
Syd Barrett went — big childhood hero of mine — so I really wanted to go there.
So, I retook my A Level in Art [...] and so I got into art school the next time',
adding, with a hint of compunction, that 'very few working-class kids go to art
school, there is [a held belief that there is] no future in it, it doesn't lead to anything, it doesn't lead to a job'. This belief in the disconnection between the joy
of art, the study of art and the credentials needed for a good job continue to
trouble him and his railing against the determinism of social class is a big
dynamic in his everyday thinking. At this point in his life, at art school in the
early 1980s, Peter mentions his interest in religion, becoming what he describes
as a 'biblical literalist [...]' which he 'felt was part of my identity', but this did
not scan with the perception of art school 'freedom of expression and widening
of horizons'. Such 'cognitive dissonance' did not sit well with him, evolving into
the moment where he felt had to make a decision on whether it was art or
becoming a minister of the church. He finished the foundation course and began
work in administration while thinking about his future. 'The art thing was very
deeply supressed in me by that stage [...] I did a few drawings in my sketch
book' but that was about it, he says. He reflected on his belief system, questioning things and, he concedes, 'I began to be more comfortable with my doubts'.
He started to question *certainty*; his politics were continuing to develop *alongside* the faith, but he remained dedicated to equality and fairness, the 'sanctity of
human beings'. The 'interrogation' of faith transmits into his contemporary

woodcuts via the slogans that he uses within the myriad of shapes, colour and texture; he cuts plywood, placing text into the centre, enjoying the ambivalence in his words, imploring people to pick up his slogans and question them, creating a dialogue that effectively involves the artist as an absent respondent. 'I'm quite interested in interpretation, in hermeneutics, because, having come from an evangelical Christian background – which is why I dropped out of art school the first time round – I am very keen on people challenging their own thinking and trying to work out what texts mean and what possibly different interpretations can be of the text', he says, adding that he likes the plurality of interpretation, stating this is something that has assisted his development in life, and as a guiding principle as he has aged. This itself is built upon the catalysts of death, lingering paternal presence and the notion of legacy. His father died in 2008, two years after he chose a career shift to 'get out of my comfort zone' into regulation in London.

> **Peter:** This was one of those moments in your life when you kind of reassess things and I was just reflecting on, I suppose, my own mortality and what do I want to leave behind when I go? What do I want to spend the rest of my life doing? Is it this? What were the things I really enjoyed when I was young? It was bird watching and art, so I kind of became a 'born again birdwatcher and artist'.

At this point in his life he went into the local art shop, bought some materials and 'set up in the spare bedroom and started making a lot of paintings'. His kids questioned his sanity he says with a smile, but he carried on, unsure of his quality, but he *carried on*, adding, sardonically, that he sold more stuff when painting in his spare room than he does now based in his bespoke studio. 'Rekindling the spark of the artistic practice was kind of a response to my Dad's death; I really think that was the trigger for it, that's where it started again', he states. Describing his visits to London galleries by way of recovering from his grief, he unintentionally, but profoundly, began 'to feed that creative side of me again'. Soon he was in at a high-profile art school and he has not looked back, completing an MA within the last two years and consequently taking a teaching role at the School. He is humbled by the family support and the sacrifices they have made after bereavement created the fork in his road; he felt that his father had never achieved his *own* potential, 'playing it safe and [doing] the factory job', so Peter was inclined to ask himself 'what talents have I got, and hadn't I better start using them?'. Much like Hubert Shelby Jr (2011 [1966]: 244), he sensed that he might get to end of his own life and regret not having taken the chance to shine. It was a 'no-brainer'.

The roots of creativity can be considered internal and creativity, according to Peter, emerges from personality and is expressed through a variety of outlets: playing the guitar, painting, carving and seeing it as 'a deep river, flowing underground all the time, always there' and re-emerging via painting and as a response to his father's death − 'it was a long time underground', he adds. The creative muse is an omnipresent, living force − the hidden river metaphor indicating a connectivity to life: flow, liquidity and the concealment of identity. It is as if the 'real Peter' had been suppressed. Thus, he does not see himself as part of a creative industry (see Flew, 2012; Hesmondhalgh & Baker, 2011) but, instead, *considers* his art as a process, an *arrangement*:

> **Peter:** Making any piece of artwork is just a succession of decisions [...] where the line goes, what colour goes where, so you get very absorbed in that and it becomes quite a meditative process [...] the emotion for me is when you do that first colour, and you put it through the press and you lift the paper up and you see it, you see what you've made, revealed [...] there's quite a thrill in that.
>
> **PM:** How do you supress the routine?
>
> **Peter:** The routine is something you really want to avoid [...] It's partly about trying to keep it fresh and responding to instincts and stimuli in a way that is enjoyable and interesting.

Routine is anathema; he prefers to be free of structure to create space for thriving invention. This approach is, at once, counter to the idea of 'editorial moments' (Becker, [1982] 2008: 199), as well as the notion of routine being, in itself, a resistance to the fluidity of late modernity. This paradox is considered by Bohm (1998: 17) who suggests that rebelling against conformity is *conformity itself*. This is not *creative* to Bohm, but arguably *reproductive*. Peter states that routine is based on instinct, intuition and a fair bit of chance and, per se, may well be reproductive, but heterogeneous.

The art that emerges dissolves the incentive to think solely about potential sales; career is more about *recognition* via the reception of the art with the public, he says, and what the 'end result I'm working towards and what I want it to convey or mean to an audience', bringing the focus onto communication, engagement and perceptions. He likes the idea that people develop their own interpretations on seeing his art; he says he has no message, 'I'm not trying to preach anything, it's more about opening a conversation or a dialogue' with the end product being 'read' by people, and this, he concludes, 'is part of the motivation in starting'. Peter wants dialogue − it is the evidence that the artist is ostensibly communicative on many levels − through the paint, the form and the conversation that this creates with himself and between others. As a result, he is quite happy for the 'meaning to be in the hands of the viewer' and, countering this, I suggested that the artist must be understood to allow people to 'get' the artwork (Foucault, 1980). Peter is not so sure about this, claiming that his 'fingerprints' are not the intention on anything that he produces, but concedes that everything he produces includes 'a bit of me' in the transaction − the investment is from him, for him, displayed in the work but subtle. It is not about being legitimate, or authentic or 'complete, more akin to it feel[ing] like what I should be doing [...] making these things, taking time to make my way in the art world; making pictures at least true to my own interests and my own self [...] something I couldn't do in any other way'. It's self-fulfilling, but is it destiny? He pauses. 'I could just stop all this', he says, 'but, this is a harder route to take [...] it feels like, this is my 'really me', this is fulfilling what I think I should be doing with my time and my life'. Time, once more, penetrates the dialogue – the pressures of time, the 'ticking clock', time as a consumed entity, speeding and speeding *up* as the experience of life compresses time (Draaisma, 2004). He considers that his new role is time consuming but that time and effort is *investment in creativity* despite the fact that he insists that his art has little value, that the nature of art is that it has 'no utilitarian purpose'. However, the subject of time is present in a great deal of *reckoning* – usually associated with the demands of 'making a living' or managing family life. The subject of *economy* is also never far from the surface – both economics and the economies of time investment. Things have not changed down the eras in Peter's opinion – maybe the technology – but it is still about using the time constructively. He thinks there will always be people who are prepared to put in the work, speaking of people he knows who spend painstaking 'time invested in' creating art. The opportunities and mechanisms of work change with time, but he suggests that 'the expressions can be different but [...] there will always be those people who will do that, not for economic gain but because that's what they want to do and that is who they are'. He has an optimistic belief that one has to invest time into developing art to *achieve* art and no corners can be cut. Despite having lost a bit of the vitality or recklessness of youth in his approach to beginning his creative processes, resulting in age and time combining to create a hesitancy or deeper consideration, he retains a faith in the 'possible'.

> **Peter:** When I was younger I was far more certain about stuff than I am now, in terms of belief and social attitudes [...] whereas now, I am much more open to accepting that I might be wrong and I probably am on most things [...] ways of seeing and approaching things. I think that gives me a more tentative approach to what I make, so I don't go into it with a certainty of what it will look like, or what it will achieve or what I am trying to communicate.

Art and creativity are not a sanctuary (there is 'no certainty' in what he does), seeing it as 'more [of] a celebration of uncertainty [...] it's quite an exploratory thing', hinting at the inductive nature of art, the excitement of not having complete control and, in this instance, recognition of the anxiety connected to development of works for *exhibition*. Peter does not really know what is coming when he begins, but he insists that he is confident that something will emerge and *exist* at the end of the process. To him, the only certainty he detects is the existence of Peter Driver the Artist, a confidence in one's identity being unyielding. There is not an on–off switch here, inspiration comes at unusual times, unexpectedly and randomly (often in the middle of the night, dream-like and urgently recorded for posterity). If ideas have a 'significance and power', he says, then they are adopted.

In contrast to the privacy of ideas, Peter is sure that art *is* social and has, at the heart of its essence, a productive, creative dynamic that is public, visible and communicative in both rudimentary and profound ways. He sees himself as no different to a writer or a musician; they are all writing for an audience 'unless it's a secret diary, but I've never understood the idea of a secret diary unless you secretly think someone else is going to read it sometime'. His emotional triggers have become more mellow with age and this is complimented by a slower pace of working; the work comes from a curious 'frenzy of creative explosion' trans-mogrifying into 'a sense of calm consideration' on completion. This articulation of energetic externalisation of something stored up is arguably indicative of an urgency to *remember*, rather than to start afresh, to *consider* and to apply reason and care. Peter is adamant that the process is about getting closer to an end result – the burst of energy launches the work and the fine-tuning and adaption come from this outburst. He does not suffer from boredom as a result, with his art he can 'go days without leaving the zone'. It is simultaneously meditative and explosive, exciting and calming, reaffirming and original. This in-between state of 'uncertainty' – as he puts it – seems to be where the anxieties and frameworks of the outside world are left behind but where there remains a historicity of learned structure. I ask him if his art has an 'aura' when he develops the work in his studio.

> **Peter:** Everything comes from somewhere, so all your visual ideas, and visual language, is developed because of the context you live in and [...] how you pick up cultural signs, so whether it's put together in a way that's never been done before is pretty unlikely really. [...] Is it the idea that is the art and then you have to go through a whole series of compromises to turn it into a physical realisation of the idea? [...] I kind of think that the original idea is the original idea and it doesn't become the art until you have actually realised it in a way that can be shared with the world.

It is an interesting interpretation of the idea, suggestive of *creative* compromise with oneself rather than with other people or things and I counter that, if this is the case, then maybe the aura is lost once people see the art – like the words of a closed printed page of a book are in darkness and uninterpretable, so you are only able to interpret what is your field of vision, via the biography, thus the aura of the art work is only ever translatable in the moment of creation, not by the moment of interpretation – everything is circumstantial after the moment of creation. The aura, I say, can only be with Peter until someone else sees the art?

'It speaks to me because I made it', he says, 'so I've got a lot of investment in it and [...] it's a small part of me. [...] Originality comes from [...] the uniqueness of every individual [...] all work is kind of autobiographical, it's all a self-portrait of some sort'. Fictional characters, he says, are the author 'working out [their] understanding of the world and replacing it with the personalities that [they've] acquired, thought about being or have come across'. This intrigues me and I ask him about how an artist makes that emotional, biographical narrative become something *visual*. 'All of my artworks are fragments [...]', he states. 'Each individual piece is a fragmentary expression of myself, my understanding of who I am'. This is realised as if perceiving art as viewed as a variety of vignettes that make up something of a grand thesis.

> **Peter:** Everything I make, I am aware of its fragmentary nature, that it isn't everything I want to say, that it isn't everything I've *got*, this is just this little bit [...] it's just one more step on a long journey [...] the artistic output always seems to happen on the periphery of something else; so they spin off in the corners some-how so, the stuff I make, [...] everything I make is kind of [...] a bit around the edge.

The 'bit at the centre' is ordinary, everyday life. 'This is the big, amorphous thing in the middle which occupies the bulk of time and thinking so that the artistic act is kind of around the edges', he says, alluding to everyday life – the routines, drudgery, repetitiveness and so on being a black, nebulous mass that one seeks to escape from, somewhat akin to getting in a car and driving from the city to the countryside. The key to such escape is skill, talent and initiative.

4.1. Art and the Projected Self

The communicative essence of art is not only through the language of the image, as Roland Barthes avowed (Barthes, [1953] 2010a, 2000), but also in the process. In other words, *who* does Peter do the art *for*? The 'commercial' and 'financial' are never far from consideration via inter-narratives of expenditure, the *recouping* of outlay and so on. I ask him if there is anything remotely ethical in his strategy of costing, to which he replies that his pricing is ethical, not exploitative. 'The time and the investment and the effort that has gone into something, I want to charge what I see as a fair price', he states. Is this softer attitude a result of age, or simply just ubiquitous? He smiles wryly and states that if he 'still had a mortgage and young kids to feed [...] I'd probably be making more commercial decisions about what I did and how I did it but, to be honest, I'd probably still be working full time in the public sector and paying the mortgage'. The *free* artist becomes the *commercial* artist when bills have to be paid and responsibilities met. He tries to balance these needs with something he calls a *holistic commercialism*; he defines 'organic' commerce as a kind of 'see what happens' approach whereas hard commercialism is about a sincere career plan, which he retreats from. I suggest he is 'free' to practice as an artist to which he replies, 'I was just really jammy [...] it fell right for me to do it'. Sales do come along and he is sanguine in his appraisal of the purchaser: purchasing is only people choosing – and his work is protected from the commercial whims, fashions and oscillating tastes of consumers, remaining uncompromised by the actions of making it or what he made it *for* and *as*. Sales come afterwards and he reiterates a dislike of working to commission; *this* ability to *shut off* is a virtue that he defends diligently.

The moment that shutting off *is shut off* is when the exhibition is realised; Peter has taken part in a few 'shows' and there is, at the time of our last full meeting, an event in Southampton approaching coupled with a 'home' exhibition at the Reading site. I visited his Reading show – a mixture of his traditional wood- and lino-cut prints and some conceptual contrivances that both augmented the traditional as well as expanding its reverberation and reach via abstractions for the viewer/participant. He is clearly comfortable with exhibiting; there is a detectable excitement beyond his otherwise friendly, sober exterior. This is pride as well as confidence, earned and maintained but not arrogant or self-effacing either. This adds a hint of resourcefulness to his personality and an esteem to the art on display. In the approach to the exhibitions he admitted to being gripped by a natural trepidation about reception, attendance and the pressure to be 'new' and invigorating in his work. I suggested that the exhibition is performative and he agreed, 'the exhibition is the gig' he stated. I was now a member of the audience *looking* at an array of greatest hits and new numbers and enjoying both in equal measure. The exhibition is where he feels authenticated by public opinion. It is how he illustrates what he is 'up to' to an 'ecology of the art world'; there is a wide, diverse audience out there and his authentication here is superior to one by an elite. His work is democratised through exhibition; it is not about ego but desiring the opinion and the critiques that will chime, ostensibly, with his own view on what he may achieve. 'I don't think I'm going to be able to change the world with my work', he says, but 'it's hard to distinguish between the art and me; it's about both'. He insists that he is happy for people to appreciate his work while being unaware of who he is. 'It's not about me', he reiterates, 'it's more about me fulfilling my purpose as an artist'. The exhibition is therapeutic and it is a point of natural discontinuity. The work, he says, 'has been in the show, people have seen it, so that kind of rounds off that episode of life.

Peter is interesting in that he ascribes to an idea of controlled segmentation here; the flow of art is unremitting, but he is able to partition the performativity of batches of art, partitioning and grouping art almost like a musician would make an album collection. In many ways, as I have intimated – as does Peter – it appears that the work segments itself naturally, like cycles and phases in life. There is also a conceptual essence at work here, almost invisible to the eye but emblematic of age, experience and an additional sense of time being partitioned. His insistence that authenticity is bestowed by the masses rather than the elite is reminiscent of Williams's notion of both knowable community and the normativity of culture, experienced via a structure of feeling (Williams, [1958] 2017, 1961) in that the knowledge of art and the artist are intuitive, silently communicated, thrusting and perpetuated 'beneath the surface' but always, somehow, in a kind of opposition to the elite, the establishment, the status quo of managed and installed taste and monitored by people like him. On the surface, it is *rebellion and resistance* (while, it must be added, he enjoys the opinions of *everybody*, including the elite) but underneath it is mere empathy, acknowledgement of values, a subtle nod to those who 'understand' the velocity and trajectory of the life chance that was offered to Peter at an unexpected juncture. Exhibiting is the platform for such communication that arises once or twice a year where the mystique of the artist comes down from the garret and into the knowable, social, empathetic communion. Life is experienced in 'episodes' and exhibition is a way of marking the passing of such instalments, revitalising the identity and remaining in touch with the past.

Beyond the public, remains the omnipresent *private*. This is a laconic inference to the 'unseen', the 'backstage' (cf. Goffman, 1959) and the *managed identity* and *anarchic possibility* duality that a creative person may cultivate. In many ways, this is where those feelings about dichotomies in life are given structure; Peter is able to interpret the (shared) 'texture' of life (Hoggart, [1957] 2009) via his own experiences of struggle and transition (subjectively) and translate them into art and communication (objectify). The structure comes from the process, but it is what happens in-between these states that gives the art its *character*. The empowerment that he experienced in 'going back to college' is an important stage in Peter's transition in midlife, the experience giving context *to* midlife and to the value of self-discovery through education. He tried, when arriving at art school in his late forties, to treat 'the other students as complete equals and that I wasn't superior to them because I had been on the planet longer', he says. In amongst the fresh-faced new students was another male in his late-thirties.

> **Peter:** we sat together on the first day – and I suppose we were together all the way through the course really – such a different background to me, he's a street artist, a graffiti street aerosol artist, really, really talented and very well known in that scene [...] that was someone really good to get to know and be alongside.

The immediacy of meeting and bonding with someone who produced a different, less conventional form of art made an impression on his comprehension of the wider artistic oeuvre, community and broader approaches to thinking about art. This was an immediate interaction with an art sub-culture (McDonald, 2001) that had gone (slightly) mainstream in the formalisation of the process of making art. 'Counter-cultural', he says with a smile. 'You don't quite fit into the normal system of employment or self-employment, it's slightly *different*'. If anything, Peter was doing the same thing but his own formalisation was to do with joining up loose ends, achieving satiation, self-efficacy and the desire that lay like an 'underground river' inside him for years. His own 'counter cultural' instinct was to eschew the formalism of office work and embrace the power of possibility. There is, consequentially, no doubt that the manifestation of another mature student who was, just about, in midlife made a difference to how Peter integrated socially, communicated artistically, made sense of his work academically and, most importantly perhaps, made sense of his decision to re-engage with art as a pathway in life. The routines of his previous working life helped too. 'The difference for me and the students who were doing it at the *normal age* I guess was that I was commuting from home and treating it like a day job', he says. Unsurprisingly, he applied himself with a natural vigour and enthusiasm to the task at hand, not really noticing his commitment in attending all the lectures and seminars and doing all of the reading required (and the practical work demanded) of a conscientious student, spending lots of time in his studio area; this, he says, is 'because I didn't have to do all the other [social] stuff that younger people have to do when they go away to Uni for the first time'. He felt he could concentrate on getting on with the 'work' immediately. He also had a sense of comparison; he could look back and connect everything up, create his own structure of feelings about his decisions, his situation and his trajectory. He had new freedom of expression too. Before it was a mimetic process articulated via manipulation and enjoyment but, he adds, 'going to art school has really broadened my horizons about all the things that are possible and access to, and looking at, a much wider range of stuff that's been done over the last century'. Art school has helped him order his influences, values and approaches to art and make sense of, and use of, his age.

> **Peter:** The visual aesthetic, it comes from things that you just pick up by osmosis through your life – so there's a kind of a bit of a punk aesthetic going on with some of my art, 'fuck it, that will do' kind of approach which comes from having grown up in the seventies and late-seventies. [...] that approach and that mind-set certainly has had a lasting effect on me and how I make work.

The *release* of education, the boundless enthusiasm and vistas of possibility lend themselves to a 'punk' art (in aesthetics and 'approach') of the conceivable and of the homological re-invention of meanings in creativity that can be utilised creatively and applied sociologically (Beer, 2014; Hebdige, 1979; Laing, [1985] 2015). He recognises the breadth of time and its relative value to the midlife artist – 'young and vibrant' can be authentically challenged by 'midlife and knowledgeable' if the stakes must exist this way. For example, he suggests that things such as album covers and magazines have drifted through time and remained with him, the observations over the decades being stored up and emerging as useful 'capital' in his development of a signature style; thus, compared to young, vibrant artists, the influences have seen him 'develop a different visual language because of having been around for much longer and seen stuff [...] visually from a different pool of energies'. I ask if younger artists have a more *innocent* language to which he replies that this could be the case, but that he still sees himself as naïve as an artist, his approach is still developing. The naivety is mainly due to a stubborn uncertainty, but an uncertainty that has developed more in later life.

The liberation of art school therefore came as both a tangible relief and an enlightenment of the possibilities in front of him metaphorically (the credentials to practice and be respected) and literally (his carving and printing ephemera). His graffiti-artist colleague was at the art school to 'get some kind of accreditation in the conservative world of art' and Peter was keen to experience new culture as well as new ideas that lead to a qualification. In the past, the interest was about going to galleries, looking, doing a bit of thinking but with the inevitable outcome of distraction. 'I hadn't really spent a lot of time looking at it and thinking about it before because I hadn't really had the time to do it', he says. Time speeds up, compresses and distorts focus in a world of work, commuting, deadlines and circuitous routines of finance, the embedded desire for 'security' and the sense that time has somehow passed, the *moment* has passed. Art school was, if anything, therefore a welcome and holistic experience.

> **Peter:** It's being initiated into any culture; you kind of find your way in and you learn as you go along [...] absorb it more than learn it, I suppose. The amount of didactic teaching is limited on an art course, it's more about exploration. [...] There's the language of techniques and processes and styles of working and there's also the critical language of understanding what the thing is trying to do. [...] It's made me more aware [what] should be *good art*, whatever the hell that is!

The language, of course, is structural, learned, articulated via accepted mediums of education, self-expression and mutuality, as well as reflexive and occasionally temporal. His 'awareness' of art extends to his own perception of his authorial signature on his work; to him it is a natural pause, not 'forgetting' per se, but a way of letting ideas 'rest, taking time to consider the meaning of things'. This, of course, is not compliant with the central dynamics of the 'mezzanine' state of creation (that 'aura' inducing suspension of the outside world) because it implies narrative consideration and editing (see Becker, [1982] 2008: Ch. 9), but it does still situate the *working* as part of the mezzanine – the work is *undertaken in isolation* from the outside but it follows that it is *considered in the outside*. Thus, Peter has to 'sometimes leave things, walk away from them, re-evaluate it with a bit of hindsight later, because if you're too close to it and you've spent too long worrying about it and you can't see it, you're too invested in it'. This, again, suggests massive forfeiture of the ideological self into the art itself, but also a suggestion that the process remains hidden from an aesthetically-defining public. Art, therefore, remains a process that is authored in private and rarely affected by external influences beyond his own biography. Does he ever get an opinion from others? Not really, he insists. 'Now I am studio based rather than in an art school studio where you are surrounded by other people making stuff, where there is much more interaction going on, people will wander by and offer you opinions whether you ask for it or not'. This is indicative of the retreat into individuated creativity, the drift from the institutional sociality towards the individuated, isolated generative scene. The structure of art school *gave him the confidence* and now he draws on the biography, experience and wisdom of midlife — and the maturity to make and believe in one's own decisions — to get a sense of value and legitimacy of his own artistic outputs. This is very telling. There is only him, the administrator and myself in the whole building — at times like these he considers that he is 'paddling [his] own canoe'. Art is a 'less social' way of working, isolated and rarely communal, in contrast with the notion of the *artists centre* in which he works; the studios are separated with big, prison-thick, white walls that do not even transmit sound through their denseness let alone encourage face-to-face communication, decentred, refreshingly abstract and 'not the same as working in an organisation where you're kind of somehow all on the same page and working on the same thing together [...] it's a bit more individualised'. I suggest that his routines in life oscillate between 'silence' and 'bright light' before reverting to 'silence' — the *art to life to art process* that he has chosen. 'Yes', he laughs. 'It's very much more varied, so you get weeks of working on your own, doing your own stuff and then you'll go [...] to someone else's show or you'll go to an art school degree show and you'll spend an evening trying to communicate with *everybody*'. This accentuation of *everybody* is suggestive of an urgency of the *moment* — to communicate quickly, deeply, decisively on things before going back into the 'silence', the creative space where he is able to control the variations of intensity; however, *is* it a binary choice? 'I'm seeking purpose and meaning', he says, revealing an inner-dialogue that he has so far skirted around. 'It might not be the art specifically, it might just be that art is the thing that I wanted to do and it's because I'm doing what I wanted to do'. With this choice comes the power to determine his isolation, his individuated-generative process. The long-term thing, to him, is about being 'engaged in something that I want to be doing and this has significance for me, regardless of whether it's successful or not'. It's not 'inner peace' but 'constant inner turmoil, where you are striving and wanting to make and achieve and do more and better'. 'In many ways', he concludes, 'it's not relaxing at all, it's just hard work'.

Peter has identified the 'space' that is otherwise theorised here as a mezzanine — the invoking of the inner turmoil and the harnessing of its creative energy. This is a particularly salient contention coming, as it does, as an exposition of turmoil where one is continually striving for improvement. Thus, it is an active space, but finite and temporal and determinate. It has no other outcome but self-improvement and a sense of self-authentication as an artist. He hopes to give something that is authentically him; a sense of society, shared humanity and be himself through his art — real stuff to eventually share with people. In Peter's wood and lino cuts he has a tendency to integrate words, creating a thrusting, interactive lexicon that adds a significant layer of meaning to his art when it is released. He senses that he 'leans' on a lexicology of politics, philosophy and art, on *words* to help people understand his art, mediating his outputs with a subliminal sense of vulnerability that intimates a lack of self-confidence. The artist Ed Ruscha applies this method too; Peter is mindful of this, respectful of Ruscha and ingratiated into this mode of 'discursive' art. It remains to be seen whether the wording is metanarrative or focussed communiqué. I sense that it is the former, at least initially. He says that he is 'trying to get away from the idea of the artist as some inspired genius who is somehow separate and 'other' from the rest of mainstream society'. No more 'starving genius in his garret', he adds, corresponding with Janet Wolff's assertion that this vision of the 'genius' is outdated, sociologically lazy, inaccurate and anti-materialist (Wolff, 1993, 1983). Peter is thinking, looking around his studio in the cool air of a summer's afternoon. 'A lot of people still have that idea and that idealised view of what an artist should be', he says, '[that] they should be somehow above and beyond and outside of the mainstream of society. I'm more inclined to see it as just being someone doing their job, doing what I do and trying to integrate it with everything else and everybody else'.

This whole process is, of course, social as well as functional. Peter is getting ready to get on with the rest of his day. This will not be the last time we meet, the exhibition is approaching and I have a few scheduled visits to undertake (including a walk to Greenham Common where he tells me that the old nuclear missile silos are visible, *listed* and somehow have an artistic-architectural quality despite their nefarious and subversive historical symbolism). For now, though, he is pensive and strokes his beard. Art, to him, is intrinsically 'human' – not necessarily 'humanist', but human in thought, construction and assemblage and rooted in ideology. The *physicality* is part of the attraction of the *process* and the *final piece of art* in his view. It is an outcome, something that has emerged from the in-between space of creation, between the real midlife world and the possibilities of the future. Seeing that something 'has been made by somebody [...] has something more human about it, because you've got the immediate connection with the person who has made it', he states. Art, in an individualised society, to Peter is 'a way of sharing and communicating common humanity [...] this is my experience of the world, you can have a look at it'. This is the communicative function of art in society and it has taken Peter a long time to arrive at the juncture where he can make space to make it, but now he is here he has a lot to convey.

Chapter 5

Down in the Woods

Wytham Woods lies directly to the west of the city of Oxford, nestling in undulating countryside and brushing against the edges of the villages of Wytham, Eynsham and Swinford. Bestowed upon Oxford University in 1942, the woods provide opportunities for ecological and artistic research within a scene of beautiful bluebell glades, thick, sensuous woodland and open rural vistas encompassing irregular dense grass, scrubland, pasture and walking tracks that double as vehicle access routes. These isolated driveways are occasionally punctuated by the chugging familiarity of a Defender Land Rover driven by Robin Wilson, the academic Anthropologist creator and Director of Oxford University's Wytham Woods Visual Arts Research Project that has its home deep in these woodlands.

Robin, upright, well-spoken and convivial meets me in the car park and drives us initially to view his Oxford Anagama Kiln Project. It is here, on a very breezy day in autumn that we 'catch up', blending art and life as we close the years between us last speaking as contemporaries at Durham University in the 1990s and our present-day, middle-aged emphases of art, creativity and the passion for *potential* while crouching and crawling into massive Japanese kilns. Robin began the Visual Arts project himself, growing it from a straightforward letter to the University of Oxford proposing a postgraduate-led research unit dedicated to an interdisciplinary approach to art, creativity and culture into the extensive project that it is now, encompassing the involvement of a large network of participants in Oxford and beyond, chasing funding and new ideas, producing research papers and involving outreach and open days and finding joys in the simple, though sophisticated, *creation of things*: art and ideas that combine to give Robin and his colleagues a sincere sense of purpose. Our day together on this occasion involves the admiration of the scale and power of the Bizen kilns that are situated in an opening in the woodland and watching the magnificently talented Takuma Takikawa (flown in specially from Japan to apply his expertise and talent to the construction) *building* the latest addition to the project before retiring to the remote, secluded studio with its exhibits of lino prints, woodcuts, charcoal drawings and watercolours, magnificent iron presses and the usual ephemera of an artist's bolthole. As a strong breeze picked up around us, rattling the wooden walls of the cabin as we drank tea next to a wood burning stove, we began to unpick the deeper meaning of the arts, the creative process and the *value of doing* to this particular middle-aged man, moving beyond depictions of 'why' and 'where' and into something much more fundamental. A free-flowing discussion commenced, focussing on precisely how Robin had found himself here, deep in the woods, making things but resistant to any-thing that may counter the freedom of the artist as a creator that fights a consist-ent and unrelenting *entropy* that exists all around us.

It immediately transpired that the Wytham Woods project came into being because of big changes in Robin's life; the rhythm of an academic career was interrupted by a need to care for an elderly relative, a hiatus that lasted two years and, when free to resume a role beyond domestic caring, he had an opportunity to evaluate what he *could do* and what he *wanted* to do. He approached some uni-versities with a proposal to start up a research unit dedicated to art, creativity and intellectual pursuits. 'Participant observation is a thing', he says, acknow-ledging his anthropological training while explaining the raison d'être and the essential kernel of the Wytham project, 'but let's create a site in which the art is informing the academia and then I can do the two things that I rather like instead of the one thing I like'. Research and art combine to create a one-off opportunity and consequently the project is emblematic of a new start and a fresh perspective on his overlapping interests of research, creativity, praxis and culture.

The roots of his creativity come from an embryonic intellectual interest devel-oped in childhood that was limited by poor eyesight, something that quite often curtailed participation in social-bonding exercises such as sport. Appreciation of books and — unusually, given his eyesight — visual art stimulated his interest early and he is sure that the process of delivering his ideas onto the page from his formative years has remained a stimulus into middle age.

> **Robin:** Drawing is something that I could do even at three or four, I could write and read when I was three, and I always had pictures in my head which, if you get them out, other one's appear [...] so, I've always had ideas [...] but they have always been visual things, bundles of things that you can twist and turn in your head [...] and by siphoning some of those things out, new one's come and you feel that there is a pressure behind you for all the new stuff to happen so I am actually speeding up, not slowing down.

The process of creativity is accumulative, it has momentum, speed and an increasing capacity that generates enthusiasm, outputs and ideas — a joyous and challenging accretion that may never be quite satiated. There is an acknowl-edged correlation between the identity of his childhood self — a *developmental* and *expressive* self — and the work that he undertakes as an adult, managed and innovated through time, articulated via anthropological research settings and transformed seamlessly into the contemporary pursuit of art.

It was in these anthropological field sites that Robin began to see the poten-tial currency of art and craftsmanship when utilised as a *method* to assist in his early career interdisciplinary research that combined the anthropological and the natural scientific. While abroad, sometimes in potentially dangerous settings, he would use his own artistic skills to ingratiate himself with the gatekeepers and the locals via wood carving and story-telling – a direct involvement combined to assuage and placate. The conversation created a dialogue, narrative or dialectic via the praxis situated in the immediate and transitory – a performative setting that Schneider and Wright describe as something of a 'web of temporary social relations [...] spun between anthropologists and research subjects' (Schneider & Wright, 2010: 10). 'You are creating a sense of what the political situation is by doing the craft', says Robin. He needed to use quickly acquired languages to both articulate his presence and to avoid danger and this communicative skill set was 'much more skilled and creative and worthwhile because I was learning about *them* so, if you tell somebody about them[selves], you learn; it's a reciprocal conversation and so I find I was learning a lot about these guys'. Sitting with men, elucidating a mutuality via dexterity, is arguably interpreting the culture as *both* semiotic and behavioural, based on learned routines and facilitating an opportunity to apply what Geertz (1973) would call *thick description*, or potentially going *well beyond* the inference and assumptions associated with the theory and into more integrated understanding; here we can see the *role* of art, the dynamic of acquired and circumstantially performed skills and the wider *essence of the social* as a combined language comprehended as a cohesive and reassuring element, universal and penetrative. The carving is analogous of what Tim Ingold would describe as *excavation*, 'a way of knowing from the inside' (Ingold, 2013: 11). Scraping away at a surface, revealing more and more detail though 'knowing' the other culture via art is arguably a tried, tested and historical method of ingratiation and mutuality (Laning, 1971: 18). Art therefore is both demonstrably subjective and social, a combined utility that acts as a lubricant of *sociality* and is blind to circumstantial cultural contrasts. The contrasts *remain*, but the art, the craft, the skill is universal, revealing and enlightening. It seems that these formative anthropological experiences inform Robin and his approach to art.

Back in the woods, Robin speaks a great deal of how he situates this combination of intellectual approaches, incrementally built over time via such experiences, a varied education and sheer necessity (language skills), into the attractive, swirling miscellany of his present-day arts project. It seems that such heterogeneity can be transferred from carving with the locals at the mines of New Guinea and put to good use in the vibrant art worlds of Oxford, but there is also the need nowadays to be pushed, stimulated and challenged by people younger and older than himself. The speed of learning – experienced in the field – transfers to a *requirement* aimed at those around him.

> **Robin:** I want bright people around me [...] so I feel that I am being pushed forward, so I feel very young here because there are eighty year olds who [have fast minds]; [...] everyone I deal with, their minds are flat out, whatever their age is and that appeals to me [...] and mine is faster because theirs is faster and everyone pulls each other up and so that is an attractive thing to me.

Such reciprocation is a recurring theme of our conversation, the sense that freshness is something that is found both externally as well as internally, that there is a sense that the creative process cannot be realised without the combination of *stimulus from outside* that rouses the internal engine. He proposed what became the Wytham Woods project at a time where he had 'nothing to lose', resulting in being able to 'create your own thing' from a platform where he was able to transform unrequited negatives in life into positive learning experiences. To Robin, the perspective of having nothing to begin with is a perfect starting point for creativity and innovation – an absence of what we might consider entrepreneurial risk-taking replaced by a sense of freedom and absence of risk.

> **Robin:** I wasn't sat there thinking that if I do this I'm going to lose my pension; [...] I wasn't losing anything, because I'd lost it, I'd taken the *choice* [...] it was, without question, the best choice I ever could have made [...] with a completely clean slate, quite late in life, I could propose anything I wanted *to* anyone and I did.

The circumstance of losing a close family member, having cared for that person for some time and the absence of a role to go back to, left him with the 'choice' he speaks of; a freedom of choice that he transposed into praxis. In creating the research unit that has grown into a large project, it clearly comprises the combination of people and thinking and action that facilitates the process of creative energy transforming into creative *building*, per se.

> **Robin:** There is something in my head which sees an end product which we are nowhere near yet which is some kind of global network of happy people doing craft, doing intellectual [and] arts and craft pursuits, not necessarily overlapping or competing but all through reciprocity, creating a pleasant sense of fairly intensive creativity, but one in which you can pick or choose the level of articulation and reflection that you want [...] I'm saying there are different *intensities* of creativity and at different times [...] there are times when you are creative and times when you are not and wanted to create an intellectual space where groups of people could work like that in a non-judgemental atmosphere.
>
> **PM:** Could you only have conceived of this project as a middle-aged man?
>
> **Robin:** No; take out the circumstances that have allowed it to happen and [...] this is actually utterly ideal [...] this hits every single button I want to do; everything.

Wytham Woods is clearly the retreat that makes for a sense of happiness, practical creativity and innovative thinking, but it is also just a venue. Robin travels and gains inspiration through what he calls a 'haptic' and spatial method that compliments his intellectual thirst for originality and new experiences. Thus, he finds it hard to objectify art as something that emerges from a specific moment; there is no similarity with, for example, The Ruins sense of 'aura' here – instead the creation of an original piece of thinking leads to an original work of art, arrangement, a *linear creative process*. Is he lost in the moment?

> **Robin:** That's the enjoyment in creativity and that's the bit I don't understand [...] there is a feeling when you are creating – I'm not sure you are *lost* in the moment – I think it's like performance [...] getting the right words at the right time and performing fluently [...] word perfect [...] it's like creating a perfect image or a perfect pot or throwing on the wheel perfectly, you're not lost in the moment, what you feel is suddenly on *top of it* and what you feel is a sudden perfection of performance while you're actually doing it.

He speaks of a recent conversation with a neurosurgeon, explaining that he learned that part of this process is in developing pathways in the brain which you get through touch and movement in space. This is also achieved in music, he explains, 'but you don't really get it from sitting in a sedentary place and [using] a screen; you have to touch and squeeze and move'. You have to be in command of the combination of space, skill set, thought patterns (i.e. what you want to get out of it – a kind of 'visioning the outcome' approach) and go with the flow – a kind of tightrope walk where, should you consider what you're doing in too much detail, you fall off. This, in many ways, is achieving what Giddens (1991) would call a sense of 'ontological security', a subjective state of order that needs no further inspection as it functions.

> **Robin:** You have to be in it, but also distant from it and it creates a slightly altered mental state [...] so whatever that hypnagogic state is, that's the moment of real creation [...] you phase in and out of it rather strangely, even if you are brilliant at what you do, there are times when you hit it right.

Creativity, therefore, is an experience as well as a series of actions; it is, in effect, a state of mind that, without a real sense of order, captures thoughts, biographies, stories and scenes and codes of communications. A mixture of sketches, memories and smells, sunlight, geography and other stimuli gather together, often just simply glimpsed on a page but opening up the cornucopia of influence. 'This', explains Robin, 'is how you *hit it*'. Creativity is experienced as a moment of enlightenment that can often be induced by a memory in its many guises. But what about *identity*? Roughly examined, what can the experience and the action it provokes via such memory stimulus tell us about the 'author's' identity? Does this nebulous concoction of ideas, experience and will weave itself into the art that is created?

> **Robin:** I think the outcome is immaterial; it's nice to have a nice pot, or a nice academic paper or a nice song or happy people having watched your play, but I find the process of creation is an internal inscription; that's why this sketch doesn't matter if you can or can't see anything in it because it doesn't matter, I can see something in it.

Thus, the identity and the meaning are highly subjective, personalised, private and subject to change depending on all of the oscillations in personal mood, environment and time, being a prosaic force that neutralises the reception of any artistic work, keeping the meaning and the value *intrinsically attached to the author* at all times. Robin explains this ownership as an imprint of satisfaction, perfection in the moment and a testament of meaning at the time, in the moment:

> **Robin:** To me [a carving] conjures up an entire month of field-work, so the process of creation – when it works – is an internal inscription which lasts. A sketchbook is quite a good analogy for that; you're not trying to represent reality, you're writing on the inside of your head and there is a froth that happens to be sketches or a linocut or pots or whatever and in that sense the creativity, to my mind, isn't a pride or a sense of achievement in the thing itself, albeit the thing itself, to a certain extent, is an aide memoir of the internal thing that has worked. Some things work and some things don't, in the same way that you're trying to craft a sentence that conveys exactly what you're trying to say.

Artistic output – a creative amalgam of many approaches, crafts, thoughts and skills – is the result of something that has somehow *come off*; there is a strong narrative of determinism and experimentation that underpins the process, a sense that art can be something that does or does not work, but nevertheless something that only makes proper sense when it *does* work, when it does emerge from the moment of perfection. Again, this is understanding art and creativity as a moment where an aura of functionality, perfection and untapped energy become such a variegated, almost anarchic combination of the senses, materials, sounds, passions, words and memories to create an ultimate, transitory sense of *presence* and cogent, coherent *satisfaction*. Thus, as Robin says, it is not actually being 'lost in the moment' at all, but simply in *command* of the moment; coherent, confident, natural and willing. He shows me a small saké cup he made, fired recently, plucked out of the kiln at 1300 degrees and plunged into water to create a certain textured surface effect, known as an 'ash glaze'. 'The thing itself is sort of a touchstone to the internal process', he says, 'but the product is very much a less intense reflection of the creative process than the creative process itself, which I've found is an interior thing'. The *process* has the penetrative value; it is the place where the identity and emotion fuse with the externalised development of a given artefact. The saké cup means a lot less that the satiation gained in making it.

> **Robin:** It is the same as when you run your hands along a book-case of books that you've either read or partially read or *want* to read; you don't have to read the contents of all of them because as you go along the spines you get the flashes of the stories and the stems of the stuff that's in them, just by seeing that; that's what I see these things as.

The art, the pots, the sketches and the linocut prints are, essentially, *attempts* to articulate a sense of being there, of *doing*. This driving life-force in such creative art is a binary system of both *effort and chance* as well as the practical articulation of skill and opportunity. The dexterity of the moment is clearly important. This is the interregnum in a process where the artist is able to draw on the 'capital' he or she has acquired and maintained over time (Bourdieu, [1984]; 2010). What Bourdieu might articulate as the 'field' of artistic production is the art world that Robin and his colleagues loosely connect with (including Oxford University and its galleries, museums and facilities to create art), but it is the social capital of Robin himself that explains the moment where he is able to essentially 'change gear' to make a work of art make sense, emerging from a tenuous zone and becoming coherent and expressive and, most of all, *explicable*.

> **Robin:** Sometimes [artworks] are accurate representations of what you wanted to say, and sometimes less so which is like the sketch-book; sometimes they just don't work, and that's where *technique* comes in and that's where, you know, you can physically make tangible the thing that's in your head and I think that's what's making the difference between art and creativity.

Such technique is not a universal skill. There is also the desire. The drive to *make something* and make something *mean something* is part of a wider process that involves layers of action from inception to completion. This is a process that involves having to step out on a limb, to take changes that are related to environmental, financial and ontological risks – in other words, you need to make a pact with yourself that you are ready for failure or the work to be banal, unoriginal and depressingly *ordinary*. 'Creativity involves risk, whereas some forms of crafts [...] where you just stamp, and you stamp, there is just no risk', he says. 'I think that risk is an essential part of creativity, that it's not an absence or not. Creativity can be seen as arranging some cups in a certain way, in rows, as triangles, at different heights and so on'. It's creative, he adds, but it's just an *arrangement*, an *association* in a visual perspective. The risk of getting arrange-ment wrong is quite low, but it doesn't mean it doesn't have any risk. He elabo-rates on the theme by stating that people put their clothes on in a certain way, acting 'creatively' with combinations of colours and styles that exist as an arrangement. It is only when you turn up at the event you are dressing for to find everyone dressed differently that the riskiness of your creativity is exposed.

> **Robin:** The arrangement of pre-existing things constitutes a creative act, albeit the intensity of the arrangement is less than the creative act. [...] the thing that I'm arranging now, I know that the clay [...] came from Japan, I know *where* in Japan it came from and I know what it took me to get all of the stuff together; [...] the *intention to create* was higher in the making of it than in the *arranging* of it, but they're still the same thing.

To get to a point of departure – the beginning of the creative act – the mechanisms of arrangement must be planned, the risks taken in assembling what is needed and then (should you 'get there') the creative process is the moment where the risk is perhaps intensified and the risk of failure is exposed. The pressure to succeed is high, despite – as Robin says – the creative process being just that, a *process* where things are *assembled* to be utilised and hopefully *emerge* as something original and satisfying given the fragility of the whole process to 'get there'. If anything, *this* is where, as Robin has previously said, 'you hit it'.

However, when it is 'hit', what next? Where does 'Robin' go? This is not an invitation to consider the moving on to a new project, a new focus of creative intensity perceived as phases of the same wider project of the self and of the art. Instead, this is about where Robin leaves an imprint – as he calls it – on the 'inside' of the finished artefact. The author must leave something of himself on the article we behold, and it is, perhaps, better to acknowledge that when we consume. Consequently, I am interested in what Robin considers there is 'of himself' left when the print or the pot goes on exhibition or is sold? His answer is thoughtful and deep. It is, to him, a process that, essentially, continues forever, explaining that each pot he makes can be arranged, manipulated, broken, gifted and so on.

> **Robin:** The act of creation continues when you see it, it's just that the intensity [...] the creative act isn't just the physical, technical [...] it is in the firing, it is in its *use*: if I give this pot to you, I've no idea what you're going to do with [it] but [it's] going to become part of where you keep paper clips or whatever, and that continues given the way that you arrange it on your desk. The manifestation of the creativity and the intensity differ, but the creativity passes to a certain extent to the new beholder [...] but as long as it sits in my imagination I am still creating it for myself [...] the creativity doesn't reside in the *thing*, the creativity resides in our living heads [...] so long as the potter is alive and remembers and inscribes something of their self, in their own heads, in the making of this it continues to live as a continual act of creation for them whether they can touch or hold it or not.

Creativity is a process, a rhythm, a routine and an endless line that exists in distances between the author and the reader, user, beholder and so on. 'The creative thing does not reside in the physicality of it', he says, 'it resides in the *notion* of it, but then it also resides in the *thing* itself'. A work of art, he adds thoughtfully, 'is not an act of memory, it's an act of *forgetting*'.

> **Robin:** [i]t's like a tombstone or a photograph, they're not memorials in that sense, they're relieving you of having to worry about the death of somebody, because it's encoded somewhere else, you know you can refer to it [...] so, by making stuff tangible. When you write a paper you *forget* it, and that's the *point*! It's *getting it out*, getting that idea perfect in your head and out, not so that you remember it forever but so you can forget the damn thing and move on to the next one. So the creative act is a process of *forgetting* [...] allows the creative process to push forward, [...] in an unsentimental way the creative act allows you to move forward [...] the point of creativity is that you *rush past* people [...] clarifying ideas and moving them *out*!
>
> [...]
>
> **PM:** Does it give you something you can hang onto? Security and sense of purpose?
>
> **Robin:** No, it's the other way around: everything is standing still, this gives me the opportunity to rush forward. [...] I see the art as not creating permanence [...] because permanence is a fallacy anyway, everything is in constant flux, the constant entropy which we are fighting, so in order to fight entropy you have to create otherwise everything falls around you.

I suggest that there is a point about midlife sequestered in there somewhere and we both laugh, pause to sip tea and a moment of thoughtful silence descends as if this choreography of the moment was inevitable. Robin breaks the silence. 'The art drives you in a period that otherwise might be a comfortable, settling into the acceptance of death; I've got no intention of going quietly', he says. Most people are obsessed with material things that illustrate an 'end point', whereas art has no discernible equivalent. To Robin, there is a requirement of every artist to have courage to summon enterprise and abilities in a resistance to the dying of the light. Creative people are instinctively resistant to capitulation in life where 'a lot of magnolia paint and a nice Audi' are the spoils of victory. This is an illusion he says, 'whether it's music or dance anything; *that's* fighting the battle and creativity is a way of living every single day knowing that every day could be our last, and one day will be'. It is a very determined and defiant standpoint, but one that summarises the resistance, via art, to the banal with clarity. Creativity pushes you through a period in which middle age is a temptation to do little, to rest, stop resisting; there is little incentive to start new things, to gain new experience; creativity is a technique to invest in one's own capital and midlife is a stage where the light burns with the greatest ferocity. Beyond the applied meaning of the things he makes, the functionality of such art and the *notion* of art is the dynamic of the creator in life itself, where he is, how he feels, how midlife functions as a dynamic of the creative whole. 'I don't define myself by age', he says, adding that routine is reflective of life, not the *stage* of life. Things happen, he infers, by a synergy of chance and desire. 'It just so happens that I am this age, but with a different set of factors I'd be there either later or earlier', he states, before adding that:

> **Robin:** [I]t's not an age based thing, this is life. I would have done something complicated like this at twenty, except at twenty people stop you; at thirty [...] you have more rhetorical tricks, you have more social capital, you have more financial capital [...] my degree of agency is higher and is increasing all the time and so I am better able to make my world in my own vision, [...] it took me longer to get the agency I would have had at eighteen had I come from a different background, so age is relevant in only that it has taken an accumulation of years for me to overcome a set of factors which would have essentially led me to becoming a lorry driver.

Circumstances, he suggests, 'wiped away some things that meant I had fewer things to lose'. His previous academic trajectory was not providing adequate stimulus; there is a sense betrayed in Robin's narrative, that he felt somehow *incomplete* and his oscillating fortunes essentially helped him to fill in gap that existed beyond his educational journey.

> **Robin:** [I]t's like building a glider, you've got to have all the bits together before it will fly and I think middle age, certainly from thirties to fifties, you start to have enough bits. You might not have the will, the body, the energy or the mind to do it, but if you're fortunate enough to have those things you have the time to bolt together your [glider] and it will fly, or not, or other people will shoot you down or whatever, but at least you can give it a shot; this thing [Wytham] could be shot down at any moment.

Midlife, to Robin is an irrelevance. It is a stage, defined extraneously, lacking meaning. What he experiences is simply 'life', a phase in the journey, an opportunity to blend together knowledge, experience and chance and make something of it. In this instance, it is his Wytham project and the multitude of functions and outputs that the project offers, but it could have been something else. The situation is just *that*, a *situation*, and it is 'quite different from some people who conduct career changes in middle age because they are feeling middle aged, I haven't done that, not in that sense'. The phase is simply indicative of a determination to achieve and see something come into being and thrive. He closes by stating that 'middle age is important because, if you're fortunate, determined and your energy and intellect remain [...] the passage of years gives you enough time to bolt stuff together that has value that you can now operate'. Middle age, therefore, is an *opportunity*. Robin is aware of the influences and experiences that channel into the making of something in his studio or his kilns in the woods, but he is also highlighting a tension between the idea of the individual and of the collective. I became increasingly aware that Robin saw art as something that is highly personal but also democratic, as the work of high-individualisation as well as a product of the social and somehow owned by the future and the interpretations upon the work that people unknown may apply. To Robin, the art is something that is extracted from the 'inside' of his own consciousness and his risk is to make that nebulous series of ideas become realised in a thing. As such, the process is riven with a multitude of risks – all being a curious mixture of the personal and the public. If anything, this is probably why fine art is the connective tissue between the idea of the individuated-generative and socio-generative arts. Robin needs his thoughts to create – just like any other artist whether it be musical, literary, fine artistic, cinematographic and so on – but he also needs his network (Becker, [1982] 2008) to help him realise it and make it live on. Thus, like song (Berger, 2016), Robin's art – like Peter's – leans forwards into time with the assistance of a willing audience who continue to extra-create the artefact. Literature, arguably, has less malleability (it is interpreted, but is not somehow *practical* like fine art or music) and 'leans forward' less obviously; however, the *practicality* of art drives Robin onwards, fuelling his creative self and instigating a sociality of art with others around him via people and institutions, events and communications. In his midlife moments, Robin is able to make sense of the art as simply part of a sense of self, of momentum, of practical purpose in the realisation of vocation. His intellectual journey from geology to anthropology to creative art is, in many ways, a natural evolution and one that is reflective of a personal transition rather than a response to systematic influences (and expositions) of social class, finance, symbolic capital or institutional control.

This is therefore not art understood via the base-superstructural Marxist analyses of ideology, economics and indirect influences on production and reproduction of such ideologies (Eagleton, [1976] 2002); instead, we are observing an instrumental, late modern, almost neo-Weberian series of relationships that function to connect the artist with the sense of self, the highly individualised riskiness of our stage of modernity and the idea of *situating* oneself, making oneself *distinct*, acting not in opposition to the structure or, indeed, socially and culturally reproducing it conscientiously like Paul Willis's 'lads' (Willis, 1977) or by applying a cultural homologous meaning to artefacts as a form of resistance (Hebdige, 1979; Willis, 1978). Instead, this embodies releasing the art to others while retaining, and somehow 'owning', its *spirit* as a statement of both original intent and retainable, omnipresent and indestructible value to the sense of self. Thus, identity is branded *onto the art* and its mechanisms of creation (its machinery, its materials and its form) and functions as a simple exposition of time, space and location. Art is an enterprise to be 'project managed' carefully, with the creative process existing before physicality is assumed, during the making-real of the artefact and continuing on into the future after the art is formed and departed. Creativity is a process of pre-history and post-partum, of physicality and the metaphysical. Art, therefore, is duality of identity and process, a custom for situating oneself in time and space, a personal diary of self-development and expression as well as the management of ideas and their transformation into *things*. To Robin, the function of his art is ostensibly to renew, initiate and confirm that what may have lay dormant or piecemeal in earlier times and to continually invigorate and challenge his self-defined boundaries that may seem intentionally instinctive and intuitive to observers but multifarious, fluid and unpredictable to the creator himself who seeks continually to explore new ways of 'hitting it' as each day passes. One can sense the excitement bubbling at all times.

As we drive back down the track to the gate to the car park I state my belief that the woods must be amazing to experience in hoar frosts or snowfall; Robin turns to me and says that coming to work each day at the studio allows him to experience, observe and understand the seasons up close and with a lasting and cogent sensory value. I make a mental note that this presents itself as a useful metaphor for the shifting qualities of art as viewed by the protagonist who drives the Land Rover: somehow the passage of time is indicative of those changes in ideas that he spoke of, in the gentle, linear shifting from one pattern to another but always retaining a familiarity and a sense of cyclical renewal. In these woods, it somehow feels right.

Chapter 6

Inspiration by the Sea

Dominic Jago opens the front door to his cottage-cum-studio and smiles. Flicking back a mane of shoulder-length hair, his eyes intense, body tall and angular and exuding a languid confidence, he greets me. The soft intensity of his body language mirrors the strokes of a painter that is somehow in tune with his textured, home counties, privately educated, cultured voice. We are soon sitting in his studio, almost literally a stone's throw from the south coast beaches where he began his journey into a life creating works of art, walking along the shore collecting driftwood and shaping small items of furniture from its jagged and rough form. I can hear the seagulls outside as we talk; Dominic wants to show me his work and he wants to talk about it. He is a lively and compelling person, a sensitive and welcoming host and a man reborn in his mid-forties. After years of wandering through school, college and career in search of true vocation, he is happiest by the sea, painting and photographing people and nature, sculpting and sketching and writing. 'I just found it therapeutic picking up bits of wood [...] and I started making bits of furniture', he states, gesturing towards a small table at his side that embodies his conversion to art from a career in tutoring life skills. He shows me some smooth, sanded wood that he also rescued from the ocean, stating that he saw the flotsam, once dried and levelled, as having potential. '[I] had the idea of painting on them [...]', he says of the oddments. 'I just squeezed paint out of the tubes and made some paintings'. Such an epiphany on a local beach has now developed into a career of creating fine art and undertaking occasional forays into photography that has helped confirm his identity and lifestyle as an expressive producer, professional and member of the diffuse and occasionally dissonant artist community that exists in his adopted town.

Drying, sanding, crafting and painting of driftwood would take his mind off other matters, such as working out what to do next in life; the sandpaper and dust, smoothing the wood all day and the ordering into a practical form, to *make something* out of them achieved a practical *outcome* to his labour as well as developing a sense of purpose in his actions. 'I didn't want to buy a coffee table, I wanted to *make one*', he says, summarising the thought processes that lead to the creation of the small table that he gestures towards with pride. Everything was to be done by hand, adding an ecology to his sense of creativity that began to develop into a sense of destiny; 'something kind of clicked; it somehow ignited something dormant [...] an artistic sensibility started to come through', he says, sensing he had space and 'the right to explore this [...] a synchronicity [...] something completely unexpected'. In the past, there was a lot of 'open energy' he says. 'It wasn't a conservative way of thinking about life, the whole thing just rolled on, [...]' seeing his immediate family moving around, trying new things, unencumbered by a requirement to stay still. He became an artist because of 'that way of living, the spontaneity, the expression, the sense of just playing with life' appealed and presented itself as an option.

The thing that initially emerges when speaking with Dominic is an *immediacy* in life that transmogrifies into a sense that the artist, in this instance, is content to embrace the combined elements of risk, success, business and critique with an energy of the *entrepreneur*; this is a person who is following a path into art as a vocation who is clearly prepared to challenge his own expectations of *life* and challenge *art* as both a way of *doing life* as well as playfully and constructively challenging art as a fixed form. There is immersion here; he *lives* as an artist as well as practicing as one (he works from his home studio; there is no private, physical space to detach from his work) and I get the sense that Dominic does not 'do things by halves' inasmuch that he envelops his whole energy into the pursuit of a self-defined excellence. This is a privately delineated form of 'capital'; Dominic doesn't tend to compare and contrast, he just *projects* and, despite the exuberance of freedom that he feels, there is still a sense of risk that pervades his thinking and his actions. Before we even get started with talking about the form of his art, his method and the routines that he applies to creativity, we are discussing the edginess that he perceives in *being* an artist. Such states of being require, in Dominic's opinion, a requirement to channel a pessimism into a laissez-faire approach to creativity – one must recognise the versatility of art and being an artist and embrace its potential.

> **Dominic:** [It] is a big risk to work as an artist – even if you've been to art college – [...] in some ways you can be no better off, it's a difficult world to earn a living in. [...] It is the capacity to take risks [...] and as an artist you are in some ways always in a high-risk situation [...] and I enjoy that.
>
> **PM:** Business entrepreneurial spirit transfers to something we would consider more artistic, looser, reactive?
>
> **Dominic:** Some entrepreneurs are probably very careful [...] risk averse [...] systematic [...] things happen spontaneously, and I like that aspect of art; basically, you have to just get up, start playing with it, a certain energy that goes with it.

Credentials equate to nothing; there is a genuine meritocracy in art based on talent and guile. There is a requirement, therefore, to take risks, do innovative things and somehow 'beat *a* system' rather than *the* system insomuch that the artist is a creator rather than a qualified professional. While, he states, 'it is limiting to publically define myself [as entrepreneurial], partly because it comes with all sorts of connotations of capitalism [...] capitalist bastard, self-centred, precocious [...]', he understands the hierarchy and he relishes the adrenaline of experiments, of being outside the elite and competitively contributing as part of the amorphous art community in order to make a living. The art establishment arguably partially resides not too far down the coast in places such as Cornwall where Woolf's Godrevy Lighthouse sits off the northern coast at St. Ives not far from Betjeman's Daymer Bay – but, here, he sees himself set aside from all of that; he is a 'maverick' in his own words. There is a latent toxicity in being entrepreneurial – as if the art itself is at risk of being tainted by its machinations – but Dominic does recognise the value of being an artist as something of a saleable image, the embodiment of the authentic expert (Giddens, 1990) situated in the right geographical *place*. Identity flows from this – or is generated from it in double-hermeneutic fashion (Giddens, 1984) that situates identity as both shaped by (in this instance) career choice and career choice shaped by his 'maverick' identity. Which came first is moot; the thing that shapes a lot of Dominic's thinking is the longevity of his art, the fact that the object will outlast its creator and that somehow the work of art has a biography on the same level as its initiator. Thus, the link between expression and emotion is strong and personal and he makes sure to give himself a lot of time to connect with what he is trying to paint. He adds a layer of thinking to what he sees – for instance, empty chairs and the people who have sat in them are envisaged in his paintings in the context that the chair itself has a biographical story and this framework of thinking is present in all that he creates; it is, to Dominic, all emotive. 'We all own objects that outlive us and they go on to other people [...] sometimes you can just paint a load of objects and it just captures something about the transience of time', he says. Thus, creativity can be considered the process of giving something like the chair a new biography, a new set of meanings. 'It means something to me and means something to them [the beholder]', he states and this, in essence, is Dominic's stance on creativity and identity – namely the connection of his own sense of transience in time, his connection to things *in* time and his desire to breathe life into such things to give them an additional life beyond him.

Dominic's identity, therefore, is connected to the 'passing on' of that abstract biography. People come to his exhibitions with a 'fear of art' that is best understood as that moment of hesitation that sees the beholder not knowing 'what to do in front of a painting'. This collusion is hidden, it is reflexive and instrumental and, in some ways, Dominic is required to bestow ownership of the emotion of the work onto the potential buyer, allowing the owner to shape and control the meaning. He is exhibiting work as we speak, in a gallery down the coast and 'while we're sitting here', he says, 'there's people looking at my work that I will never meet'. The art exists in its own right, separate to its creator but something hangs on. 'I'm not sure how much the art makes me change my view of myself, I suppose I have a vague knowledge that I created it [...]', he says, but 'nothing is eternal [...]. You know these things are only going to live so long'. The art takes on its own life in being received by the eyes and minds of other people who exist outside of his field of creation; Dominic retains a sense of connection–surrogacy really–that he knows will continue in his absence from the artefact. To him, the *objet d'art* is a legacy, albeit a finite, almost *mortal* one that figuratively mirrors the life of the artist in a sense of renewal, fitness, suitability and the vagaries of the situational that we must all maintain.

A strong theme emerges from our various discussions – whether on the beach, in the studio, walking up the High Street, over food, in the car and so on – that envelops Dominic's dual sense of connection with his outputs and their afterlife. To him, the notion of completion of work is important – a therapeutic sense of the realisation of completion, rather than the physical closure. 'It is an interesting moment when you must decide that it is finished', he states, but reiterates the sense that it is difficult to work out when something *is* finished – but here lies a basic intuition on what the *art is*, when it is done. Signing the painting completes it; he holds his breath when he does it. He then varnishes the canvas, but this is not the birth of the painting, it is perhaps the moment where it *comes of age*. As he explains above, art is always in a state of being restored, revitalised, repositioned socially and intellectually and situationally. When he completes a work and he considers the 'rituals involved with these things' such as in choosing the frame and its colour and only then, he states, it is ready, complete and primed for exhibition as a simultaneous closing and opening of the same chapter in his life and the art's own biography. 'I've created something and it wouldn't exist without me', he says, and 'art is a risk because you're putting something very personal out there, publically, and people can say that it's absolute crap; people *do* sometimes [do this]' and it can be dispiriting. This flow of feedback ensures that the art and the artist remain *one thing* despite the artwork being abstracted, awarded its own life, its own biography beyond the author. This organic connectivity is arguably never broken, despite separation of creator and artefact. In explaining the process Dominic produces a portfolio of sketches, cuttings, photographs and written ideas and discusses the way that visuals stimulate the creative process, suggesting that the randomness of image 'illustrate that the creative process can go in any direction really'. He gives me a detailed commentary of meaning, metaphor and narrative of such materials and I posit that *ideas are formed* before the *form that the art will take* is decided upon. Dominic is adamant that things come together from a cornucopia of thoughts and actions, channelled into considered ventures that crystallise the form but, in the beginning, he says he was completely naïve of these process. 'It was completely innocent [...] but I quickly recognised that there was a technical side to art', he says. When he started to finish his first serious work he 'was quite shocked' that he could do it; he hadn't realised what he was creating, it came as a surprise. 'It almost brought me to tears', he says without embarrassment. It clearly was a profound moment of self-realisation.

With regards to the environment of creativity, Dominic does not demarcate the spaces between domicile, family and his vocation; these poetics of space are joyously, deliberately blurred, but there remains a lingering sense that the domain of art and creativity is separated from the function and delight of family life. While existing under the same roof (not conscientiously sought by the two other artists that I spoke with), there is a sense that Dominic is merely 'working from home', perhaps instrumentally and very functionally (the cottage was once the home of an artist and the hooks and nails for the purposes of hanging, drying and *exhibiting* canvas are all over the property), but necessarily – one feels — designed as a lifestyle choice (Chaney, 1996). 'I want to live art, you know?' he says, continuing by adding that 'life and art [...] there is no space between them'. There is always a sense, he says, that 'I am somehow always in those *spaces* — I never really leave being an artist'. The work 'comes home' with him, while remaining *at* home and he is insistent that separations between work and family are crucial: things cannot get in the way when you want the space for art and, at other times, leaving it behind is paramount. 'Having to pack up' is more difficult at his house he says because, in the past, he could shut a door, walk home, take care to understand the binary spaces of art and home. Now art is *in* his home, it part of his everyday existence.

> **Dominic:** Here, I can finish a painting and then, you know, suddenly, just before I go to bed, I think I just need to check this or that and then I think 'Oh God! I just need to touch that up a bit!' and then I'm there, in my pyjamas touching up a painting at midnight and I just can't go to bed until I've made an alteration to it.

However, there *is* a space between creative art and *doing other things* — he finds that he cannot 'paint in the morning and write in the afternoon [...] I can paint for two weeks and write for two weeks or, *better*, paint for six months and write for six months' but there is a routine that does not permit an overlap. He experienced what he calls a 'grieving process' in having to drop a writing project and to go back to the art, but he managed this process by immediately signing up to exhibit at a forthcoming exhibition in the deep South West, setting course for a concerted period of painting, concentration and commitment. After the cycle is completed, there is great catharsis in clearing out, cleaning, 'chucking stuff out' and then starting again, readjusting to writing, *changing*.

With dedication comes loneliness, but Dominic is philosophical about his isolation, aware of that requirement to stand back and get space; sometimes *living the art* means living it alone and seeking to live it that way. I put it to him that art is a lonely form of creativity but he retorts that there are too many varieties of practice, too many ways of considering praxis as art. 'Is a choreographer an artist? Is a playwright? Is a director?' he rhetorically asks.

> **Dominic:** I mean, what is an artist? You get some forms of collective art, for sure and at other times though, if you're a painter [...] I have done quite a lot of easel painting which [...] has become increasingly old fashioned in some ways, but it still exists — it's still hanging in there — but, that can be, that *experience* [...] working alone in a studio for months on end, literally me wrestling with my art work, that *is* lonely, yeah [...] a difference between loneliness and *solitude* and I think; as an artist, you have to be able to cope with periods of solitude; that doesn't mean you're lonely, if you see what I mean? If you suffer from loneliness whenever you're alone, then you shouldn't be an artist.

Solitude is a *gift* to the artist – a place of thoughtfulness, inspiration and ideological purity; nothing can penetrate its ephemeral value and, while it is symbolic of modern life in its disconnectedness from others, it is also a place where such disconnection can be inspiring. However, solitude is only half of the story here. Dominic balances his view of the value of solitude with the continual appeal of *involvement*. Art, to him, is a process that involves a combination of the mind, skill and influence that lies beyond the canonical. Art is seen as something that emerges from affiliation with others, being therefore inherently social and borne of communications. The subjects that frame his work emerge from sociality; he is something of an *artist ethnographer*, drawing heavily on his own emotions, experiences and values and connecting them with a sense of the political, structural and cultural (Ellis, 2003). He explains, for example, that he is a male artist that only paints women, is interested in 'gender politics' and seeks to illustrate his educational and experiential capital via a sensitivity of context in the associative work that he seeks to communicate to the beholder. Having elder sisters has helped shape this approach. He was 'brought up in a very female environment [...] that's the artist in me, who watches what is going on all the time'. He watched his family 'living out their lives' and sought to get some of this practical observation into the narrative of his works; he says he wanted to 'communicate female power', to make his work speak as 'an antidote to oppression' and speaks a lot about the 'crossing [of] boundaries' but is non-committal when I ask him if it is a political or psychological stance. In response, he states that men often find his paintings 'push something', a border – perhaps – is pushed here, an arbitrary border willing the male admirer to cross the border. Dominic seems interested in these reactions, it seems to give his painting and his soft-ideology meaning, value and edge and the hidden (auto)ethnographer in him and his work is beholden to the responses that it creates.

6.1.   Art Becomes Life

The process of artistic creativity hinges mainly on the sense that the artist is seeking a form of both expressionism and control that is entwined with a quest for vibrancy at the midlife stage. Thus, the humdrum of everyday life is resisted rather than harnessed, but in a way that considers the quest for *stability* in a changing world as being dull, routine and amounting to some kind of *surrender*. This is felt keenly in midlife, in-between the vitality of youth and the expected decelerating patterns of older age. So, what does this resistant, *second-wind vitality* look like? What rules does it have? How does an artist remain vibrant, original and inspired? The answer lies here in the sense of contribution to wider discourse, plaudits and the power of art to be personally and socially transformative.

The 'artist ethnographer' is evident in the collection of cuttings and photographs that Dominic placed back into the portfolio; but there is no anxiety of influence here because he considers all art original. Earlier, I cited the work of Hallam and Ingold (2007) on creativity, improvisation and the perception of originality, centring mainly on the notion that art is essentially discursive, organic, evolving and features, at its heart, the belief that *art must be original* is ripe for challenging. This can be achieved, they suggest, through understanding the inherent value of *improvisation*. This lends itself to that idea that all art is, in fact, innovative; to Dominic, leafing through his folder of cuttings, the genesis of (at least some) art emerges from the story that a picture is telling him and, whether subconscious or not, the folder facilitates 'hours looking at these, [getting] so many ideas' concluding that 'plagiarism is pointless [...], no-one needs a dud copy'. Is aura sensed via originality *in* him or *transferred to* him from others?

> **Dominic:** I've done paintings of female figures where I've done it as [...] constructed in thirty or forty lines, expressive lines; you can't possibly control the process completely, it's down to something [...] like a millisecond will change the painting completely so whatever comes out, that is completely fresh to what you did in that moment.

He begins to sketch out a drawing of a young woman, using lines drawn in simple pencil, while suggesting it is about 'value' and not 'emotion' to him. There is a sense he wishes to convey that the 'line' takes on its own life, moving through time externally to the controlling human emotion that allows it to 'live'. Lines, says Tim Ingold, incorporate 'all [...] aspects [...] of human activity' and exist as a form of silent language of movement and growth, occasionally *linear* but mainly organic and transient and communicative' (Ingold, [2007] 2016: 1–3) and Edward Laning adds to this when he says of the manifest functions of the artist,

> Ours is not a language of words, but one of lines, textures and tones. [...] Ours is a language addressed to the eye as the poet's is addressed to the ear. We are not involved in copying nature, but in constructing a reality parallel to nature. (Laning, 1971: 11)

Such 'lines, textures and tones' are arranged in a certain way, reflecting the arranger and not the random lines of nature (Ingold, [2007] 2016). Lines, therefore, tell stories and promise potential, expansiveness, *hope*. What Dominic explains is ascribing to this 'history', series of thought patterns and expressive language and is also an articulation of a simple artistic routine, a praxis that suggests an aura that *can be imagined as a sudden experience of the moment* with no future and no past – immediate, transitory, unrepeatable and plausibly *unintentional*. It is, as Ingold would suggest, a language separated from art (ibid.: 4). This laissez-faire *result*, emerging from a controlled, rational choice to *make* art, is where the aura lies. This, like with music and with writing, is the moment that the magic exists, where intent turns into action – almost, as it were, the point in-between the thought and the drawing. This is what makes 'aura' so hard to define, replicate or, indeed, capture as a creative capital. 'Art is like that',

Dominic asserts, 'a lot of things are so tiny – the adjustment of the hand when you're painting – that it's impossible to completely replicate that, you know, you are catching something [...] about me *being there'*. The artist is present, as is the spirit, as are the materials and something happens. The original *is* 'in the moment' whatever consequently occurs in 'editing' phases because whatever ends up on the canvas, board or paper is what existed in that *moment* of creation. The original, thus, is a product of the moment but Dominic concludes his point with an interesting, almost metaphysical, dimension to the subject of originality. The original, he says, *can* be changed. Pointing out a painting on his wall he says that 'if you shine artificial light on it, it will change completely [...] it completely changes at different times of day [...] at night it takes on a completely different form [...] in a way it's always changing'. The painting can have an aura and life all of its own dependent on its environment, beholder and timespace. Art, therefore, like the artist who creates it, has its own in-between states of *being there*.

This interpretation is transient, circumstantial and subjective. I explained to him that I have seen many interpretations of 'art' crystallised into a few minutes in a lecture theatre and was both thrilled and troubled by the seeming resistance to works of art, such as when I exposed my student class to Tracey Emin's *My Bed*. There seemed to be a sense that aesthetically it was lazy, that it illustrated 'no talent' and that, consequently, 'anyone could have done it'. Overall, there was a sense that the students thought that they 'knew what art was' and this, most certainly, 'was *not* art' (Newman, Goulding, & Whitehead, 2013; Silva, 2008), echoing the 'old-fashioned' belief that the author of *My Bed* was a charlatan (Cottington, 2005: 72). This quasi-structuralist stance requires some *poststructuralist* fairy dust applied for the art to *communicate* with the beholder, to break down the border. There *was* an attempt by some of the students to open themselves up to the *chance* that it *might* be saying something, that emotion might well be there, that the 'bed' might be relating a story to those who wish to listen (or imagine). It might be revealing something about Emin or feminism, or politics (Jabri, 2002) or, in this case, possibly a narrative relating to life following a departed partner or simply to do with the 'detritus of her life' (Gompertz, [2012] 2016: 381). It can be realised in 'confessional' form (Fanthome, 2008) and representative of – and recognisable as – a chaotic autobiography with post-feminist essence (Cottington, 2005: 72, 91, 94), couched in materialist celebrity culture via a configuration of mediagenic 'celebrification', a process arguably diachronic and mutually courted (Rojek, 2001: 186–187). This reading of art is dependent on the emotions being piqued and the psyche being open to the *possibility* of art. Dominic hands me a print of a bowl of cherries he painted and explained, in deliberate detail, the process of sourcing the cherries, organising them in a bowl, achieving the right light, the somatic act of drawing the outline of them and then painting them. To some people, he suggests, this is doing 'something really carefully, really diligently', careful organisation and the sense of industry that goes into it (maybe the students were missing the arrangement of the Emin installation!). Dominic opines that some people don't care how long it's taken an artist to do the painting, it is what it *means to them* that seals the value and this, of course, depends on the viewer's appreciation of art via genre, history, personal taste and in the situational context of impact.

This appreciation transcends the aura of creation; appreciation is the difference between survival and financial or spiritual destitution or the development of a reputation or obscurity. Finance is often not too far away from the thoughts of a professional artist, but finance and creativity have a strained relationship. This is something of an abstract currency, an in-between state of tension between the need for purity and the recognition of authenticity bestowed upon a piece of art via the financial transaction.

> **Dominic:** If you want to make money, then I don't think art is the thing you want to do; it's very difficult to do anything but survive as an artist [...] If you're spending a week on a painting, selling at five hundred quid, you're making two hundred and fifty pounds [after materials].

Galleries take a cut, he says. Framing is expensive; materials are expensive and 'it's not really something you'd go into thinking "I'm doing this to make money", I'm just being entrepreneurial to survive'. Dominic is absolutely sure that, somewhere, a 'business head' is what you *need* to survive through the production of art. 'You can't just create *anything* and expect someone to buy it [...] you have to think about [...] if you *want* to make a living', he says. You consider the 'fashions of selling' – what the punters want: colours, genres, things that go with 'sober interiors' and so on. There's a lot of abstract art in his locality, and people do make a living down there, 'but you've got to think where you place yourself, you can't just sort of think "I'm just going paint anything, someone's going buy it", you've got to place yourself in some kind of market'. This 'market' situates him firmly both within a commercial, but also a generational, oeuvre. This is where he can excel – the midlife artist connecting with the midlife buyers looking to populate their second homes with fabulous things to look at, to discuss with friends, dinner guests and erudite interior decorators. People buy expensive canvases to prove something to themselves and others. It's about economic status and narcissism but the effort is in persuading the moneyed people to buy your work. Lots of good art, he says resignedly, is being missed 'sitting in artist's studios when it should be on people's walls, you know?' However, it is also about *social class*. Sociological late modernism arguably functions as a force of disembedding (in this instance) the art from the process of creation, the place of creation and the subjective 'ownership' of the artist and, instead, recontextualising the art as a social lubricant – something that encourages sociality, controversy, humour, narcissism, status, ego and power. It's about 'capital' and 'credentials' and potency and those with financial capital *consider* the potency with a form of precision.

> **Dominic:** Upper middle-class are risk-averse [...] they are wary [about buying]; they are worried about where it's going to fit and

what people are going to think about it [...] when they have their
dinner party, what their particular clique is going to think about
it, that can go on. When you buy art, it is a way of constructing
yourself as a person socially, because [...] most people don't buy
a painting, put it in their study and look at it every day and medi-
tate upon it, they put it in a public place, people come round and
they want people to see it, they want people to know the story
about how they bought it and what a wacky, scruffy little artist
they bought it from [...] 'came across this gallery, found this fantastic painting' and so on!

It's all about making a connection between the incremental construction of
an identity within the buyer, the beholder and their social group and the flexible,
reflexive articulation of the latent character of the art itself. Art therefore is a
lubricant of sociality here; it is all about the experience of the chase, the exhibiting at home and the story-telling of the buyer. Dominic, is simply providing a
social text for consumption and he has no control over what the narrative of the
artwork has after he has sold it, except it's nothing to do, necessarily, with
what's going on in the painting. There is a belief that having a piece of art hanging in a gallery gives the art its authenticity, validating the work via its presence
(Bourdieu, 1996). Augmenting this assertion, Tröndle, Kirchberg and Tschacher
(2014) state with assurance that the audience makes no reference to this way of
thinking about what they are looking at (ibid.: 327). The fact that the art is in a
gallery does not authenticate it as art, or good art. It is simply on display.
Dominic is right to consider the viewing public as detached from the art; he
observes that they are sometimes looking for a piece of the artist as part of the
story and, in many ways, this might be a good way to describe the lack of connection between the finished product and its creator. The 'buying public' are
looking for furniture and a fable, not necessarily aesthetic wonder and accumulative investment. Art, says Dominic, is bought 'by people with money, and people with money – unless they've inherited it – [...] the art they buy is part of the
whole lifestyle, the whole *system* and it can be a very effective way of changing
your status within a group, for sure. And *people know that*'. On the pleasures
(and anxieties) of exhibiting his work, we discussed the possibility that exhibition
is not just about canvas, oils, frames and fancy lighting. We veered off to
explore whether exhibition was a conscientious baring of the soul, or the *identity*, of the artist and what is, and what is not, for sale. Explaining an 'open studio exhibition' that was held at his own house and the concept that involves
potential suitors of one's work visiting the artist at home, viewing the works *in
situ*, he explained that such visitors were there to look at *him* as much as his
work and to experience the visit as part of some kind of 'art story' that they
could potentially attach to a work of art if they eventually purchased it. He
therefore became convinced that visitors are interested in 'buying the *story*' of
the visit as well as the paintings: coming around to see him and to see the art
and the story of physically entering the artist's studio in the house and so on.

The essence of this approach is very much the case, according to Dominic, with famous artists when people buy their art.

> **Dominic:** I'm not exhibiting myself.
>
> **PM:** How do you hide yourself then?
>
> **Dominic:** Sometimes people want to buy *you*; they want to construct, they want to know who you are and they want to buy your story. [...] Quite often you are not there when the art is sold so [...] the gallery has go to tell a story, I suppose, about you.

This is a good example of the fragmented identity of the artist taking, as we do, that art is a multi-faceted process that involves ideas, skill, action, physicality, *performativity* and involved perceptions of others. Dominic's identity is only supremely his own *in the mezzanine*; once the flanking influences of interpretation are applied, he simply becomes *part of the art*. Famous artists become something of an omnipresent 'performance' that lives within their works and, despite insisting that there is no division between his own life and the artistic works that he completes (and sells), he recognises that performance comes with fame and, without fame, this performativity dynamic of the artist and the art is insignificant. If anything, the purchaser is attaching their *own biography* to the artwork, bypassing the anonymity of the artist. The identity of the artist is, therefore, usually locked in the creative tense. This gives the mezzanine even more power to deliver the liberty to create to the everyday artist; once the artefact emerges, it is fair game for the manipulative factors of economic capital and its associative power. He realises, therefore, that he must be undiscerning regarding sales – it's none of his business, he says, he just sells to whoever buys. Echoing the thoughts of Betts and Bly (2013) on the 'investment' culture in art, he adds that he sees no value of credence in increasing the cultural capital of arms dealers via selling to them, but he hopes that art (in general) might penetrate their consciousness with something positive, making them reflect on who they are and what they do. You cannot be judgemental, he insists, but you need to retain hope. The value is knowing that the painting exists somewhere else, is appreciated and is generating new thoughts and history with autonomous people. It is a post-partum anxiety, he admits, that pricks his sense of perfection in the art that he has sold.

§

Dominic has always considered himself a creator of things; from his epiphany on the beach through to his current exhibition at a local gallery, the sense that to create is close to an awareness of life force is prevalent. 'It's impossible to imagine not creating things [...] it would literally be like death [...] it's not about *being* something, it's about creating', he says. Art is not an inner peace but something that signals vibrancy, excitement and sensual anarchy. 'I'm more interested in transformation [...] for me, chaos sounds more interesting [...] because in the chaos there's change, there's potentially growth and transform- ation and something more expansive, otherwise it feels claustrophobic', he asserts, making eye contact all the time. *Peace* sounds claustrophobic to him. Peace sounds like *death*: static, silent, lifeless. Nothing in life is permanent, reliable or indispensable to him. Life and art is not about throwing caution to the wind – he's never felt he has *had* security to abandon. The 'life of the artist is a spiritual path; it involves a level of commitment that goes beyond just doing a job', he muses, but adds that he is unsure whether this is merely delusional.

> **Dominic:** I think you're working with things that are not very tan- gible [...] you have to work through a medium where something abstract is given value. To believe in that, you are trading some- thing abstract [...] working with a medium where it's not obvious; you can't eat paintings, you can't make a film from a painting, you can't drive paintings, you can't play a game with a painting; what is it? It's quite intangible.

Art does not connect him with anything in particular; the process, lifestyle and philosophy flies free of its potential moorings, connecting him only with a discernible faith in the authenticity and validity that sales give his work. His art world isn't bohemian or clique-like in its essence – he cites Picasso as a great example of an artist who lived in a commune (Gilot & Lake, [1964] 1990) and 'they needed each other, but I think now, I'm not sure it exists, I haven't experi- enced that'. These days, artists tend to 'meet at joint exhibitions [...] but we are isolated from each other'. They don't *live* together; it's a bit competitive, less col- laborative and the modern focus on the 'virtual' exacerbates this 'separation', diminishing need for face-to-face communications and in arranging gallery space and exhibitions. '[U]nfortunately the digital image is important if you want to sell art because people [...] want to look at your work [via] your website', he states, buying from the gallery having looked at it online. This introduces another barrier (or *connection into* the network of art), resulting in artists divided from the public via gallery and website and art itself; the artist is distant from the narratives of the art, divided by time, distance, gatekeeper and screen. I posit that we are living in an age where peer review is diminishing. When art is exhibited, he says, 'it is social; if it sits in my home studio and no-one ever sees it [...] then it isn't' despite some galleries being 'sniffy' about who exhibits, they set the rules and sometimes the rules are seen as based on taste, have a discrimin- atory feel and stern gatekeeping that relies on self-regulating discourses. 'It's bullshit; a new set of rules and regulations', he states with not a little exasper- ation with such omnipresent, arbitrary barriers to realisation. It follows that he likes the potential for art to touch the masses, especially via television (Williams, [1974] 2003).

Dominic: Programmes on mainstream terrestrial television on art are still really important; I think the galleries that have large numbers of visitors are really important; I think that, even down here [the galleries] serve an important role to make people take a bit of time to look, to value something that is not normally valued in everyday life. [...] [People are] taking a little time to absorb something aesthetic [...] open their minds to concepts of beauty, and I think that does have [...] a positive effect on society. [...] it doesn't matter if you haven't got any money, you can still go into a gallery and look at art [...] I don't think that art is essentially about money.

For Dominic, it all comes down to the juxtaposition of destiny, circumstance and age. The narrative of affirmation is here, as is the sense that he attaches the notion of midlife to the unspeakable idea of a steadfast meaning of art. Midlife is certainly not anchored in the perception of a phase; instead, Dominic is keen to create a sense of agelessness, fanciful and impractical at times, but reinforced by the eclectic sociality of art. 'Sometimes I do recognise that I am supposedly middle-aged, but I don't look my age, so quite often, people assume I'm in my [...] thirties and [...] when I meet people who are in middle age I don't really relate to that identity', he says before adding that 'I'm forty-five, so that's in the middle, isn't it?' We laugh, but the point at the heart of the consideration is that midlife is only something of a state of mind, despite the *effect* of time on mental faculties and physique. The vagaries of midlife, essentially, must be resisted to keep a clear vision of vocation and to allow for continual renewal. If anything, midlife is tainted by the suggestion that one is stuck in one's ways; the alternative way of viewing such hiatus is to say that, in this in-between state, one is able to continually morph into other things. It is a 'free space' with endless opportunities. Dominic's paintings have a self-articulated narrative that embodies this intermediate space to locate and exploit.

Dominic: I don't really live a very conservative life, which I would associate with [midlife] [...] I'll always create art; I don't think I'll reach a certain age and say 'Oh, I've had enough of this art thing', you know? I always seem to be reinventing myself, and sometimes I [...] think that you get artists who write and people are writers who paint or create art and sometimes I think that I am a writer who creates art. [...] You are framing something in a moment in time; so, where a story is taking place *over* time, art is of its own space [...] it's a way of telling a story, but it's better to read a book in my opinion. But, with art, you *can* catch a moment in time.

However, midlife is also a phase in life where people obtain freedoms to acquire new status that had been, until then, always tantalisingly out of reach for many. As we wind down on a sunny afternoon in summer he reflects on the chances that some people get to practice their dreams, ambitions and intent. People inherit money when parents pass away; some people see their children grow up, leave home and look for new stimulus and, thus, seek to 'redefin[e] themselves at another stage of life [...] a break with being a parent, being a mother [...] a completely fresh start'; some people simply perceive the mainstream of life, the rat race, the humdrum and routine and seek to reject it before they become completely subsumed in its claustrophobic whole. It's a pivotal place to be, but midlife is not − by definition − a universal opportunity or, indeed, a time to be satisfied.

> **Dominic:** It maybe is something that is [...] a vehicle, an avenue that is open for people to follow; I think it's something that's particularly attractive. Your archetypal artist who turns to middle aged person, who *turns to art* in middle age, is not your archetypal character; a bit of a maverick in some ways.

It is an 'opportunity [...] to avoid being dragged into the mainstream' and the mainstream is oppressive. Being an artist is to operate on one's own terms, within a space *separated from* the mainstream of labour, from the immediacies of conventional family structures and roles and from structural ideology, that may be exploited for the opportunity it promises and for the value in which it is held and continues to guarantee.

> **Dominic:** It's an opportunity for me to operate outside, an alternative [...] an alternative *lifestyle*. [...] I'm always ambitious; I'm quite pushy; I don't think I'm always going to hang around here [...] the artist [...] is a state of mind, that's never going to go.

This is Dominic; subtle, not easy to define, fluid and expansive, revealing. As I leave, he hitches a lift into the town centre in my car to beat the rain shower that has threatened to soak us to the skin and with a quick farewell and a thump of the passenger door he is gone, up the steps and blending into the shopping precinct crowds as I watch him go.

§

Art is seen here as a calling in life. It is the place where decisions are made, where communication is possible, where private ideas (until now 'locked in' to the imagination) are given voice, articulated onto canvas, paper, wood and acrylics and where the creators are able to consider their labour as a way of compounding their values as human beings. Art is considered a 'learned language', acquired young and articulated alone. The solitude − seen as a *sought-after* inner-turmoil − is communicated across distances as an experience of the world, creating a sociality, a sense of connection and being reciprocal, boundless and variable in intensity. Creativity is an extremely personal 'record of time', the dialectic of change articulated well by Robin when he spoke of *being there and doing*, taking risks in a constant state of flux and harnessing the ability to *forget* as intrinsic stages of inventive concatenation flow. Creativity is all about renewal of things and the self, equating to midlife being both a phase and a location of *opportunity* – a sentiment eagerly shared by all three artists here. While art may be personal and creativity quite private, solitude is not equated to *loneliness*; solitude is *productive*, but meaningfulness of the work comes from sociality causing art to shift in meaning from creation to eventual ownership. Art is intrinsically *ethnographic* in both conception and articulation: original, immediate, situational, changeable with environment – never capturing a pure original, the labour of art hidden in the image, the identity of the creator transposed into the life worlds of the 'inheritors'. This is how art *feels* to these men and how it is sprung from the necessity of calling, the vitality of creation and the therapeutic ritual of release. While 'creativity' is sourced from the 'outside', all feel that their outputs are segments of their being, the 'making real' their call to action, their ideas, their values. Sales are just 'consumer choices', exhibition is about acceptance, validation and the cessation of phases in the creative cycle – but what of art itself? Art is *intuitive* – it is a code, a real structure of feeling, a way of life.

I have introduced and interpreted the artistic routines and perceptions of three men who approach their art in differing ways, have different proposed outcomes and have contrasting circumstances. It is evident that each artist is engaged in a creative dichotomy – namely the passionate, *tempestuous thrust of creation* and the *post-creative meaning* and *utility* of such art. Such a balance of turbulence and serenity are not evident in the characters and outward personalities of the men involved, instead these people are committed, focussed and confident without oscillations in the intensity of action or mood. The art that 'comes' is responsive to the habitus and field while drawing on a structure of feeling that situates the creation of art a little beyond ideology via the nature of its creative nexus combined with a perception of 'space' bestowed by midlife. In fact, this previous point is detectable in every artistic routine present in this book, but in *fine art* it has a curious combination of chance and finality, urge and determinism rolled into one – the artists thrive in the possibilities presented and the understanding of risk in such possibilities. There is, in essence, a 'no going back' mode of working; despite the opportunity to destroy unconvincing output, everything is *considered* output, *everything is creative* when in the 'zone', in the chaotic refuge from the banal 'everyday'. The in-between state of creation here is one that is terrifyingly unstructured and wonderfully unpredictable, but beautifully executed and aesthetically exciting. Like Tim Ingold's ((2007) 2016) 'lines' and the demonstration of drawing by Dominic Jago that I have explained, the lives of these three men illustrate a sense of destiny in an acknowledged unknown: this is the essence of the midlife artistic identity and the routines of the fine artist.

PART III: LITERARY MIDLIFE – SOLITUDE SITTING

The critic and poet Al Alvarez observed, fairly recently, that we are entering into an era 'where literature itself seems in danger of being upstaged by biography' (Alverez, 2005: 68). Alvarez was not discussing the glut of celebrity biographies that, more often than not it seems, eventually find themselves forlornly displayed on the shelves of 'bargain bookstores' but, instead, how the writers' own biography is so completely woven into our own interpretation of literature so as to be inextricable. 'Imaginative literature', he suggests, 'is about listening to a voice' (ibid.: 15), a voice that speaks directly to the reader, private, distinctive and timeless. There is a transcendence of sensibility between the writer and the reader but there is, as Alvarez also notes in the case of the author Jean Rhys, a possibility that the writer is reshaping his or her *own* biography – the frailties and foibles – into something that is more acceptable to the writer. This is a reordering, in neo-romantic context, of experience, the unpredictable inner-self, the freedom of sensuality in feeling, reacting and creating (ibid.: 70–78). Authorial *routines* – the technique of creation – are central to our understanding of how authors create their works and what value they gain from their endeavours. Writing can be about the reinvention of self as well as the utilisation of imagination – and the development of 'voice' – for public diffusion. Voice, for a writer, is therefore both an inner narrative as well as a public presence.

When considering the intricacies of 'authorial routine', I am not the first person to consider Anthony Trollope's *Autobiography* (Trollope, [1883] 2016) as a useful starting point and neither will I be the last. Trollope's routine was almost mechanical in application: a certain time of rising, a certain amount of words to be written before work, a certain drink to be supplied at the same time, every day and so on. In fact, what can be overlooked when marvelling in his methodical approach is the fact that he also combined writing with a full-time job. Here was Trollope – on his way to becoming one of the literary greats to emerge from 19th century Britain – undertaking writing as an aside to his midlife occupation as a post office surveyor; for a man for whom, by all accounts, routine and structure had been difficult to achieve in working life, writing was bound by strict discipline. Throughout the ages, authors have had 'ways of doing' their writing, impacted by matters of life in general such as situation, location, state of health and the stop-go punctuations of mental fragility, notable in the case of Virginia Woolf (Lee, 1996), and it is fair to say that such writing routine may have been redolent of the broad effects relating to, and *onset of*, midlife itself. Woolf's routine was atypical pretty much throughout her career – writing in the morning, exercise in the afternoon and reading in the evening (Whitworth, 2005: 18) and, additionally when in a writing *phase*, she would engage in what might be considered an unconventional schedule of vocal recital of ideas and lines, self-critique and the separation of writing and typing – between armchair and desk (ibid.: 21). She 'tuned-up' her ideas *avec cigarette* before beginning to engage with the flow of inscribing by hand (Harris, 2011: 64), attempting to find rhythm and form for those emotions and senses, those 'waves in the mind' that she suggested existed long before the words that could combine to explain them (Woolf, 1989). Sylvia Plath used her time in a certain way too, recognising that opportunity to use the silent intervals before dawn was a circadian prospect to separate creativity from the duties of motherhood (cf. Cusk, [2001] 2008) and concentrate exclusively on the art of writing, influenced by her (much documented) simmering anxieties, her environment and her ambitions; her routine transmogrified into, *inter alia*, references of 'red eyes' in the 'cauldron of morning' (Plath, 1981: 240) used arguably as metaphorical source domains (Demjén, 2015: 97) to illustrate the tiredness, the dawn breaking as the children awoke thus relocating her from the transience of the autonomous poet into the simple maternal protagonist (Sigmund & Crowther, 2014: 89).

These days the writing routine may well be divided between the vagaries of online writers' forums (van Dijk, 2014) that involve sociality, creativity and critique and can, on occasions, lead to publication and the individuated-generative creativity of solitude. The writing routines themselves are arguably simple to predict because they tend to involve the combination of time, space and opportunity and usually involve sedentary contemplation that can lead to that state of 'focused flux' (Callahan & Stack, 2007) where ideas and inspiration and action combine. The dynamics that emerge prior to the 'sitting down' are what is of initial interest here: the biography, the thought processes, the involvement in the *social present* and so on. Writing, so solitary an occupation – even when working with co-authors – and so reliant on subjective reflexivity with ideology (Eagleton, [1976] 2002), is also somehow unique in that it does not *present* imagery or sound to a beholder but, instead, invites the *reader* to 'fill in blanks' via use of their own imaginations, habitus and capital (Bourdieu, 1977; [1984] 2010) and utilise awareness of the immediacies of their own circumstances (in other words, *where* they might be while reading, how they are *feeling*, what the weather is like outside, whether they are hungry, tired, elated, bored and so on). Writing invites the reader to 'picture the scene', but what *are* these scenes? Writing is a gift to both writer *and* reader, shared but not mutually recognised in form; writing, and the *act* of writing, the processes and the routines, are what is of interest in the following portraits and, ultimately, where it facilitates a sense of self and a sense of ownership. Does writing fiction transform midlife identity?

Chapter 7

Living a Dream and Dreaming a Living

In the heart of the city, outside the entrance to a well-known bookstore, I meet Annette. There is an immediate bonhomie, with only a hint of a little hesitancy in reflecting this as being the first time we have met, despite conversing through cyberspace for a long time, sharing thoughts, arguing about politics (from the same side) and observing the outside world from behind a screen. It feels 'right' to finally meet, shake hands, smile and natter. It is time for coffee in the bookstore; we have lots to talk about before our communication slips back to missives from the keyboard. Annette is a writer with a new book out, in the shops, *in the bookstore we meet in*; however, I want to speak to her about what having the book in the shop *means to her*, rather than what the book is *about*. I want to discover the emotional traction of writing (how it is done and what it represents) and how it can help to transform life for someone in their fifties.

Annette hails from elsewhere but made the city her home, coming here to University, dropping out, staying on and establishing a career in administration. She spent nearly 30 years in this career, working up to middle management level until the recession bit and voluntary redundancy was offered. She took the chance to change things in her life, supported by a husband and her own fragile confidence.

> **Annette:** I really liked writing and I really liked reading but I'm from a working-class background and it never occurred to me that you could be a writer; I don't know why it didn't occur to me but I thought writers were just this special species and maybe you could only be one if you went to Oxbridge [...] but all through the years I wanted to write, tried to write things, never really got anywhere.

Then she read *Harry Potter* and wondered if she could 'write for kids'. Entering her early forties, she realised that this was what she wanted to do more than anything else. 'It was like something was going inside my head', she says, 'and I just started writing'. Her early work got good reviews, no *publisher* but *did* gain her an agent. Her fourth novel, after 12 years of writing part time, got her the breakthrough. This was the time she realised that a career change could be utilised to best effect. 'I really like being on my own [...] with books, with paper and with pen', she adds. 'I could just do that for the rest of my life'. Now was the time.

A career change that embodied cutting ties with the certainties of employment to live on your wits as a self-employed writer was fraught with anxiety.
'When I was a kid I was a bit of an outsider [...] I was a bit bullied and therefore
I never had much confidence so I think [...] some of that feeds through', she
says, adding that some of her characters are outsiders and *different*. This
embodies her resilience and her resistance – the 'outsider' status (Becker, 1963)
makes for a more sensitive, reflexive and robust self, a stronger identity, no sense
of entitlement, expectancy or *loss*. Annette has always operated in an individuated sphere, but being an outsider is a *strong* sense and one that can reproduce
itself in thought patterns and the consequent text.

She speaks of her routine and how its isolated essence sees her plucking ideas
out of the air while walking, swimming, lying in the bath or in that dreamy state
very early in the morning. 'Before I'm even properly awake, an answer to something I've been trying to sort out will kind of come to me, or a character will
just appear', she states while adding that she occasionally wakes up in the night
and writes something down, reinforcing the belief that a writer never stops
thinking about the story (Atwood, [2002] 2015; King, [2002] 2012). This method
is the culmination of the years of literary, bibliographic dedication, emerging
from a childhood where books were central, but this is not nostalgia (Bauman,
2000), instead it is the separation of imagination and 'real life'. 'I remember that
feeling of reading a really good story, the magic of it, and being able to go somewhere else [...] maybe I'm trying to recreate that feeling for myself', she says.
The writing and articulation of such thoughts give her the sense of satiation, a
'feeling' of both adding to the literary canon as well as satisfying her own urge
to tell *herself* the stories, entertain herself with her own random thinking and her
own imaginative agilities. Jonathan Wynn, exploring something similar via a
discussion of Bakhtin, spoke of the point where literature can become, in effect,
'memories of one another' tacit via 'spaces [...] haunted by other moments
[...] – other voices, other texts, other sub-texts – resulting in ethnographic heteroglossia' (after Bakhtin, 1982; Renfrew, 2015). This process, experienced by
Annette, is lonely but *active* and intellectually industrious, drawing on memory,
texts and experiences; the process seems to be, even at our early stage of discussion, resplendently surprising to the author herself. It is as if she feels that her
own abilities have emerged from somewhere hidden to delight her, tantalise and
astound and are displayed prominently when writing, emerging into the arena
and expressing themselves with the variety demanded by such *heteroglossia*. The
writer is emerging as that 'outsider' that she identifies as and, charged with a
soft mission to create, she separates herself from the 'writer' within – this is an
individualised labour, dependent on sensual stimulus and the *space* to be
inspired within an 'anytime' framework, pressured by requirement but loosened
by the *non*-requirement for sociality or the functionality of location. Her vision
of herself has a rhythmical symbiosis – the rhythms of life and the rhythms of
writing, interlocking, experiential and real but separated by the lived and performative experience. Annette 'goes somewhere' to locate her 'feeling' to write
and allows her age, experience and cultural heritage to speak through her.

Writing was not *quite* a *career change*, it arose from an unexpected career *opportunity*. Redundancy, she insists, was a 'lucky coincidence' that actually followed her first professional writing contract. 'I did agonise over it, but I realised that I'd never have a chance like this again', she says, stating that the opportunity to leave doubled as a liberation in her mind (making the decision to leave easier), permitting her to proceed with the writing that she now needed to do. Writing became viewed as a 'job' in itself and is, she says, 'a personal and emotional thing [...] I'm not quite there yet, but I am starting to think of it as a business as well'. However, lingering in the back of her mind is a sense that the role of the writer somehow belongs – by entitlement – to the 'other'. There is a sense that coming to writing at her age, with her background and her incomplete formal educational route, lacks the legitimacy the trade somehow demands.

> **Annette:** I'm still at the stage where I still feel a bit *fake* [...] when people ask me what I do I can actually legitimately say that I'm a writer but there's a little voice in the back of my head that's going 'you're not really! What are you saying that for?' [...] I do feel like this is what I was meant to do – maybe I should have realised it earlier – but I do feel what I am doing now, this is *me*, and I never felt like that about [my previous career].

Her outsider status is reinforced and challenged by belief that she might be too late to catch up and make an *impact* like the rest but, she adds, 'whereas now I feel like I have found what actually I am, [...] I still feel a bit of an outsider'. The networks of writers in her genre are friendly and reasonably welcoming, but she experiences social closure due to her age and her relatively 'late' entry into the field, making penetration of such spheres more difficult to achieve from the outside and creating a problematic maintenance of legitimacy *when* outside. When eventually *inside*, a further struggle to develop is encountered; she is not quite inside the restricted art world (Becker, [1982] 2008) as yet and, when I ask her if she believes this to be, conversely, *freedom* she thinks for a moment before replying that maybe it is, as she has never really felt a sense of true comfort in the closed circles of *anything*. 'I found out who I really am', she counters. She *identifies* herself as a writer. Her identity fits with the sense of purpose that exists in the literary field and she considers that the isolation and fluid routines combine well with her desire for originality and the sense of exploration. This mutability cannot compromise her belief in her outputs and she is reassured by her own potential because she *did not expect* to be in the position of writing for a living. 'I never thought I'd make it, so I never gave it much thought', she says. Thus, no sense of pressure, no tradition to uphold and no palpable sense of risk exist, instead an interesting inferred juxtaposition of fluidity and solidity. The fluid routine, the space and flow of thought and the timeless essence of writing – anytime, anywhere and anything – combine with the physical structures of walls, screens and the metaphorical barriers of silence that separate writers from each other. The hidden writers in society do not know each other, she intimates. Online peer review sites can be 'a bit fruity', occasionally vicious in their competitive thrust, not functioning well as a forum of *support*, but the life of a writer is protected by those barriers and spaces of separation.

§

In the creative spaces of writers there must be some kind of prominent or clandestine routine, a sense of *destiny* regardless of materials or thoughts at hand at the outset. How does a writer envision the end of something from the outset? Annette illustrates that her writing technique and routine have matured over time.

> **Annette:** I had a vague idea of a storyline and I just wrote to see where it took me [...] but I've now found that it's not the most productive way to write because I end up with all sorts of stuff that doesn't really link to the other stuff in the novel [...] so I've changed the process a bit.

It is common for this process to begin and end in this way; plotting becomes a central requirement to avoid disorder in structure of writing. While a certain disorder is required to achieve the necessary stimulus to *write things* (the imagination needs randomness and surprises), the plot needs rigid structure. Again, there is a sense of the hard and the soft essence of individuated-generative creativity here. 'Structure is so important', she states, 'that's something that I discovered [...] I'm really haphazard; I avoid it for as long as possible and then I have to sit round and do something'. She says that she finds it hard to get started and eventually loves the editing but the writing in-between is paradoxically less enjoyable. Perhaps this is hard routine playing off against soft, intellectual creativity; the creativity is in the thinking, the ordering of disparate thoughts and random imagery, writing itself hard labour in comparison, compromised and less easy to enjoy. It starts 'when I've got a deadline', she says. 'I need that pressure, otherwise I wouldn't do anything'. The *creative process* is about 'making sure there is a structure', mindful of the habit of unwanted detours in narrative. It is a creative discipline. Are the detours better for creativity? She answers in the affirmative, but the tension at the heart of her authorial routine is clear. The thinking phase and the writing phase are two entirely different things; one is soft labour, free and dreamlike and the second is hard labour, driven by requirements, rules and pressure. The two streams of production do not mix well, if at all. However, the machinery of the writing process ceases with a 'clocking off' that results in something of a 'buzz' where 'I can go off and do something else and not feel guilty about it [...] feel like I've really achieved something', she concludes.

Annette has illustrated a division of time between what might be considered 'leisure' and 'work'. This leisure time is dreamlike and open; the routine is pretty much absent, making way for a pleasurable, constructive randomness experienced as imaginative engagement for the development of storyline and characters or the elucidation of location, mood or nuances of plot. The 'work' time is more rigid, routine and focussed but is not considered a time for free thinking or the creating of variations or alterations of the 'agreed' plot. The labour of writing is divided between thought and toil; it is as if both activities are *separate in character* and *different in impact* on the same creative self that commands both areas. The author requires the ability to switch from one pattern of labour to another without confusing both fields. Time figures strongly as both a physical division for the purposes of labour (writing, deadlines, time of day, etc.) as well as in a more abstract milieu via the contextualisation of time as a period of creative work or as a free-thinking, flexible 'zone' where one can think and 'uncover' ideas. The writer must learn to contextualise creative time *as* creative, recognising its signals when they happen, thus understanding method and feel and value.

> **Annette:** It's there all the time, it's just having the discipline [...] Stephen King once said that all ideas are pre-existing, are already out there and all it needs is somebody to start uncovering it and when I write I sometimes feel that [is] the case because you start off with a little bit and uncover and then it's so obvious [...] it's hard to believe that it didn't exist in the first place.

Such disembedding of time, or the *removal of boundaries* (cf. Giddens, 1990), is redolent of the late modern flow of information and the patterns of life we inhabit, the transference of ideas between time frames, times of day, night, sleep, activity and so on. Thus, the boundaries of work and leisure are muddled deliberately, allowing for creativity to co-exist, transferring imaginative thought from moment to moment without transferring such ideas from person to person. The disembedding, perhaps, is physical when manifest on page or computer screen but remains symbolic and representative of a solidly owned and protected constant in life. As social, economic and political life liquefies and becomes consequently abstracted (via technology and social geographies) across time and space, writing represents something traditional, simultaneously *non-technological* (thought) and technological (practice), but essentially timeless in essence while anchoring the creator to a *place in time*: a room, a café, a library or a myriad of other potential locations. Writing is something that *travels* with the creator, enhanced by movement, variety and sensuality, available at all times. 'There is this centre-bit of me, the writing and the books, [...] the only constant bit [...] holding me together', she says, 'otherwise I would explode from all the stress of too much change [...] just being able to go into that space and write' makes all the difference.

This *poetic* of space (Bachelard, [1964] 2014) is illustrative of how writing can be added to the amalgam of wider creativity as a capacity of the *mind* that exists by definition as an individuated-generative method and should not be considered as some valedictory or retrospective dynamic of the wider creative process (i.e. post-invention — retrospective — considered, in this instance, as the 'dreamlike state' mentioned above), but understood as a central energy of space. This is teleological in context; there is created a dialectic of division (ibid.: 227) where the interior speaks and where the 'prison is on the outside' (ibid.: 236). Such dialectics of invention are based on inner-narratives of innovation and omnipresent self-editing and are lonely but invigorating. Being 'outside' allows oneself to get 'inside' without obstruction. No one, in other words, can affect or unduly influence the train of thought and the construction of ideas – *apart from the author herself.* Art is isolated, but is it *lonely*?

> **Annette:** Yes, it is [...] but I don't see that necessarily as a negative thing [...] you never know that you're good enough and you've always got all these doubts [...] 'I'm fake, I'm not good enough, all of this is just a mistake, I had a good piece of luck, it's nothing to do with being *good* or anything like that' and that is very lonely, very difficult to share those emotions with somebody else [...] it's right there, in the centre of everything.

Authors exist in a transitory, liminal and individualised place; 'It's got a singular core', says Annette. It reminds me of Sylvia Plath's journal entry in which she fears 'the death of imagination' and suggests

> that synthesizing spirit, that 'shaping' force, which prolifically sprouts and makes up its own worlds with more inventiveness than God [...] if I sit still and don't do anything, the world goes on beating like a slack drum, without meaning (Plath, [1977] 1979: 217).

The creative spirit relies on work, dreams and articulation and, she continues, 'the poverty of life without dreams is too horrible to imagine' (ibid.). Annette has inherited that spirit from somewhere, playing with its possibilities in her head, digging deep into the realms of fantasies for ideas and, having always felt that she was somehow required to 'hold back', she now feels 'I can just be me; maybe there is a sense of relief?' Such relief is palpable; now there is no exterior dialogue, no narrative of connection between livelihood and the adherence to rules, structures and expectancies (beyond the necessity of writing itself and the commercial thrust of professional author status). However, with relief comes that sense of dislocation and the risk that lies with individuation. 'I get quite anxious [...] to give up that job and that security, but I've done it', she says. If security is now effectively absent, what does self-employment *feel* like? 'I had to embrace [it] and get on', she says, adding that 'I also know that I might have to get a proper job at some point but I don't care what it is [...] this is my career and if it ends tomorrow, it's still my career, mine'.

This is resistance – she has taken possession of the status of author and, whatever life throws at her now, such status will always be ensconced, defended and unbreakable. This is no Marxist resistance; if anything, this is classically late modern in that it connects the individual to a sense of simultaneous status anxiety and status perception. 'If your *books don't sell* [...] it is a very transient vocation', she says. It is suggestive that the risk is involuntary and, as Beck (1992) intimates, this is often the case in a society whose norms, values, trends and patterns of production are changing so rapidly. However, there is a positive outcome from this seemingly anxiety-producing scenario namely that individuals can take control of their sense of self (a *self-reflexive biography*, Beck, 1992: 135), framing possibilities and guarding hope and strategy. The writer's destiny is in her head and her approach is empowering when all around us the taken-for-granted ways of doing things are melting away.

§

This sense of duality — a representation of both the *thought processes* and the *method/action* of writing (and its dynamics as both profession and riskiness of reception) — may illustrate the route to, and the *routine of*, writing for Annette. There is that sense that the accident of writing is appreciated and that the free-dom to create is defended and acknowledged as potentially transient, but what about the *relationship* that the writer has with the originality and the value of her ideas? Where does the writer 'go' when she is creating and how does she seek to communicate her ideas to a readership? 'I think you've got to accept that nothing is original [...]', she says while acknowledging that the writer has always got to guard against getting 'too close' to something else. We all read and under-stand that language is universal, 'democratic' and has a history and she tends to agree that there is always a likelihood that something you *think* is original is similar in theme to something else. However, the anxiety of influence (Bloom, 1973) does not rank high here; there is no sense, in her rational thinking, that the shadow of the oeuvre is present when she thinks, writes and edits her work. She does, however, speak of drifting into what we might call 'another place' when she writes. This is the elementary form of fantasy, a dreamlike state becoming less of a dream and more of a location that she can be aware of set-tling into for the duration of writing.

> **Annette:** I definitely go into another place; sometimes I can start writing and [...] then sometimes a few days later I might read back what I did and I can't remember writing it, it's really weird, I'll feel that someone else had written that.

On the publication of her manuscripts she also senses distance from her own work, an experience that she likens to the disconcerting sensation of forgetting chunks of driving time on a motorway. The work is projected into the public domain and while the ownership of the words as they are ordered remains hers, the interpretation is myriad. It is arguably that moment where text is democra-tised, the author is 'dead' and the reader has control (Barthes, 1977) despite biography of both creator and reader being gently merged to contextualise the text (Foucault, 1980) and raise the question of 'who' is speaking (Bennett, 2005: 19).

> **Annette:** I think the [reader] will see [the reader]; once it's out
> there it's not yours anymore, [readers] can put completely differ-
> ent interpretations on things, can't they? [...] I could read a novel
> and think 'oh, this is what the writer meant', but the writer could
> have meant something completely different. There might be the
> writer in the book, but I don't think that's necessarily what the
> reader would take away; the reader would take away what's in
> *them*.

This hermeneutic process is where the writer loses her power, but she retains
a signature on the text. This is arguably difficult for any writer (or artist) to
manage; it is where the monogram of identity is lightly erased from the work,
where the story becomes interpreted by strangers with distinct biographies and
emotions and, therefore, the work is somehow 'lost'. I explore the idea that there
has to be something of Annette left there on the page, in the characters and the
construction of language, phrases and punctuations but she's not so sure while
simultaneously recognising the potential for her own biography remaining present subliminally in her text. Despite this, she is comfortable with the notion of
sharing the text with an anonymous public. The 'thing' that grounds her and
helps her focus when life alters is ejected from her grasp – the manuscript, the
story – and sacrificed to the vagaries of the market and the forces of criticism
but she knows that, ultimately, the 'real meaning' of her stories continues to rest
with her alone. She states forcefully that her routines – imaginative, practical
and strategic – are not connected to servicing the market, adding that 'I don't
think you should write to the market because the market changes so much any-
way [...] I just happened to write something that fitted what people are looking
for'.

> **PM:** There is an element of chance there?

> **Annette:** Oh definitely; luck has such a bit part to play in it [...]
> I think it makes being a writer very hard because there is that
> element of luck [...] most things don't take off. [...] I do worry
> about failure.

Reviews affect her mind-set more that she likes, resulting in the paradox that
'getting too much feedback can be damaging, you can end up trying to please
everyone [...] you end up losing what's really *you* about it'. It affects her artistic
output, the way that she prepares and the way that she uses her dreamlike time.
'I don't want to think about the outside world when I write; it's just me and the
page really', she states. This is an articulation of how protected she feels within
her routine and how protective *of* her routine she remains. Those barriers of
walls and silences protect against the barbarism of the 'prison outside' of the creative mind. The freedom to *be*, to write and to blend life into art is available if
one observes the value of the dreamlike state and resists the temptation to participate in everyday life beyond the necessities of standard requirements –

family and partners and children, the weather and the coffee pot and the walk to the corner shop for a loaf of bread.

Writing, like music, is prone to the essence of permanent rehearsal, continued revisions and the sense that the manuscript can be seen as 'a pathway [...] that can continue indefinitely and it gets to the point where you have to let it out [...] and let it go'. Annette senses that, when writing, the ending is not the end at all. A sense of soft regret lingers in the aftermath of a publication and she is to be found regularly considering that 'I would have re-written that scene, what was I thinking?'. There is evidence of enduring reconsideration of the story, that things could be *different* every time, but when she recites the narrative in her own mind, there *are* considered fluctuations in style and in tone and nothing 'reads the same' to her, time and time again. It is a matter of chance that she senses the narrative is 'right'. 'It can depend on the mood you're in when you look at it', she states. You can *see* something different, *hear* something different, sense the *change* that is possible in the text based on mood. Literature is interpretative, both linguistically and emotionally (Searle, 1979) and Annette suggests that age changes the tone, colour and impact of literature. 'You read books at certain times of your life and what might resonate with you at one age, and you read it later on, and think [this isn't doing it for me]', she opines. Things change over time and, articulating a detectable Modernist essence, age bends the perception and reception of the text. The theme of transformation emerges from our various discussions; I am always aware that, perhaps covertly, Annette is battling with the tension at the heart of the belief in the 'sense of motionlessness' (Creighton, 1985: 92) of middle age and the desire to retain the sheer excitement of a midlife opportunity that she never really saw coming.

> **Annette:** Sometimes I wonder what would have happened if I hadn't started writing and what I *think* would have happened is that I never would have would have [left] work, I would have probably stayed there until I was sixty and then done whatever and just kind of *meandered*, and now I feel like [...] it's the next phase of my life and I've got something that I never expected to have, like a new purpose.

Such purpose is resistance and writing is giving 'two fingers up to middle age!' However, there remains a palpable sense that midlife has given her a different perspective on approach, audience and *style* of writing.

> **Annette:** If I'd starting writing at a much younger age, it would have been really different to what it is now [...] I don't think I would have written for children, I think I would have written for adults. I'm not sure why I think that, but I think I would have felt more like I had something to prove [...] but now I've got the confidence.

Midlife has provided a key dynamic in her method – namely instilling the confidence in herself. I asked her what it is that 'drives her on', to which she fired back with immediacy that *continuity* is the key, the sense that she cannot now even imagine life where writing is not central. 'I think it's the thing I'm good at and when you find the thing you're really good at you just keep doing it [...], she says. 'It's an excitement thing [...] you can create something out of your own head onto a bit of paper', she adds, and this exhilaration is a central continuity. The contentment – and, in effect, the routine of confidence – is hard to crystallise, but it functions as a resistance to the expectancy of invisibility in midlife. This is something that Annette concentrates on in her narrative; such invisibility is not simply illustrative of a period where people synthesise into opaque dullness, indiscernible in the street, vapid fashion, anonymity at work and so on, it is also where men and women identify differently with the challenges.

> **Annette:** I do think it's something about resisting middle age [...]
> as a middle-aged woman you can just disappear and that you *do*
> disappear is really weird. When you're thirty people notice you as
> a woman, when you're fifty people just don't notice you so
> I think some of it is 'I'm still here and I don't want to disappear
> and I've still got that youthfulness inside me and that desire to *do*
> *something*'. [...] A lot of people start writing in middle age, that's
> what I've found.

This points to writing as a resistance in pure form, the point where the 'pen' becomes the weapon against the invisibility of midlife. It is all about attitude, 'I think giving less of shit about what people think of you', she says. 'I think that is one of the benefits of middle age, that you stop worrying about all that'. Does this belief feed through into her creative routines? She offers an alternative take on whether caring has an impact, continuing to link it to age but also offering a focus on the perception of quality and the role of ego. Some of her output she considers 'silly and fun' and states that a younger version of herself might consider it a tad 'stupid', but, she counters, 'I am at that stage of my life where I do not really worry about that, it is a decent freedom really'. Such freedom is contextualised by a desire to move faster, to write more, to achieve things at a less leisurely pace. Invariably, such thinking is driven by the perception that life is speeding up and that things simply must be done. She is adamant that it is not *regretting* things that have happened, it is instead more about the possibility of regretting not *trying* things that are new and untested and this, she says, is where the 'mojo' originates – the challenge to do something new.

> **Annette:** I do wonder if it's because we are not old-old, but we're
> getting old and we start seeing people we know die, people we
> know don't make it to sixty and we think 'bloody hell I might as

well do it now because there's no guarantee that I'll be here this
time next year.

Life will always be about telling stories, she says. It is about creating an
active fiction. She says that this can be viewed on social media in the way that
people construct fictions about their own lives, embellishing and exaggerating
matters of the everyday to give the impression of functionality and happiness.
'[T]hey create a story they want the rest of the world to see [...], it's just that
I make a longer story with more characters and more plot but it's like we're all
telling stories to each other all the time', she says. I am intrigued and ask
whether we — everybody, in fact — are *living a fiction*. 'Yes', states Annette, finishing her coffee and placing the cup in the saucer, 'but maybe books take us
away from that; because when you're reading a book you're reading a book as
you, you don't have to pretend to be anyone else'.
   I close our meeting by considering a question that I asked of the artists and
writers (but not the musicians) in all of the meetings that occurred. Could she,
I asked, have done this one 100 years ago?

> **Annette:** One hundred years ago, I don't think someone like me
> would have had the opportunities [...] I don't think it would have
> happened [...] somebody of my background would have been a
> miner's wife or something like that I might not even be very liter-
> ate [...]
>
> **PM:** The modern world has given you that chance?
>
> **Annette:** Yes, but I wonder if it will be the same for people in the
> future though, because we seem to be going backwards.

Echoing the minutiae of Woolf's, *Room of One's Own* ([1925] 2011), Annette
leaves me with a poser: the late-modern world may be opening up opportunities,
but this a *brief* window of opportunity. The perfect 'storm' of progress, technology, fluidity in employment markets, leisure time expansion and the broadening
opportunities of women have blended to give her the chance to make substantial
changes to her life in her fifties, but she senses that the door is closing, the scene
is shifting, the momentum is lost and the reforms are regressing. Her class is not
a skilled elite and her class can never transform itself into a functional elite
either — it is a residual, predictable 'place' that she comes from, lost in dreamy
aspiration to cultural emancipation but never achieving much: functional and
undervalued and obstructed. She does not put a fine enough point on her comment (and one feels this is tantalisingly deliberate — no solution to this slightly
melancholy comment is given, but awareness of an antipathy of the possibility is
rife), leaving me with a portrait of a lady who is pleasantly amazed and contented by self-discovery, retains a natural anxiety and self-doubt due to her own
perception of being an 'outsider' and is enjoying the latitude delivered to her
(and, it must be said, courageously grasped by her at a time when many would

have opted for the security of wages and the sagaciousness of familiar routine) at this stage of her life. She feels she is 'living a dream' despite omnipresent apprehension but, she concludes, 'I'm so much happier'.

We part outside the bookstore and head off in opposite directions, both in search of a bus or a train and in search of the tranquillity of the dreamlike state of writing in midlife. I sense that Annette is complete now; that her outsider status is perfectly instrumental and wonderfully apt for her midlife creative self.

Chapter 8

Shifting Rhythms and a Sense of Purpose

Katherine Webb opens the door at her house deep in the countryside and smiles, welcomes me to her home, shoos the cat away and puts on the kettle. It has been a long time since we last met and it is good to see her again. The more things change, as they say, the more they stay the same; we last conversed in her kitchen in her previous house about eight years ago and, as one might expect, a lot has happened in the intervening years. Katherine now has six published novels to her name and has passed the age of 40, but she remains positive, ambitious and mindful of her craft. Midlife is not changing her, but she now perceives 'gaps' in her work as time that create a latent anxiety. It is as if writing — and the routine of writing — is such a *central* facet of her life that when the complexity of late modernity penetrates her thinking the writing must be summonsed to soothe, to fill time and to make her feel complete. She is complex, interesting and overwhelmingly human; her thoughts and the routines of everyday life weave together to create a 'reality' that precipitates fiction — imagination creates escape that creates fiction that creates escape. It is all in a day's work for Katherine.

Growing up in rural southern England, she speaks of a 'very stable home life [...], which is great and quite rare I think', and an educational journey that began in the village primary, progressing via the local comprehensive and eventually into Durham University. She recognises that her creative identity was a slow burner, influenced by many things from childhood onwards, developing as she grew up and after she had left home — but the origins of her artistic self are found in her youth.

> **Katherine:** Neither of my parents were creative, particularly. My mum's a really big reader and she definitely got me reading really early. [...] I wasn't a very gregarious child [...] I never had big groups of friends [...] I played on my own a lot so I think that is possibly early signs of [being] very imaginative.

She never thought about writing for a living until signing up for a Master's degree that did not eventually provide the depth and breadth of intellectual stimulus she had hoped for, turning into 'a bit of a failure to launch really. I wasn't ready to leave Durham [...] so I got a job in the library and I started to write a novel'. After travelling abroad, she came home with a completed manuscript, bought the *Writers and Artists Handbook* and 'went through it, sent off submissions' to agents, got rejections in the time-honoured fashion, began a second novel and was then, she sanguinely reports, 'in a holding pattern for the next decade'. Her first novel to be published was her seventh completed effort.

> **Katherine:** I've never been very proactive; I've never sort of had the mind-set of going out and seeking help with anything, I tend to do things by myself. [...] So, I had a very slow self-apprenticeship in the writing. [...] I did join a writing group around book six [and in] doing it professionally you *have* to be able to take editorial.

This is the first indication that a slightly cloistered childhood has led to an individualised, solitary adult emerging; this solitude, with no ties and no reliance seems to sit comfortably with her as both an instrumental requirement of the writing routine as well as the space to invent, think, imagine and plan. The writing group, she says, proved very useful – the criticism and the feedback was good, encouraging and helped to shape her process but as she has no other career to speak of, she concentrated solely on writing, taking jobs where she could 'leave at the door at 5 pm [and] come home and write in the evenings'. With the passage of time came the notion that the artistic brain needed time to be 'free' while the body is in bondage.

> **Katherine:** Thirty came and went and was starting to get a bit anxious because [my occupations were] a means to an end – and I think this is why artistic types often end up in these quite menial jobs because, actually, they require no input from your brain at all so your brain is free and is off and in different places altogether and is cooking things up whilst your hands are ironing eighteen [pairs of] shorts, or whatever they are doing!

No additional stimulus was required to inculcate more creativity. 'The creativity is there and it is the *most* part of my brain. [...] Everything I have done [work] has been a way to *let that happen* in my brain', she says. Office work and attendant team work 'where you have to be fully present in the room, I have absolutely loathed it [...] I don't like doing that to my brain', she states, adding that 'my brain does not want to be in a room concentrating on something, it wants to be off thinking up stories, concentrating on a story that I want to be writing'. Her jobs gave her the 'space to be creative', time to switch off and – most importantly – provided a binary set of options where the creative self and the routine of writing could be totally separated from the mundane requirements of the everyday world. 'It's a defining thing for me; it's what I do and what I *am*', she concludes. Being creative and having the discipline to construct a binary life has positives and negatives, but she is very proud of being able to turn on and turn off the 'moment' and feels lucky she has a mind capable of achieving this. However, a tension exists at the heart of even the most acquiescent of such binaries, to tune in and tune out of creative 'spaces' is a welcome precept, but there remains a penetrative, omnipresent constituent for the professional to observe.

The art that she produces nowadays is subjected to *commercial forces*, a subtle merging of 'creativity' and 'business' that may compliment her binary creativity. It is possible to see this as a hard clash of heads resulting in a forced collaboration 'on the presentation of work', but Katherine sees it as a perennial occupational dynamic. Painters paint and sell but publishers have the right to get in-between the artist and the art. The cover of a book, for example, is crucial; there is an occasional discord between the cover art and what the author 'sees' — 'It's like having someone else dress you for an important occasion', she says with a smile. The 'commercial' is connected to art and illustrates where the external can penetrate the internal world of the literary artist — the outside world, with its idealist forms of social reality ideologically affecting the writer's routine of production, intellectual thought processes and emotional connectivity with the narratives of the text. In Marxist terms, the superstructure is being manipulated by the 'base', with the writer a semi-detached agent of the process.

If there is only 'semi-detachment', then what does this 'state' feel like? How does the writer connect the idea of writing to the sense of self, identity and authenticity in the varied and shifting boundaries of late modernity? 'If I go a couple of months between book ideas I feel incredibly worthless and depressed [...] there is no point to me unless I am working!' she says. 'I am getting these terrifying spells after a book where I have no ideas at all and I don't know if that is an age thing, I'm finding that I need time now to recharge and to let ideas just happen'. I ask her if she is *confident* taking breaks from the creative routine, to which she replies that she somehow *ought to be*, but that she has 'large gaps' in her brain that are difficult to fill when she is not writing. Her thinking is a curious mixture of the serious and the blithe, but her creativity is closely entwined with a conscious state of identity that, once more, illustrates the binary context of her vocation.

> **Katherine:** I don't try and think about my own identity; I do feel a real split between me and the real world! [...] I generally feel a lot more alive and real when I'm writing and I'm thinking and I'm creating than the rest of the time and possibly that comes from [...] that sense of separateness from the rest of the world; I generally have a feeling of watching rather than taking part!

The use of the words 'alive' and 'real' and 'separateness' are striking — firmly locating the routine in dislocated spaces of free-thought and articulating the recourse to the fruitful yield of the imagination — but this is not hermetically sealed. The biography, experience and senses all play a role in the development of literary narratives, ostensibly created from scratch but all portraying signs of the author, her life and her moods. The characters that she develops in these sequestered times are, she says, *'entirely* separate to myself [...]; certain biographical things do creep in there, it's been pointed out [...] I identify as female [...], certain things creep in when you aren't thinking hard enough about your story I think'. There is also the curious sense of dislocation with *text* that occurs after the text has been completed; a sense of displacement from the outside world when creating (the routine) and then a sense of dislocation with the finished work.

> **Katherine:** I completely inhabit the world of my novel when I'm writing it and I completely inhabit my characters − especially my central characters − but then, the second it's finished, it feels like someone else wrote it, I've got no connection to it anymore, it's always like it's something that's got severed when it's finished and it's gone off into the world and suddenly I see it for what it is; it's a piece of work.

There is anxiety that the work is gone, irretrievable for corrections, lost to the interpretations of others who have not taken part in its creation. The author is 'gone', detached, disempowered and forgotten as the narrative is placed firmly into the emotional, sensual and experiential domains of the receiver (in this case, the reader), transferred from 'that unconscious flow that can happen [...] it's a kind of [...] interpretation of what was in my head [and when] it's finished, it's gone and it's whatever anyone else makes of it at that point'. The author imagines something fresh, in that aura-filled moment of conception, and then struggles with the latent apprehension over loss of clarity of her own images via the interpretative process of writing itself, resulting in an almost transliterative process where the beauty of the 'art' simply transmogrifies into a 'work', potentially belying the real meanings originally intended, rendering the work somehow 'alien' even to its own creator. This is indicative of the anxiety not of *influence* but of *trajectory*, a thrust into the future of an idea, an image, a plot or a broad narrative that needs to survive the vicissitudes of its own birth − hypothetically chimera-like and unstable − and survive in the autosuggestive, myriad interpretations of the diverse outside world. Writing is about stepping aside from the 'real world' and it is fun, blitzing mundanity within the instinctively antithetical solitude of her study, looking out on her garden and the countryside beyond. She needs time alone, stating that 'I need to be by myself for hours at a time [...] it's something that a lot of introverts need [...] time to *recharge* [...] if there's someone else in the room then that's the focus of my attention and that just steals energy from the creative side of the brain'. This is an individuated-generative process, a routine that suggests sociality will simply sap the energy and the spirit and regretting her original optimism that working as a professional author would result in shorter writing timeframes. 'It will only percolate at the speed it will percolate', she says of her writing. 'It doesn't matter if you've got eight hours to write, I can only write for about three or four hours a day and after that it's game over and I have to wait for the next section to become clearer'. Patience in creative life is omnipresent; you cannot hurry the process and the author must have patience *in* herself and *with* herself. She says that 'there is a lot to be said for the menial, repetitive task [...] I don't tend to go out walking, I do tend to go on mad cleaning sprees, or mad painting sprees [...] paint a wall [...] something!' The routine, repetition and isolation is transplanted from the social to the personal, public to private sphere (Goffman, 1959) and acting as an antidote to anxiety. From dull, individual routine can come the self-determination and deliverance of imagination and resultant writing.

The routine is therefore based on recognition of the banal outside world and the recognition of the contrast with the liberation of the individuated-generative process delivered through writing. The author is able to 'see both worlds', to cherish the moments of escape and to value the challenge of 'translation'. This is the domain of resistance to the banal (sometimes by forcing herself to recognise the banal through menial tasks and habits) and furthermore experiencing the thrill and release of writing. It is resistance through ritual, but this ritual is escapist, imaginative and serene rather than chaotic, unpredictable and adrenaline fuelled as the artists and the musicians experience. Thus, the individuated-generative resistance is *escape*, while the socio-generative resistance is *explosive*, harnessed by sociality and exhibitionism. Katherine, like Annette, is seeking to exploit her 'outsider' status by somehow relying on the value of such outsider *thinking*. It is her gift to 'step outside' the boundaries and explore the inherently possible. The routine is rarely compromised by this. 'Some days [...] I'll sit there at the desk and nothing's happening and I just won't let myself move [...] eventually I will write, even if it's just a paragraph and that unsticks what is stuck', she says. She cannot switch on and switch off her creative self, she states. 'I don't sleep well; especially if it's not going well, and I wake up and I think of things in the night – just tiny ridiculous, petty things [...] in the scene I wrote that day and I come down and I do it!' There is no disruption to her creative *thinking*, her main motivator being that there is no break from it 'until it goes away', the book is completed, the relief tangible. 'When I hit send [...] I've got it down, got it out, relief [...] the pressure comes as much from me as from anyone else', she says.

This 'late modern' dynamic that sees writing as a *constant*, a 'thing' to hold onto when change exists all around us is attenuated here by the broader dynamics of ambition – the mindful determination to see to fruition the ordered narratives of the imagination. Katherine is not conscious of sensing her writing as something to be used instrumentally as a barrier against the anxieties and unpredictability of the risky late modern world. She says that she feels 'distant to things', often deep in thought. It *is* a *constant*, but not perceived as a utility. At times where she is challenged – such as times of affective change – she says that she 'can just sit down and write and it's a breath of fresh air'. Authors with kids and jobs have greater challenges ordering their lives; this dislocation is not without its own in-built anxiety, aware of the transitory and varied nature of life in general, career, lifestyle and taste. She is also aware that her own decisions shape her approach to her lifestyle and her writing. There is a freedom in this, a sense of self-efficacy and destiny that is enlightening and reassuring.

Katherine: I sometimes worry that [...] they are living fuller lives than I am living [...] I'm dedicating so much of myself to writing, I sometimes worry that I'm a one trick pony, you know? That's all I've got. [...] Different personalities in different authors mean they take it in different directions; I've always been quite intro-verted and quite a loner and so I'm quite happy to dedicate the most part of myself to that, that is my comfort zone and that is how I feel that I am doing something important and worthwhile and I do sort of sometimes [...] think 'am I really missing out?' [...] Am I just setting myself up for a really lonely life?' and then I have to think 'well, don't second guess it, this is the life I've cho-sen for myself, you know, so go with it!

8.1. Writing and Emotion

Katherine's writing has developed over the years and her personality has mel-lowed, suggesting that she sees getting older as 'settling into your personality a bit more', but does this affect the way that she writes now?

Katherine: You get to a place where you just see things differently I think — you mind less about things, you're more philosophical about things, [...] you're more wistful about things and you're able to look back with a bit of nostalgia, mainly, but to see that what you felt then and how you felt then was a result of *you*.

She worries that 'this more reflective, more introverted approach to stories' might isolate her readers, but understands that this may be symbolic of her own journey and her gradually changing direction. The readership who follow Katherine's development as a writer over time are also arguably following the linear pattern; as the emotions of a writer naturally change with age, her readers may find such transition comfortable because they are also adjusting. 'I get a sneaking feeling that readers want to know in advance what they want to be reading', she says, illuminating a point that people might want time to stand still, remain stable, predictable, communal, obtain certainty in their own late modern lives through the medium of fiction. While Katherine takes care to diversify her themes, she perceives that her novels 'are getting darker [...] less optimistic'. This is not a commercial strategy.

Katherine: It's about how much input is required from the reader, whether the beauty of the prose is enough to sustain the novel rather than the drive of the plot. [the readers] just want to be told a story and they don't want to have to be patient and they don't want to have to do too much work themselves filling in any gaps, [...] but it's not black and white, it's a huge spectrum of grey [...].

There are a lot more people at the 'pop' end of things, but fewer people will find the 'Beethoven end' of things as emotionally fulfilling. [...] I mean it's all good writing, different writing, there's a place for everything and a reader for everything [...].

This is arguably a defining perception of the late modern reader's desire for escape, comfort, certainty and re-assurance. Katherine's words are not, when one takes a moment to consider their depth, a critique of either readers or writers, they are instead a recognition of the desire for emotional fulfilment in the process of reading. This is similar, perhaps, to how one could describe that reading Flaubert ([1857] 2003) feels like the literary equivalent of placing your head on a fresh feather pillow; the quest for excellence in writing, finding that rhythm and penetration in prose that creates such a smooth meta-dialogue as *Madame Bovary*, is the mission of Katherine and other writers. They write for different audiences, but they seek the same quality in final product. If anything, Bourdieu, so much the fan of Flaubert, would agree that the value of a novel is in its

charm [...] in the way it speaks of the most serious things without insisting [...] on being taken completely seriously. Writing offers the author and the reader the possibility of a mature understanding which is not half-hearted. [...] One may 'live all lives', in Flaubert's phrase, by writing or reading, only because they [*sic*] are so many ways of not truly living it (Bourdieu, 1996: 33).

Thus, writing and reading 'fills in a gap', communicating to others and oneself the value of metanarratives and the value of the imaginative voice. In her early writing, she was trying to compose in a literary way; putting everything into it, but her 'own voice' (Alvarez, 2005) started to alert her to its presence as she got older. She desired complete originality and never sets out to imitate. 'The idea comes very organically, it percolates and it grows and it spreads', she says emphatically. While writing prosaically can lead to being typecast, an anxiety of influence (Bloom, 1973) that has destructive impacts on readership and reception (Willis, 2018) and commercial ramifications, Katherine is more concerned about the 'pigeonholing' of genre (Frow, 2015), stating that 'I have been fighting against it and I've come to the conclusion that you just can't fight it, you'll get nowhere'. It is best to produce quality output within the field of literary production to which you have aligned.

Katherine: I'm just writing a story and I think the way to convey emotion is that hopefully readers are investing and are empathising with your characters to the extent that they will feel their emotions along with them. I think if you're *trying* to convey emotion [...] you can spot it a mile off — it's like that manipulative string music on TV when they want you to cry!

She asks herself if her characters 'come alive' but recognises that it just does not get through to everyone reading it. 'You would have created people that they care about and that gets them invested in the story', she states, arguably aligning such creativity with something of the realist tradition in literature. This emotional investment in the reader is a gift to them – transferring the ownership of the character from author to the reader, reflecting (perhaps) something of their own lives in the text. This is where the risk and unpredictability of the outside world is corrected, formulated and reimagined in literature and where, arguably, the reader is momentarily admitted to the individuated-generative domain, spending time with the thought processes of the author without having any emotional, physical or philosophical connection to the autonomous writer. For a moment, the reader and the author are in the same place – and that 'place' is in a world that has no risk, no fears and no fluidity (at least for the duration of reading – see Eagleton, 2013). Amazon reviews interest her in understanding what might not have got through to readers in her prose, but she also looks at reviews of books that she has enjoyed in order to understand a variety of reader perspectives. It is reflexive and proactive and the strategy is connective with readers, authors and the thinking that exists externally to the manifestations of story, narrative, prose and physicality of the book itself. If anything, *feedback* (in the public domain) gives *life* to the routine of writing. This discursive process connects the super-isolated 'dreamlike state' of writing to the lived realities of the populace and Katherine values it greatly. We talk about what I call the 'surviving *Ulysses* scenario' (after Joyce, [1920] 2000) that involves the *finishing* of such works being considered the *achievement* and *in* finishing the work it takes on something of an elevated place more associated with *challenge* rather than *connectivity* with the story or, indeed, entertainment or *enjoyment*. We talk about the associative 'why *didn't* I like that?' scenario – the great book, revered by so many over time and leaving the reader cold, discombobulated, disconcerted. *Why* didn't I like it? Was I *missing something*? It is all a coping mechanism in Katherine's view. She draws us back to the image of the isolated writer again to make the point, painting a picture of writers dislocated and requiring connectivity – albeit occasional – with those who make sense of their writing. That way, she infers, the circle is completed by 'watching' both real life and the emotions and thought patterns that are present there with the writer and *among others*.

> **Katherine:** I have met a lot of writers who are self-contained – and I think of myself as quite emotionally self-contained as well, not given to big outpourings, someone who would retreat from strong emotion, rather than throwing themselves into it and I wonder if that's part of an artistic trait, an 'authorly' trait, a writing trait – that *stepping back from it* is that watchful part that is almost taking notes on your own life and how you are feeling and, [...] rather than just living it one hundred percent, it's a bit of you that's watching.

This is an emotional pause, a stepping-back, the author 'runs a reel' simultaneously with real, *lived life*, creating a way of recording emotion without necessarily evaluating it, feeling it in the moment. The writer and her audience must eventually *commune*, but the book, physically, is an eternal boundary (or barrier) that allows both the writer and reader to play with the autonomy and interpret and re-interpret values and meaning at will.

8.2. Writing and Life

Literature, like life, is performative in role, but such performativity is complex – whether it is literally *performed* (Brook, [1968] 2008) or simply evocative of imagery and action in the writer's and receiver's imaginations, the performativity of the text is arguably central to its value and its linguistic instructiveness in a *reader's mind* (Austin, [1962] 1976; Culler, [1975] 2002: 125) and thus brought to life – or *used* – by its iterations (Derrida, 1978, 1988; Glendinning, 2011; Royle, 2003). Literature can be affective via drama and linguistics (such as constative and performative utterances – a kind of *instructional text* that is either persuasive but not committal or quite the opposite). Writing, text and its acceptance as literature *here* is dependent on Katherine telling a story and involving the reader rather than the text being instructive in any way. The literature *performs*, but it is ostensibly *narration* rather than *instruction* here. *Writing* is thus rehearsed and then performed by an author, crafted, released and then *read by an awaiting public*. The narrative ostensibly involves the reader by inviting imagining of physicality, movement, sound, intonation, senses, colour and so on – thus, the text 'performs' via the narrative. Those routines and processes of audience dissemination are fairly uniform across the arts, but what is the specific modus operandi in the *literary authorial* convention? The ideas must perform for the author prior to committal.

> **Katherine:** I don't know, when I sit down to write, what I am going to write [...] it's a free form, organic, *in the moment* kind of thing. Not all authors work that way; a lot of authors plan and [...] when they then sit down to actually turn that plan into prose there has to be some kind of switching off of the conscious mind to allow that creative mind to just talk – I can't see how else you could do it.

The story is intrinsically 'there' and the writing of it is arguably the 'drudge work' where putting into words what is on your mind onto the page is considered labour; 'the story itself is done in your head when you sit down', says Katherine, but the crafting of the story is the skilled part of the process requiring the most attention. Katherine likes the *research*, stating she is 'extremely old school; I do 90–95% of my research from books [...] foraged, second hand, from libraries, and then I go and visit my locations as a follow-up to the reading that I've done [...] I might check a few, tiny facts online as I'm writing'. Some library web resources are very useful, 'but generally speaking, the kind of thing I need to know is what it was like to live there at the time', she says. Using the bibliography and following the trail of knowledge the ideas start to gain life, form and the sparkle of possibility. The formulation is imaginative; it is fun, *performative* in many ways, the setting for the playful act between ideas and characters, the consideration and realisation of potential and the ordering of plot. It is, like writing a play for stage or screen, the *elementary creative phase* of a project. After the writing is done, edited, re-constituted and released then the next phase of performativity is experienced. Katherine simply wants to write, experience creative solitude, avoid being 'out there'. She feels too old for social media, left behind by this revolution in communication, isolated from it and relatively happy to keep it at distance, but the commercial realities of authorship are paramount in the reckoning of remaining an author and are consequently unavoidable, but was it ever any different?

> **Katherine:** You talk about exhibiting as an artist, well there's so much exhibiting by authors now – writing a book is not enough anymore, you have to be able to promote it and you have to be able to go out and speak about it and meet people and cause buzz.

When the novel is finished, it is 'done' much like, she suggests, a painting is considered done when the signature is added and the varnish is applied and the frame is completed. That moment *locks in* aura for the writer and allows the text to perform an autonomous function – an autonomous and individual, personal performance in many ways.

> **Katherine:** The *original* only exists in my own head and I think [...] it's not a different performance in the way a band can do a different performance every time and it will depend what mood the musicians are in, [...] what they're getting back from the crowd, what the vibe is like; [...] it's a very different relationship between reader and book, it's that one-on-one, that interpretation in their own minds [*original emphasis*].

I suggest that literature is performative because each person interprets the words, the order, the grammar in a certain way – *performing* the book rather than reading it, but essentially making a 'cover version' of the original (an original that Katherine can only know). Thus, the reader is required to *perform* the text, adding the dramatic texture to the descriptive, the sounds and the volume, the lights and the temperatures and the intonations of voice, the speed of scenes and so on. These are all in the gift of the reader, democratising the text, making it unique for every reader, performative *in extremis*, aura-filled and original every time it is encountered and, most of all, interpreted on the reader's own terms. While the rigidity of text will reflect the authorial power of the creator, the performance is passed to the reader as an *opportunity*. Katherine understands this analogy. 'Can it be said to be performative if the author at that point has nothing whatsoever to do with it?' she asks. 'Who's doing the performing?' I argue that it is, as stated, the reader. *It's like drama, but fiction does not become drama, but it is dependent on the reader's life experiences. Five billion versions of her novel, at any one time, can potentially be in existence.* This depiction of her work (like any work) individualises the escapism of the novel, the storytelling and the interpretative values of fiction in the modern world. The reader is able to contextualise the narrative in his or her own circumstances, setting it in familiar places, hearing familiar voices and even imagining characters' physicality – including faces – as something *familiar and re-assuring* as the elements of certainty in the outside, 'real' world fade, crumple and liquefy. Katherine states her own take on this theory, suggesting that in re-reading a novel that you read as a teenager there is a sense that this once-wonderful, profound experience can be so disappointing when re-encountered, revised and re-appraised with the benefit of time and experience, re-embedding the narratives and finding them disorientated, puerile, faded and reformed by changing times. 'That is just a startling, wake-up call as to how much your own mind has changed and your own experience of life has changed', she says.

This re-imagining of the narratives of fiction – and their disembedding from both originator (author) and reader (in time) – can also be considered through the modern manifestation of audiobook or, possibly, TV or radio dramatisation. This 'adaption and appropriation' (Sanders, 2015) of original text adds a layer of interpretation in Katherine's view, through voices and inflections that may not have been intended by the author. She hesitates to judge on 'that disconnect between the author and the reader' but insists that her own take on literature is that 'books are there to be read and not listened to'. This is arguably illustrative of those barriers that come between the intimacy of the author–reader relationship. This is important, sensual and suggestive of structure – capitalism arguably interjects and re-constructs the text in its own shape, form and feel for its own purposes. This editorial influence (Becker, [1982] 2008) is not driven by capitalism or control per se, but does augment the 'voice' of others *onto the 'voice' received*. The dynamic that involves the oscillation of reader and author connectivity in an age of a 'public' or 'social' sensual *dis*connection is involved here – namely the intimacy of text (people tend to read *alone*) and the application of autonomous interpretation. Late modern capitalism arguably tries to separate us, but maybe reading *is* the last vestige of connection between individuals across time and space as we are increasingly separated/connected by screens and associative disparate lives – the intimacy of reading is a way to feel connected, even if there still remains a *book between us.*

Katherine is appreciative of the fact that her books are read, performed and intellectually valued. After years of not being published she states that there remains an everlasting nothingness in 'words that are unread, what is that? What are words that are unread? They're just dead, aren't they?' A good feeling exists knowing that words are going to a publisher rather than 'working in the wilderness'. The public give her stories *life*. She writes because she has an *urge* to do so, but readers are critical and she welcomes the interactivity of such review. She would not want to go back to knowing that 'no readers are waiting', further appreciating that this is communicative, networked and connective. She likes to hear from readers, because they write about life, about experience, emotions and connectivity.

> **Katherine:** [Readers talk] about some aspect of a story that has completely resonated with them and it made them think differently about something that happened to them, or they had felt completely in tune with the character because of a similar experience, and I think to myself that book has come alive for them [...] it's not words on a page anymore, it's something that's gone into their mind and it's stayed there.

This is, she states, 'what any artist wants; for work to be absorbed like that'. As midlife emerges she is sanguine, accepting and reflective. She considers being in her forties as just another phase, the process of writing changes little. 'The excitement of having your idea, the waiting for it to grow and spread [...] and writing' all stay the same she says, but publishing is changing and, perhaps detecting a subtle cynicism in its environs, she adds that she wants to 'reflect a greater maturity' in her writing but sees a conflict approaching between maturity and entertaining the reader. 'It has to be spontaneous and organic', she says, but there is a tension between remaining with a tried and tested formula or experimentation, change, departure. She looks into the next 10 years with a mixture of determination, anticipation and some trepidation, but when I ask her if writing has a longevity or a liminality she is more guarded, less sure about the distinction. 'I don't generally think about the future a great deal, I can't imagine ever not writing and [...] I'm starting to see [...] that this is now changing', she says. Her rhythms are shifting, her identity remains in flux with the continuity of writing, the sense of the possible merging with the sense of the familiar merged itself with a sense of desire to develop and to adjust, inspiration moving in waves and, while 'feeling blessed to be able to do this for a living' she understands the potential liminality of the profession. What sets Katherine aside from many of the creative people that I met is her insistence that writing does, in fact, offer her an inner peace rather than the oft-cited dynamics of chaos and excitement. The stability is felt most keenly in the reward of having a purposeful occupation. This tenacity transfers from the conditions of labour to the conditions of life itself, re-assigning to her character and her associative sense of wellbeing from the praxis of writing and its physical repetitions. Despite identifying as a 'conventional' person, she insists that her need for structure is born of a different field. She needs to write 2000 words a day to feel a sense of progress and purpose (a bit like Trollope, [1883] 2016), lest it become considered partial or in abeyance and she sees herself as something of a 'young fogey' that turns *away* from chaos; her routine, she admits, is 'kind of a reaction' to a sense of loosely defined chaos in the everyday.

> **Katherine:** If I stop and think about where I stand philosophic-
> ally, I [...] have flashes of existential crises, I guess, the universe is
> vast and infinite, uncaring space and we're all going to die, so
> why would you do anything, why would you love anybody, why
> does anything matter? And the answer is it doesn't, and there's
> tremendous freedom in that, but it's bloody scary as well. I think
> writing and having that sense of purpose and that routine just
> anchors me back to the real world just slightly! [...] I think if
> I had too much time alone not writing [...] I would probably just
> go off into the wilderness!

Life has gifted her opportunities that, despite being diligently pursued, have
changed so many things for her and affected her whole way of being, incorporating an exhilarating combination of possibilities, anxieties, reflexivity and bursts
of serenity and contemplation and she views whatever the future brings with a
sense of the *inevitable*. She also understands, instinctively, the need for literature
and, consequently, the need for writers and the intrinsic value of story-telling,
the lexicon of human experience and also, potentially, the currency of social and
cultural reproduction.

> **Katherine:** For whatever reason, the human brain needs stories, it
> needs to be told stories, you know, that's how we relate to other
> people and how we place ourselves in this world and how we
> define ourselves in reference to others, in everything. [...] People
> need to read stories and I seem to be able to come up with stories
> that people enjoy reading for whatever reason, whether it's to be
> taken out of their own lives or whether to see some truth reflected
> about their own lives or some shared experience [...] so I don't
> feel I have some tremendous or unique experience, I don't feel
> I'm unique in any way really but I just seem to have a gift for
> making up stories that people enjoy reading, that's what I've got
> to give.

She concludes by returning to her theme of *purpose*. Writing, she emphatically states, 'gives me a purpose and I think if you've no sense of purpose that's
when people really struggle [...] and there may not be any point to what I'm
writing but it gives me the sense that there *is*'. It is therefore a highly therapeutic
thing, medicinal and purposive and serves to keep doubts at bay. It is an integral
part of her identity, keeping her on an even-keel and serving as a reminder that
'it produces a sense of calm and having a *place in the world*'. Writing is a functional thing that has been bestowed naturally as a thrusting force of purpose as
well as a calming sense of enlightenment; she sees her vocation as placing her *in*
the world rather than separate from it. The circle is completed.

§

Writing is clearly both the achievement of a long-held ambition, but also a way of life for Annette and Katherine. Throughout the conversations it was clear that, while writing was considered an 'everyday' thing that was framed by established routines that promised to furnish effort with tangible outputs, it also promised more via a hidden excitement that was couched in the sense of the unpredictable, the limitless space of the imagination and the revisable. Thus, when Katherine pointed out that writers tend to have a division between 'work' minds and 'creative' minds, it was not just the dedication to the craft and the ability to 'think beyond' the normative that blessed the writer, it was also the recognition that there was time of unbridled imaginative anarchy that one can summon that drives the process forwards. While the work is allied with the routine of research, having a strong ethnographic feel (Annette and Katherine both spoke about being able draw on a cornucopia of life experience and observations as well as continuing to 'watch' a great deal of life as it passes), and the omnipresent sense – and articulation – that creative art is 'labour' in itself (often measured in time), it is also an activity that has deep metaphysical qualities. The imagination is rich with the dynamics of discovery, recovery, boundless and exciting, resplendent in its *mezzanine* 'dreamlike state' that exists between the real world and the imagination itself; in your head you are 'free', the *discipline* of creativity comes with the ordering of such disparity but, as Katherine said, the creative mind never switches off. Writing reflects life in that it is organic, flexible, unpredictable and revisionist, is *communicative* with people both via texts and via the 'corresponding journey' of the life course, contributes to an oeuvre from the midlife phase, but also retains a deep, meaningful privacy for the writer herself. This is where the individualised 'hidden' author retains an 'ultimate truth' relating to the meaning of their work, forever remaining their unique possession, separated from society by the book itself, a *physicality* that enshrines the individuated-generative routines of the writer. The writer resists the opaque conformity and security of midlife for the thrill of the unknown. However, this is arguably the creative process that has the least 'anarchy' of thought applied, as it is, to a greater firmness in historically-founded style, genre, form and audience expectations. These are women who remain visible *as* creative women in midlife – professional, erudite and productive and exploiting the opportunity to progressively contribute to literature earned via hard work, dedication and the ability to imaginatively think.

The meetings with Annette and Katherine uncovered a sense that writing exists *within* the writer; it is not 'learned' or acquired, but naturally couched in the identity waiting to be discovered and harnessed. It is also unpredictable and varied, oscillating in quality, prone to pique at inconvenient times, sitting heavily on the conscience and the nerves. It is, despite all of these things, a joy and a gift that is appreciated. The authors would not want to do anything else with their time. In midlife, whether just entering the rough domain or established within its nebulous boundaries, the women are conscious of their maturity and their sense of mission in tandem with the shifting patterns of time felt through age and changing lifestyles. It is as if writing has delivered them into a more comfortable sense of self, the vagaries of 'youth' being ironed out into a smooth engagement with wisdom through writing. I got the sense that 'life' and 'art' (writing) were *lived* separately but *practiced* as *one thing*, creating an organic communion with the purpose of life, the articulation of fantasy and the urge to commit to paper the visions of imagination to entertain, stimulate and assuage. Walter Benjamin made an interesting observation when he stated that Proust described life not as *life*, but as a *process* of memory of the person describing the life (Benjamin, [1923] 2008: 93). We therefore, he continues, remember through many things – including smell – with the *mémoire involuntaire* being somewhat intuitive, formless and indeterminate (ibid.: 110). As life moved forwards for the authors, there is a sense that the 'many things' we remember by are woven into the actions of writing as well as the content produced. In other words, 'life' (or recurrent experience) continues to remind the writers of what they are *doing* (and why they value it) as well as informing them during moments of creation of how to *do* or *say* it. For instance, in the discussion with Katherine about the interpretation of her art and the 'performative' essence of reading, I suggested that the *reader* is required to add multiple layers of hyper-contemporary interpretive dimensions to the text itself. This can be, of course, compared to the somewhat *romantic* notion that art and culture are merely a front, an abstraction, or a substitute for social relations in the modern world (Williams, [1958] 2017: 356). In other words, we discuss an idea of social relations through – in this case – the literature, substituting connection with the 'real world' and the social relations that exist (or do not exist) within it for a dialogue via our connection with literature. Such Romantic idealism seems to jar with the complexities of the modern age, but perhaps this is indicative of our retreat from meaningful communicative action? This 'new' Romantic suggestion – the articulation of social relations through our communion with the printed text (whether on a page or a screen) – is suggestive that we are withdrawing into an individualised existence despite our much lauded 'age of communication'. The writer, if anything, is communicating with *herself* and her memories while writing. If this is the case there may be a somewhat unintended renaissance of the Romantic view that art *determines* social reality (ibid.: 359) rather than reflecting it and reproducing it and, consequently, hindering our penetration of our dispersal in late modern times. The routines of creating literature, as explained above, tend towards a dichotomy of meaning, ostensibly removing the suggestion that the author is transmitting (contested) ideology and world view (Bauman, 1999) with an intention to mask our divisions through individualised, performative reading. Instead, the art is created by isolated, imaginative individuals who are committed to their art for the sake of their own creative urges, rather than to bestow cultural reproduction on the masses. This, however, could be false consciousness on all counts.

Katherine and Annette are therefore talking about *life* and they are talking about *writing*, citing writers talking about writing (King, [2000] 2012) and, as Margaret Atwood would say, they are also aware of the symbolic (public) *weight* of *being* a writer (Atwood, [2003] 2015: 23). That is a very public pressure to deliver. They may actually be talking about themselves writing *to* themselves, but it never diverts into the realm of what might be called metafiction *per se*

(Waugh, 1984). Instead creativity arguably rests on the dynamic triangle of life-style, vocation and identity experienced, in these instances, in midlife. This is not about the *pursuit* of a certain type of perfection in fiction via form or style (Lodge, [1992] 2011a; [1996] 2011b; [1966] 2001) but the pursuit of *routine* and social and metaphysical meaning — of doing something meaningful, something that one can *do*, but doing it *well*. Writing gives their lives meaning by being plastered on the page, so to speak, *seeing their lives in their prose*. The dynamics and outcomes of the writing process are therefore, invariably, influenced by structure in the manifestation of biography, mother tongue and latent, omnipresent economy; as Italo Calvino states, it 'is certain that writing (unlike language) is a fact of culture not of nature' (Calvino, 2013: 41) but, as it is evident above, the dynamics of *being* a writer are considered more natural, in-built, non-arbitrarily hard wired into the soul rather than nurtured by the system or, as Calvino states, the *culture*. Thus, the *fact* of culture shapes the formatting of language, influencing its mode, form, pace and assiduity but it is through a sense of self-efficacy and the role of discursive practices with both the self and with others that the *fact* of culture is transformed into a negotiated compromise between culture and nature, an influence that is hegemonic, embraced but also manipulated in the creative space that I call the 'mezzanine'.

Chapter 9

The Mezzanine and Midlife Creativity

At the outset of this study, I stated that art is about transformation of material and the self; creating art is a method of asserting an authenticity of the self and identity to oneself and to others and is best understood as a process of both *becoming an artist* as well as thriving as one. At the heart of this work were the dynamics of midlife, creative methods and the meaning held by creative people towards their outputs and how such constituents of identity and life may resist the humdrum of the midlife phase. The outcome has been to understand 'art' as both an opportunity and a resistance – how praxis creates excitement, self-efficacy and the sense of the possible.

9.1. Midlife

The midlife phase, as I have illustrated, is considered 'an opportunity' and the nature of such opportunity is usually couched in the perception of choice connected to the utilisation of skill and the capitalisation of time. The creative people in this study see midlife as a chance to either 'come together' to achieve a personal goal within a unit or to 'work apart' from the erstwhile presence of family, auxiliary job or other distractions, all recognising the separation from such matters as being exclusively connected to achieving transformations in *materials* and in the *self*. Midlife is much more than image maintenance or nostalgia; it is about playfulness, wisdom, space, power and assertiveness, experience and achievement as well as resistance to predictability. The mezzanine of creativeness provides such a platform for such confrontation with the ordinary.

When discussing midlife as it is represented in the works of the writer Margaret Drabble (in this instance, up until the mid-1980s), Joanne Creighton described the depiction of midlife as being something of a 'motionless sameness' (Creighton, 1985: 92; Drabble, 1980). This sentiment is partially echoed and developed by Cathrine Degnen who argues that *older* age (i.e. the stage that ostensibly succeeds midlife) is, when theorised in the context of the passing of time, something of a 'motionless present' (Degnen, 2007: 231) where routine is not *practiced*, is reliant on the past for context and with actors *preoccupied* by such reflections. While Degnen is speaking of people beyond the midlife stage that is defined within *this* research, there is a useful comparison here in that the midlife routines that I have presented are a resistance to the inevitable regressive routines (and inevitabilities) that Degnen discusses; the artists are effectively fending off the repetitions that they may, indeed, foresee. Robin, for example, is clear in his dedication to stimulation and originality, taking his art as a gift that must be utilised, originally, at all times. It is, to him, a way of permanently seeking a form of joyous (productive) disorder in his life where stability could equate to repetition and retrogression. This finds a nexus with the ideas of Sharon Kaufman (1986) who suggests in *The Ageless Self* that something of an in-built denial of the ageing process can be detected in the thoughts of those who are ageing, with similar sentiments identified in Al Alvarez's *Pondlife* (2013) where 'denial' is arguably practiced through participation in open water swimming while *acceptance* of the increasing limitations of age is considered *through* such resistance (i.e. the swimming is done *despite* age while the mind accepts the diminishing power of the body to cope with the effects). This *resistance* to age – in its most nebulous context – can be detected in the ethnography above, where age is accepted as *progress* on one hand and *routine and banality* on the other.

Creativity is a 'midlife open water swim', the effects invigorating and creating of momentum rather than reminding the artist of a diminishing mental, physical or contributing power. It is a resistance to motionless sameness and the repetitive, routine present; this mezzanine is based, again, on reactivity and novelty as a separation from the banal zones that flank the generative-self. Midlife is experienced in the *middle of many things*, not least the linearity of life itself but also as a phase where risks can be taken, ambitions realised, and separations of duties negotiated. Art is also a 'thing' that exists between subjectivity and the objective or, to put it another way, it emerges from the 'murmur of intention' (Foucault, [1969] 1972), eventually becoming the subject of an aesthetic value discourse (Wolff, 1983: 106). This research is about the moments that exist in-between those two extremes. The artists are all 'in the middle', between things, transferring from one thing to another, transforming their lives *through* things; they are seeking space in the centre, between individualisation and sociality; they are looking for the moment of serenity between two forms of 'noise'. Midlife is lived on an everyday basis but seen here through the creative will and the creative praxis. It is this combination of intelligence (and wisdom) and connected action (utilising of skill and discernible outcomes) coupled with determination, chance and the presence of 'time capital' (freedom to *do*) that has framed the ethnographic responses of the creative people who feature. All respondents allude to two things: the history from which their creativity springs and the uncertainty of the moment of creation.

Throughout the preceding chapters it has been possible to notice the profound influence of the midlife phase of life in facilitating the autonomy to act artistically via the accumulation of human capital (social, cultural and 'time' capitals, etc.) as well as the curious sense of tumultuous uncertainty that is attached to the central tenet of the creative process – the generation of novelty. The *value of experience* (habitus), the *options* present via the phase, the omnipresent 'anxiety of influence' that sits in the background and the devil-may-care discarding of stability in favour of 'chaos' and freedom all appear to combine to frame artistic routine. The will towards the *satiation* of subjectively retained desire is coupled with the projected consideration of *personal value* towards the process of creating along with ubiquitous cognisance of the auxiliary playmakers such as location, circumstances, commitments and choice that flow together to further make possible the artistic routine that consequently helps shape identity and something of a *raison d'être*. There is also a need to oscillate between that external, quantifiable dynamic of 'age and experience' with the timeless emotional turmoil of the creative process (considered as both exciting and serene in equal measure); I am concerned with why these artists do what they do, how they do it and what it might mean to them as well as being interested in how the process is somehow shaped by the stage in life in which all of the respondents find themselves in but I am also excited by the emergence of the commitment to tumultuousness and edgy uncertainty of the moment. The psycho-social, quasi-ontological experience of the creative routine itself is central and the ethnography has deliberately couched the midlife element in *subtle* terms, permitting the respondents to 'make sense themselves' and to consider the impact that their art has on them (and possibly on others), consequently allowing them to write their own relevance into their own *thoughts* about whether midlife affects the process in any way. It is clear, of course, that being in the midlife phase has had a profound effect on their decisions, options, choices and in the way that they frame their outputs, but it is also clear that midlife is a dynamic that is partially side-lined in favour of viewing the present as an exciting *now* (i.e. do not look back and do not look forwards but 'live in the present'). This is a fine opportunity to consider the 'in-between' as the metaphor as well as the 'space', understanding midlife and subconscious fantasy emerging as the platform for newness and exhilaration. The march of time invariably creates personal anxiety on many levels, and one can sense the latent anxiety seeping through in idioms, such as Laurie Taylor's expansion of the word *surviving* (Hepworth & Featherstone, 1982) equating to a notion of *coping*. To many people in the midlife phase, coping is pejorative in context and something to be discarded, resisted and mocked. Artistic creativity may well offer the chance to discard coping, anxiety and the inevitabilities of time by escaping all three strictures and proving that the in-between state is an adrenaline-charged sanctuary.

Midlife can be rescued from a hegemonic servitude of inevitability (slowing down, conventionality, etc.) via a continued energy, industry and personal growth. This is a period where stable identity is detected and creativity exploited. Evidence suggests that 'youth' cultures can continue to shape sociality into midlife (Bennett, 2006; Bennett & Hodkinson, 2012), but the longevity of such subcultural connection is arguably an embodiment of 'holding back' the 'inevitable' rather than effortlessly embracing the fluidity of time as essentially 'ageless'. Midlife expressionism and exhibitionism can instead be meritoriously disembedded from the predictable *linear pattern of ageing* and understood instead as a *period of industry* that, ipso facto, differs from the diverged youthful surges of exuberance and latter-life *sage-like wisdom*. This can be considered not as an inevitable *phase* (i.e. midlife) but merely a *present time* where the experiences and human capital can be exploited to better effect in a 'field' of artistic creation (Bourdieu, [1984] 2010) and where continued effervescence is considered possible and actively sought. Therefore, midlife can embody effervescent *potential*, not managed *decline*, and be understood as a point in the life-course where creativity and identity/biography combine to resist the somewhat structurally embedded expectancy that it is *all about consolidation from here on in*.

There is a widely held view amongst creative people that the thrust of the creative self is to be found from *within*, that it is democratic and meritocratic in essence, celebrated as a form of resistance to the humdrum, continually new, vibrant and valuable. Routines effectively replace routines; the *negative* is replaced by the *liberating*. The spark of creativity is uncertain, unreliable in timing (if not in presence) and to be seized 'in the moment' and it is this 'space' that I chose to theorise as being supra-ideological and the embodiment of freedom, embodying resistance to negative routine and the point where identity, biography and *possibility* meet in an otherwise perfect combination. I have chosen throughout to term this space the 'mezzanine' because it *metaphorically illustrates* an *in-between* space, neither governed by responsibility or affective of the future. It has no causal consequences or any preconditions, is indicative of the late modern empowered 'I-am-I', biographically-centred self (Beck, 1992) and acts as an attractive destination away from the formativeness and determinism of the real world. Things 'happen here'; it is at once the point of departure for creativity and its conclusive state for novelty, ontologically quite naked and thrillingly uncertain in outcome.

9.2.   Creativity: Ideology and Action

The quest for novelty has a rich history, detectable as far back as the Greeks. While Plato declared creativity a process of *discovery* and consequent imitation that existed largely in ethereal disembodiment (Fuller, 2005: 109−110; Plato, 1994), Sternberg and Lubart (1999a, 1999b), Feldman, Csikszentmihalyi and Gardner (1994) position creativity as a more contemporaneous *process*, or a routine that merges ability and skill to develop *usefulness* (echoing the Kant and Bourdieu discourse on art, use, sense of aesthetics − see Grenfell & Hardy, 2007; Geldof & Marlin, 1997). While creativity is often connected to consolidating the incongruent themes of the *subject* (action, intelligence, biography, disciplinary focus − i.e. creativity in the lab the art studio, the recording studio, accounting and so on), there remains a sense that the topic/definition belongs to an incremental *educative* process (Burnard, 2006) that is realised through artistic endeavours. The decision to undertake research into creativity in midlife emerged from an interest in the intellectual nexus of the ethnographic tradition in sociology and cultural studies with the associative natural relationship of ideas relating to common cultures (Hoggart, [1957] 2009; Willis, 1990), 'structures of feeling' (Williams, 1961) and what can be described further here as the 'codes' of production (namely, why and how some people in society make things for the pleasure of other people in society − and what discernible value it provides for them as individuals and groups − and, ultimately, how they go about *doing* it). It is possible to add the more undisciplined, unpredictable influences of social, economic and cultural change theorised throughout under the aegis of 'late modernism' to this formula to create a contemporaneous slant on the anxieties of the post-industrial and 'post-Fordist' (Bonefield & Holloway, 1992; Burrows & Loader, 1994) age of relative insecurity and rampant personal and professional reflexivity (May & Perry, 2017) and how this plays out in the journey to being creative and the decision to *continue to be so*. It is possible to equate the creative process not only to the simple thoughts and actions of the individual or group, but also in greater depth via the emancipatory thrust of critical theory, tested by the forces of late modernism in that the central dynamic of hegemony (Gramsci, 1971) – namely the strategy of the working class to master its self-administrative strategies and organise (Bronner, 2011: 22) – comes under scrutiny in an age of individualisation. To be sure, individualisation can be seen in itself as a hegemonic instrument of control, but while the artists that feature in this project have seemingly found a method of counter-hegemony, the *resistance* has little or nothing to do with social class or the inferred dynamic of mass action. These are individuals who resist on their own terms, via their own techniques and in a highly dissociative domain. Creativity is an action that can embody (potentially subconscious) resistance to exploitation. Johnny of The Ruins stated that the 'five percent' of creative time that he carved out of a working week produced fruits that he only fleetingly owned prior to their dissemination to an audience that he could neither see, hear, smell or feel. 'Creativity' is therefore repositioned and appropriated as a *space* by the creator as a resistance to such exploitation. It is a state of passive insurrection, sought out, earned, defended and retained as a last vestige of power and a place where anything is possible. This is the reward, rather than the entitlement, of a creative person.

The modes of creativity and the categorisation of activity segues well with the contested, interdisciplinary character of cultural studies (Moran, 2010). The study of culture itself, with the 'everyday' being arguably contentious due to the complexities of material functionality and lived experience (Pink, 2012), individual subjectivity and the unpredictable markers of taste, fashion and utility, is further prone to subconscious individual and collective assimilative and instrumental strategies (de Certeau, 1984) and is variable in terms of penetration, applied value and participation and utilisation (Arnold, [1869] 2006; Leavis & Thompson, 1933; Williams, 1977). For culture to be seen as an 'ordinary' thing (Williams, [1958] 1989) it needs to be seen as emergent from simple actions of people, omnipresent, detected subtly and channelled into the making of things – the artefact and the identity. It is best to settle the defining of 'creativity' as commonly found within the *ordinary*, predictable 'everyday' in order to more clearly recognise how art forms can be broadly defined (playing music; painting and printing; and writing) and considered instrumental in some lives as both routine and as experienced as the moment of distraction from real life. The process of creating art can be understood as a *situated action* emerging from comprehension of a myriad of influences involving simultaneous dynamics of midlife (biography and identity), the discursive dialogue of art and society (history, aesthetics, audience, value, etc.), grasp of an understanding of 'culture' and the cultural, and a perception of reception (audience, affect and effect). Art can also be deciphered as a creative 'state' where the active player is called upon to interpret – or augment – an existing subconsciously attentive canon of work

via biography, experience, capital and skill resulting in the emergence of a problematic dichotomy. While the habitus of the artist feeds intrinsically *into the
action of creation*, resulting in art being unable to exist in vacuum, mimetically
building on existing knowledge, the parameters and dynamics of the *act* or *routine* of creation itself points to an 'uncertain now' where novelty must be divided
from history to define itself *as* novel. The 'social condition of art' is, according
to Raymond Williams, an embracing of aesthetics, psychology and history, with
the latter being categorised as a dynamic largely separated from the former two
fields and leading to a belief that aesthetics and psychology introduce 'social
conditions as modifiers' or 'construct general periods of human culture within
which certain type of art flourish' (Williams, 1981: 21). This study has veered
away from becoming categorised in such a way, perhaps owing more to the idea
of 'mediation' (or reflections of social relations in the becoming art forms) or
'forms' themselves (format of delivery) that can be subjected to a continual
change not focussed necessarily on the artists' *a priori* impulses of creation but
turning instead, as Georg Lukács states,

> towards a new aim which is essentially different from the old one
> [...] [meaning that] the old parallelism of the transcendental struc-
> ture of the form-giving subject [author] and the world of created
> forms has been destroyed and the ultimate basis of artistic cre-
> ation has become homeless (Lukács, [1971] 2006: 40–41).

Such 'homelessness' is arguably where the artist applies no determining *a
priori* (transcendental) thrust to the creative process (i.e. a desire to 'solve'
instabilities in previous creative works) and instead faces a point where existing
and potential form does not segue, resulting in the author *having to be original
every time*. This is the principal compulsion in all of the creative people featured
in this study. They exalt the unpredictability of the creative routine and I shall
return to the technique of such process shortly. There is a need to trace back the
thrust of the creative action to the point where the biography is 'feeding in' to
the state of creativity but is ignorant to the outcome. Reception, thus, becomes a
useful tool to essentially 'look into the future' to understand the 'present' (creative zone) and the past (biography, ideology and structure). The Ruins spoke
of their songs that 'lean forwards' into a future from their moment of creation
and, having established that the focus throughout this work is the *routine of creativity* rather than the *aesthetic value* placed upon products after 'completion', it
is essential to define the parameters of 'creativity' by those who actually *make
stuff*. The middle-aged artists are essentially 'riffing' on a familiar set of themes
and, despite being original in every way by continually creating something that
had not existed before, they are also drawing upon existing oeuvres of their art,
inspired by a body of artistic 'knowledge', an 'anxiety of influence' (Bloom,
1973) scenario that either means 'fight or flight' in creative terms, acknowledge
and 'better' or destroy. They also seek to be *contributing to something* rather
than beginning from scratch per se; it is another song, painting or book that

exists in a 'long line' of such artefacts; creativity and *imagination* may therefore be perceived as something that exist with binary qualities. They are not, in conjunction, as Terry Eagleton states, 'unequivocally positive' – *noble*, but also prone to the vagaries of fantasy (Eagleton, 2013: 77). If anything, the creative *process* (that includes *imagination as a somewhat crucial ingredient*) is the inert, secure touchstone of security as the oscillations of late modernity create a diffidence at the heart of midlife suppositions. The creative *process* and the creative *muse* have emblematic traces that stretch back to childhood; these personal histories, experiences and emotional imprints effectively blend together forming a creative self, that *identity of resistance*, in early life. *Creative*, as a verb, therefore need not be considered to have a particularly positive personal archaeology for the artists here despite merging with imaginative fantasy to create wonderful results.

Creativity can also be considered as being connected to what Storr (1972) would argue was a combination of 'wish fulfilment', 'play' and the 'quest for identity'. These foci are understood via strong Freudian analysis, featuring the creative outcomes (artworks, books, music, etc.) being viewed, somewhat severely, as 'nothing but surrogates; inferior substitutes for what the author is unable to obtain for himself in reality' (Storr, 1972: 30). Daydreaming and fantasy combine and are applied to a quest for a realisation of *something of the real* in an emerging artefact (story, song, painting, film, etc.) and leans on a scenario where the 'imagination is used to create substitutes for reality' (ibid.: 45), where disappointments may be effectively corrected by the creative spirit in an almost Nietzschean reappraisal of the past. Creativity, in this oeuvre, is therefore something of an affirmative method of reparation, perfection, satiation of the hanging sense of incompleteness that may trouble the creator. It is a pervasive argument that seeks to reach a *deeper and richer truth* as well as deliver an alternative reality, a safe sanctuary from the real world that satisfies our deeper understanding of the real world beyond our immediate thoughts and experiences. Of course, this can be applied to both the creation of art and the consumption of art – whether music, image or text. In this instance, in the mind of the artist entering and coping with midlife, the identity is framed as 'positive fantasy' – a state of mind picturing the perfect and the insightful, depositing pent-up thoughts, emotions, ambitions and dialogues into an artefact, communicative via the disposing of a 'back story' into the art and communicating such visions to others.

Where creativity can be traditionally considered a genesis of thought and the development of an object via such creative thrust, it can also be a process that is practiced, fluid, incremental and reflexive, educational (Karlsen, 2010; Westerlund, 2006) and organisational (Fornäs, Lindberg, & Sernhede, 1995). Music can be interpreted as disembedded from its forum, experienced 'in the moment' and via the understanding of artistic output as being connected to interpretation, sensibilities, emotion and self (Williams, 1961; Wolff, 1975). Of course, 'rehearsal' is associated predominantly with music and other performative arts, but fine art and writing can be effectively rehearsed likewise. Creative routines situate 'life' as a continual 'rehearsal' of meaning, feeling and creativeness that is realised through a moment, in the mezzanine, where the disparate influences and possibilities become crystallised and 'captured', resulting in the midlife artist apprehending a sense of aura about both their own lives and the continual joy of the expected unexpected.

9.3.   Identity and Feeling: Art and Soul

Janet Wolff provides a foundation for both the understanding of sociological narratives in wider conceptions of art and the aesthetic interpretations of art post-creation, arguing that the artist is not isolated 'genius' but is, instead, merely an actor within a large framework of production (Wolff, 1993). All the while, artists *are*, in fact, seeking a (potentially partial) *suspension* of ideology in their routines, despite being unable (structurally) to dispel the lineage of socialisation and ideology from their actions. Wolff's works retain use by situating a central dynamic of the artist as an actor that can summon the historical muse while retaining authorial ownership. This can be considered the moment where the artist is able to transpose his or her biography, habitus, capital and actions 'onto' that blank canvas in the mezzanine. However, art is so often caught up in an inexorable dialectic of production-reception-value-longevity, leading the observer to conceptualise 'art' as a process that envelops the artist, the art work and the public that exist beyond the studio, writing room, recording studio or theatre. Art is considered a product of a community, an 'art world' (Becker, [1982] 2008), and a 'scene' (Bennett, 2000; Bennett & Peterson, 2004; Crossley & Boterro, 2015), with the kernel of the creative self-intensifying and enveloping notions of aesthetics, affectivity, reception and performativity. The connectivity need not be holistic: while art structurally and ideologically (mostly involuntarily) involves influence in technique, this is not necessarily a given that it be considered a process that becomes *public*, that the procedure of creation is *designed* to connect with a sense of utility, beauty and value (either aesthetic or financial). Art can simply be about being alone, in the moment, with the *power to manipulate* the moment and to ultimately *record* it.

The effect of art can be considered as *impact that creates impact*, that tells a story, invokes a memory or thrusts a new perception upon an unwitting viewer. This hermeneutic *effect* is worth considering via the impression that reception and performativity have on the *creation* of art — that is, how the work is formed from time and emotion, 'communicates' with the invisible audience from the 'hidden place' and the individual 'practice' that the artist occupies. Jauss (1982) understood fluidity in subjectivity of *reception* via critiques of philological and aesthetic approaches, discussing the poetics and hermeneutics of text that can be equally applied to arts such as music and fine art and stating that '[h]ermeneutic reflection cannot and need not deny the horizon of contemporary interests' that condition our way of thinking about text (Jauss, 1982: 137). Ostensibly, people must accept art as *historically* created but also understood in the *now* (considered here as both the *immediate* and in relation to the *times*), closing the 'gap' between the brush stroke, the typed character or the strummed chord and the functionality of effect while simultaneously recognising initial vagaries of intent and the unbridgeable gap of homogeneity of meaning. In the course of the ethnography the role of the eventual 'reader' was never explicitly absent because all who took part were 'readers' themselves. This can be described as something of a 'ghost dynamic' in the process of creativity – namely that the 'reader' has a role but does not have an influence. This subject area has been extensively debated over time, with Roland Barthes (1977) and Michel Foucault (1980) initially explaining the nature of authorship, joined by Wolfgang Iser (1974; 1978) on 'aesthetic response' (between the poles of text and reader) and Umberto Eco ([1979] 1981) on the establishment and interpretation of semiotics *inside* the texts. While not central to the aim of understanding midlife creativity and identity, the role of the reader *is* a required dynamic in further understanding the determinants of action in creative modes. For instance, a lot of work on 'literature' from the point of writing (and reading) may well be polemical (Atwood, [2003] 2015; King, [2000] 2012; Orwell, 1970b), but *penetrative*. Eco ([2002/2004 transl.] 2005) stated that

> [t]here is only one thing you write for yourself, and that is a shopping list. It helps to remember what you have to buy, and when you have bought everything you can destroy it, because it is no use to anyone else. Every other thing that you write, you write to say something to someone (ibid.: 334).

This has resonance because of its simplicity of message – writing (creativity and end product) is 'communication' at virtually *all times*; writing is done to be *read*, is communicative and has a dynamic of the ghost reader present. In *The Sociology of Literature* (1971), Laurenson and Swingewood compounded this idea by stating that a novel deals with

> much the same social, economic, and political textures as sociology. But, of course it achieves more than this; as art, literature transcends mere description […] penetrating the surfaces of social life, showing the ways in which men and women experience society as feeling (Laurenson & Swingewood, 1971: 12−13).

Thus, literature (and art) has everyday characteristics that reflect the human emotions and senses, surpassing the simple function of entertainment and penetrating the 'back story' of the author and the 'forward story' of communication, empathy and communality. David Lodge declares himself a fan of the Arnoldian edict when considering the aesthetic value of literature as being 'what is special about it' (Lodge, 1977: xii) and, if anything, this is the penetrative, hidden language of art: the ability to summon responsiveness in the individual and group. Such sensuousness is echoed in work on emotion and music: on memory (Green, 2016); influence on 'fans' (Lewis, 1992); and lasting emotional value (DeNora, 2000). Sara Ahmed (2014) discusses functionalist theories of emotion and the fact that they state that there might be a *compulsion* involved in how we feel, how the function can be *instinctive* as well as consequently enabling *action*. However, there is also the essence of us, *the observer*, understanding what the person experiencing the emotion *might be feeling*, but it is only shaped by *our own* cultural and material histories – not by the artist, musician or writer. Emotion is also not just about instinct and action but also about what it *does* to the beholder. We need to *learn* emotion and *learn to recognise* its value and its manifestations and understand if it is *repeated*, drawn *from* something or entirely *new*. Thus, Ahmed states, '[e]motions are relational: they involve (re)actions or relations of 'towardness' or 'awayness' in relation to such objects' (Ahmed, 2014: 8). The *object* here being the created work, or the approach to the creative process while in motion, connecting the human response to the object of art. Emotion has a tendency to be theorised as an internal dialogue, resulting in art conveying the emotions of the *creator* to an *outside audience*, what Ahmed calls the 'inside out' model (ibid.: 8), joining many who have argued that emotions are not 'psychological' *per se*, but have greater traction when considered social and cultural *practice* (Katz, 1999; Williams, 2001) or the subject of an anticipated routine. For example, in the musical sphere there is a *physical sensuousness* in playing – touching the instrument, the calluses that develop on the fingers, sensing the vibration of the strings. Emotion in the listener is like this too: hairs on the neck, tears, tension and anxiety and so on (Cumming, 2000: 275). It is as if the art 'performs', projected from the creator to the autonomous audience. Thus, it is possible to relate the generation of literary work and, to a lesser extent art and music, to the concept of performativity that considers the notion that literature can *perform actions* rather than simply *reporting them* (Austin, [1962] 1976; Culler, [1975] 2002, 2011; Loxley, 2007), centring, as it does, on the notion that art is communicative, projecting an identity via process and 'ideology' of the creator to an audience (who are *in abstentia* throughout) and how the creators might view this 'performative' effect. Finally, there are aesthetics and the dialogue within the audience that the creator has no specific role in beyond releasing the work of art for the purposes of such aesthetic discourse. What has been understood from the ethnographic material is that identity is understood as a permutation of history/biography, action, circumstances, choice and fate. The creative personality is one thing and the creative identity another – the former being a will and a skill combining to make something pleasurable that did not exist before and the latter being a sense of dissonance between the act of creation and the person doing it. This latter descriptor – namely the gap between the action and the product – is a way of understanding the structures of cultural influence on the creative process. As is evident from the ethnography, work and family, age, circumstance, endeavour and will all combine to bring to a temporary creative pinnacle a series of chances that culminate in a product of the culture of the creative, resplendent within the cultural frameworks of the society from which the artefacts emerge. What are these frameworks and how can they be described to add light to the meaning of creativity?

9.4.   Towards Structures of Feeling and Knowable Communities in Creative Praxis

I am not an advocate of weighing down the beauty of anthropocentric research findings with social and cultural theory, believing that this distracts from the nexus of the thoughts and feelings of the people who make the research happen and, in this case, we may be divested of the dynamics of creation and the inspirations of the creators. However, I do consider the generic arguments posited by Raymond Williams over his career to be a suitable guide as I seek to explain why people create art and what it means to them as individuals, citizens and members of networks and how this resonates in wider society. Williams's discussions of culture via concepts of 'knowable communities', 'structures of feeling' and wider hypotheses of cultural materialism are particularly useful as I seek to explore the meaning and value of creativity in late modern times. Creativity can be seen as educative, reflexive and experiential in origin (Williams, [1958] 2017: 33–47), but Williams's focus on culture provides the best springboard.

In *Keywords* (Williams, [1976] 2014), the oft-cited quasi-encyclopaedic collection of definitions, *culture* is described by Williams as being 'complicated' due to historical developments and its absorption into the common lexicons of scholarship and everyday life (ibid.: 84). Williams began to develop a discourse in synergy with existing Marxist theory (*cultural materialism*) that placed culture at the heart of such social and economic reproduction practice (Higgins, 1999: 125), albeit since intellectually contested (Wilson, 1995). Such focus on the word 'culture' (and its broader interpretation and various practicalities), was construed by some to be an antithesis of materialism, *ergo* social rather than economic, *soft* instead of *solid* and so on. Culture is perceived as having 'its own modes of production, power-effects, social relations, identifiable audiences' (Eagleton, [1983] 2008: 198), thus enriching existing Marxism by carrying 'materialism boldly through to the "spiritual" itself' (ibid.: 199). Despite criticisms that it somewhat diluted the edicts of Marx (and Engels), Williams was principally challenging the idea that culture was exclusively super-structural, augmenting that the base was a 'process and not a state' leading to a consequential revaluation of such intrinsic determinism of limits and control (Williams, [1980] 2005: 34) and, mirroring the standpoint of new historicism (Wilson & Dutton, 1992), that such distinction was secondary. So, culture was indeed a 'complicated word', at once developmental and abstract, multifarious in its overlapping of human inaugurations and ways of life, but somehow remaining connected to 'works and practices of art and intelligence' (Williams, [1976] 2014: 88–89). It was also, very much, a *way of life*. Williams was keen to point out that, despite the superficially seductive draw of the 'spontaneous whole' or 'totality' (Lukács, [1968] 1971, [1971] 2006), the denial of determinism is to potentially dismiss intention (Williams, [1980] 2005: 35–36), somewhat akin, I posit, to likening this dynamic to a (Kantian) aesthetic formalism that centres on the disinterested (Pinkney, 1989: 17), almost *unconscious* role and *effect* in culture and art rather than the recognition of historical influence, bias, variation of skill and structural regulation of thought. So, while Williams remained committed to the value of the super-structure — especially the effects of social class — he retained a scepticism that art and thought were exclusively superstructural (Pinkney, 1989: 36). Something ran deeper than mere effect and interpretation, confronting the 'complex and oblique' interregnum between formalism and the general Marxism of cultural production (Laing, 1978: 48–49; Williams, [1989] 2007: 166). Williams set out in *The Long Revolution* (1961) to consider what Giddens described as 'the expansion of culture in its interrelation with economic and political development' (Giddens, 1996: 202), but it is his subtle precedence to the culture over society, per se, that gives relevance to this research in that the material creativity (action) affects transformations in the individual or closed group (Dix, 2013: 36). This does not *exclude* society but concentrates more on what Williams terms the structures of learning and communication (Williams, 1961; Dix, 2013: 37) and the cultural materialist development of something new from *within*.

Culture, therefore, is a complex intersection of ideas that play out against a backdrop of structural tensions. Art exists inside this void — perhaps in microcosm in the intervals in individual lives that exist between the structures of the real world and the 'illusory' quintessence of aesthetic value (Wolff, 1983). Williams addressed the perception of the creative *muse* in the early chapters of his first major book, *Culture and Society* (Williams, [1958] 2017), advancing the idea of the artist as a *special person* connected to a 'superior reality' of artistic exhibition that can be adequately traced back to the Romantic period of the mid-1700s. While discussing poetry — and the thoughts of the poets themselves — Williams was interested in the postulations of Young ([1759] 2013) who argued the possibility that art could be seen as emergent from an artist's imagination, organically growing rather than being 'assembled' for a preordained reason (Williams, [1958] 2017: 56). Thus, this organic analogy tends towards an avoidance of the association between art and ideology, art and capitalism and markets and the inherent needs of the creator to generate income from his labour to survive in late modern times. If anything, the romantic take on art embeds itself as a 'romantic' vision of art for art's sake, of art as a living thing estranged from its creator and from the meanings that artists symbolically place amongst and within their works as being emblematic of their own identities. Thus, removing this mechanical essence from the act of creation and subsequent meaning of artefacts can be seen as being in contrast to what the artist desires while being also in opposition to how the artist may wish to view the work objectively himself. It is an interesting quandary. However, it is arguable that the 'Romantic vision' was lost with the onset of industrialism and the rise of capitalism; markets entered art and commodified creativity in the same way that it commodified leisure (Henry, 2001; Roberts, 1970; Rojek, 1995), music (Adorno, 1991) and just about everything else that penetrated the everyday life of the people, not least the media (McGuigan, 1992: 178) and its effect on modern culture (Chaney, 1993: 121; Thompson, 1990) ladling in 'phantasmagoric' myth and tradition to divest the people of their awareness of common, historically exploited conditions (Swingewood, 1998: 158). While art in the age of capitalism might have fought back against market via a process of 'imaginative truth' (Williams, [1958] 2017: 61), there remained a belief that such a process was simply art acquiring a function of opposition to those dehumanising essences of industrialisation with the dynamics of an artist moving gently from hard skill to sensibilities (ibid.: 66).

The role that Williams plays in the conceptualisation of art and routine as ingrained in the everyday life of the populace is crucial here. Over time he developed ideas of 'knowable community' and 'structure of feeling' that provide useful mechanisms for understanding the way that routines of creativity and works of art are *emergent from the ordinary lives* of people and how they relate to a sense of history, the *situated* and action. Culture, after all, according to Williams 'is ordinary' (Williams, [1958] 1989). Creativity and art can be perceived as instinctive action and recognisable artefacts by those who exist in the environs of those who produce. While artists engage in a dialogue with the past *in the present*, or the *disruptive influence of the present on the past*, Williams plays with ideas that have an echo of hermeneutics and *verstehen* but are, ultimately, about the connectivity with an *oeuvre* rather than any particular thing or text. Structure of feeling, consequently, is no simple concept – slippery to grasp and occasionally couched in 'tortuous language' (Jones, [2004] 2006: 20), as something of the *result* of organisation in society and as a reflexive, incremental *process of meaning* applied to things by people, a generic *essence* and a sense of *connection* with an oeuvre either in situ or via a 'selective tradition' (Williams, 1961: 63–67). Williams argued that with the coming of the industrial age, urban capitalism diminished the 'knowable community' (Williams, 1970: 16) of the age of Eliot or Dickens or Hardy and gone was something we could recognise *within and about* ourselves and *relate to* via our use of (in this instance) fiction in the current epoch of liquid modernity (Bauman, 2000). Nowadays, we are unsure even of our neighbours – in the town or the country – and our relationships are disparate and fluid, transient and unreliable (Bauman, 2001). Thus, we may find it hard to see ourselves reflected in our penetration of fictional narratives or in the art and music that we enjoy but do not necessarily commune with. The narrators of, for example, modern British fiction may speak only of what we may perceive as fantasy – something we think we long for that promises the tranquillity of certainty, reliability and safety. However, this is not nostalgia; perhaps it is desire. Perhaps we may read Hardy and Trollope and see a desired community, a fetishist desire for bonds and dialogues of certainty. If anything, the knowable – while quite *unknowable* for those who live at least 100 years from the era, and consciously possibly quite further away still – is couched in the perception of securities borne of the modern era, slipping from our grasp in a trickle of what Giddens (1990) might term 'high modern' dynamics of automation, science, medicine and time-space distanciation (including the internet/cyberspace revolution and the development of new forms of pseudo-disconnected routines of communication that came a little later). We may read fiction of the Victorian age as being representative of our innermost desires not so much to return to a place we cannot know, but instead to revive the sense of community as a security to ourselves. This 'ontological security' (Giddens, 1991) is, of course, merely an illusionary crutch but, nevertheless, we are seeking it for a reason. Perhaps it confronts the anxieties we feel deep down and offers a resistance to the forces that we know will inevitably continue to tear us all apart. In many ways, this subconscious desire may well be the attraction of a mezzanine where an individual or group can resist this relentless march and find familiarity in the *knowable reflexivity* of creativity. The respondents in the ethnography have indicated this is so, but with conditions – effectively selective, determinable, transitory, unrepeatable but still resigned to the inevitable sense of loss. The fact that the art must be relinquished – somehow – as an end-game is overpowering.

There are ambiguities regarding the structure of feeling that can be arguably settled by the commentary of Lawrence Grossberg (2010) who explored such opacity, interior tensions and (arguable) contradictions within the theory that he describes overall as something of a *fluid theory of experience and values*. He suggests that Williams himself shifted his own opinion on the meaning of experience, existing somewhere in-between the mind and language/structure objectivism dichotomy of humanism and structuralism resulting in a consideration of experience as phenomenologically problematic. *Experience* is not *individualised* and therefore unable to mediate those *spaces between* subject and object, though its position seems to be constantly shifting (Grossberg, 2010: 22). Williams began to suggest that 'structure of feeling is the endless comparison [...] between the articulated and the lived' (Grossberg, 2010: 23; Williams, [1979] 2015: 168) that can *disrupt the meaning* between the signifier and the signified in the present and that there is consequently a 'space between presence and emergence' that is, as an 'ontological present', no more graspable *now* that it is to grasp the past (Grossberg, 2010: 24). The known and the *knowable* therefore present a conundrum of apprehension, an 'eternal contemporaneity' of our grasp of the moment' (ibid.; Pinkney, 1989), an *eternal now* that is always subject to something of an instantaneous Hegelian dialectic. Williams is aware of this, but Grossberg concludes that Williams's own idea of modernity is best understood with the *confluence of history* and the 'now' and their reflexivity, merging

> two modes of temporality [...]: history and presence [...] an endless construction and deconstruction of the difference between the known and the knowable, between culture and experience, between history and an ontological presence, but even that ontology is a historical, a contextual one, that can only be understood in its relation to a differentiation from culture as the site of history, but also of transcendence or possibility (Grossberg, 2010: 24).

Structure of feeling is fluid, between experience and structure itself and borne of mass rather than individuality. Thus, meaning shifts *permanently* due to *continual experience*, enduringly re-negotiating by using the 'past' and the 'now', merging and perpetually in-between knowing and *knowable*. Art is conceptualised/conceived, created and considered and the artist in isolation can draw on history and the ontological 'now' to invent novelty. This links directly to

Bourdieu's discussion on habitus – or, in truth, to how the habitus is realised. Utilising Bourdieu to understand the creation of a mezzanine condition I am able to suggest that the state of *aura* is achieved via a combination of conscious and *sub*conscious acquisition and consequent utilisation of skill, practicality and intuition (though Bourdieu would attest that it is unconscious rather than sub-conscious: Bourdieu, 1990). The creative 'now' relating to Grossberg's reading of Williams above is strengthened by Bourdieu's attesting that the body does not 'memorize the past', instead it *'enacts'* it, reviving it and creating what he calls a 'practical *mimesis* [...] which implies an overall relation of identification' that bypasses imitation on the grounds that imitation is a conscious effort to replicate (Bourdieu, 1990: 73, original emphases). This is a natural response, drawing on forgotten skills, memories, influences and feelings. It appears intuitive, instinct-ive and spontaneous but it is, in fact, drawn from the aforementioned reserves of knowledge derived from mimetic socialisation (Potolsky, 2006).

The generic guiding concepts of this whole work connect a sense of the acquired cultural and social capital by the midlife phase and how it may be uti-lised, albeit in a slightly involuntary *now*. The crux of the creativity that springs from the wisdom and available 'time capital' of midlife is based on the utilisa-tion of such knowledge and, of course, how the knowledge is *applied* in creating new variations of art form. The creative self seems to be founded in a mixture of explosive routine and thoughtful serenity that is occasionally peppered with latent anxiety caused by the individualised, exposed self in late modern times. The mezzanine that I speak of is multifarious – descriptive of the *stage* in life, the *place* of creation and, most potently, the *phase* of creativity and what hap-pens there. So, is it possible to get to the crux of the creative self? This process, described as something that is 'done' in the ethnography, is also a technique that requires a code, a 'way in' that is not completely obvious to the lay observer but draws on the habitus – the instinctive articulation of the partially forgotten experiences, the 'sporadic intellect' and the use of skill.

It is our biographies that synthesise to create a structure of feeling (Williams, 1961). It is our lived realities, flexible and liquid (Bauman, 2000) on a day to day basis, malleable and negotiated, delegated and altered through sociality and simple *chance* that combine to create routine responses to the everyday. A sen-sual cornucopia is built up that can 'fill in' our blanks automatically, directing involuntary thinking and occupying an operational space in the imagination – namely where we seek *effect* in what we read or see or hear (Halliday, 2013; Hughes, 2011). It is arguable that the reader of any text can only ever see a frag-ment of the 'story' that is read, the rest being applied by our biography – our library of experiences – to form elaborate pictures of dramatic scenes, internal and external locations, faces, tones of voice and so on. The story is *told*, but we own the imagination, we own the feeling. The words convey the theme, the lin-guistic and the tone but *we* apply the contexts and we all apply them differently. This works best in fiction but can be applied also to autobiography: the narra-tive is broadly similar in that it requires us to 'go along' with a trusted narrator. For example, each time Laurie Lee is 'set down from the carrier's cart' at the beginning of *Cider With Rosie* (Lee, 1959: 1), each person who reads this sees a different scene: a different cart, a different country location, different long grass, a different child and a different tone of sunlight. They imagine it *through* Laurie Lee, imagining who he might have been and what he might have looked like, but they also arguably imagine it through *themselves*, applying a hermeneutic process to the imagination of a scene − thus, we see ourselves seeing Lee as a child. We imagine what we see, what we *might see*, despite being told by Lee that this has happened, and is not possible to be re-seen in the present, as he narrates, as he recalls. Each person who reads Laurie Lee will apply their own varied brush strokes to the imagery of the idealised country life that is often dramatic, nostalgic, ill-informed and recently lost (Williams, [1973] 2015). What we are doing, essentially, is making ourselves *there*. In conjunction, the artist, the musician or the writer is actually concentrating on the *moment of the gaze*; this is where the mezzanine is experienced and where there is nothing between the artist and the potential to create. This is the moment where the *artist* is 'there' (to the exclusion of all others and all structures) and where he or she has the *complete power* to alter, affect and to *define* a work of art as completely original. This is where, if you like, the *dark matter* becomes visible, a place where the outside world of place, biography, emotion and risk are suspended, and a clear moment of possibility is exercised fully, exploited and celebrated, creating something from nothing. The concentration of the gaze and the involuntary, subconscious exploitation of the habitus is where art is no longer abstract, we become part of it. The artist, therefore, is in a privileged position to *shape the gaze* into an active alteration of the form, like 'getting into the scene' and no longer *watching* Laurie Lee get down from the cart but *living the moment with him* as active determiners of the scene itself. This is where the artists are in the mezzanine and this is why it is an exclusively individual, lonely place to be − alone with an unlimited repertoire of power and opportunities.

9.5.   The Mezzanine: Origin and Theory

I first described what I termed a 'mezzanine condition' in writing up my Doctoral thesis (Arnot, 2007: 79; Miles, 2004), following interviews with young people living in a deindustrialised (former mining) valley in south east Wales who were planning a departure from home for University at the turn of the century. Noting the kids' self-separation from working class 'authenticity' and their anxiety of perceived retreat from their ascribed social class, I noted their in-between states − the risky relinquishment of working class identity without a new identity to grasp in its place. Zygmunt Bauman wrote, after Freud, that the German word '*Sicherheit*' has the benefit of 'squeezing' the meaning of three words in English into one in German, thus 'security, certainty and safety' mesh together to create the 'conditions of self-confidence' in an individual. When one factor diminishes, the formula is weakened so appreciatively that a person (or people) can lose self-assurance and experience incapacitation, anxiety and other negative traits in the human psyche (Bauman, 1999: 17). In the current phase of history, it is pertinent to suggest that such anxiety and incapacitation is possible via diminishing employment security, economic oscillations, the lessening connectivity between skills and career and the latent apprehensions of intergenerational ambition. A body of work – now appearing dated, but still very relevant indeed in explaining a prevailing sense of uncertainty – existed in the 1990s and 2000s dedicated to exploring the nature of social, economic and cultural fragmentation as well as empowerment and enlightenment arising from the effects (Bauman, 2000; Beck, 1999; Giddens, 1991). These works, among others, theorised *fragmentation* as a process of becoming individualised (Beck & Beck-Gernsheim, 2002; Furlong & Cartmel, 1997) and, consequently, becoming responsible for one's own destiny. The sense of existential *separation* within society was (and arguably remains) rife and, perhaps, people look for relief from such disquiet via meaningful action (alternatively considered 'pastime'). There is a 'reflexive imperative' that exists in society (Archer, 2012) seeing the individual effectively compelled to make choices and inherit the consequences of such action that can have impact on subjectivity and life chances (Archer, 2003, 2007), further perceived as a consequence of the 'victories of capitalism' that creates an incremental revolution in everyday life, the embracing of post-traditionalism and the self-confrontation of the autonomous individual (Beck et al., 1994). While individualisation is a complex matter in being linked (not exclusively) to both an ideology of neoliberalism (i.e. the entrepreneurial spirit) and a series of compelled choices, it can result, if negotiated well, in significant empowerment. It has meaningful overlap with the idea of the mezzanine – namely the creation of a space where the individual is able to consider and construct a strategy for emotional and credential *progress*. The self-reflective 'incompleteness of the self [and] the end of theoretical collectivisms' that result in a social sensitivity (Beck & Beck-Gernsheim, 2002: xxi–xxii), social iteration and the management of autarchic sentiment in harness with social responsibility can be harnessed as a resistance to anxiety, routine and powerlessness. A mezzanine can be experienced as a place – or situation – where the *individual* is best positioned to utilise the power bestowed upon he or she *by* the structure in order to *interpret* the structure with freedom of ideology and spirit. The mezzanine is temporal and unpredictable, but it is available democratically to anyone who wishes to locate it.

It is necessary to consider the notion of liminality to understand 'where' the mezzanine can be located; in understanding the mezzanine as frequent, unstable, temporal and explosive in immediacy and impact it is sagacious to consider liminality as 'moments in and out of time [...] often connected with those moments of symbolic renewal' (Delanty, 2003: 44). The words 'moments' and 'renewal' drive the essence of what I am arguing, centring on the in-between, the transient, the rejuvenation of identity using the acquired skills (and physical tools) of creativity. Late modernism is concerned with ideas of identity with skills, social in context and arguably socialising in effect. 'Self-confrontation' is evident in the times in which the midlife artist asks himself or herself the question: *is now the time?* The mezzanine is an inverted version of the commonplace consideration that late modernism and individualisation give the individual less and less to 'hold on to' apart from their own confidence in themselves, achieved via self-confrontations. In the mezzanine, the artists that I have spoken with mostly agree that they are looking for *nothing to hold onto*, considering it a place to legitimately *let go*, resist banality, lose structurally-framed, ideologically driven identities by engaging with an imaginary world of blissed-out aura. Late modernism and its retained dominant ideologies relating to capitalism, globalisation and cultural homogeneity is therefore *penetrated*, *reversed* and *used* by these artists in the belief that the spirit of insecurity can provide freedom to create while the flanking routine of dullness is the *certainty* of life, a boring, predictable, anxiety-generated ordinariness that is anathema to creativity.

The mezzanine is also sensuous and mimetic in character, a zone of hyperreality where the 'real' and *a* fiction merge (Baudrillard, 1994), the artist drawing on the *authentic* and projecting *into* a fiction — something that is to *be* invented and realised but *not fully realised* as yet. Playfulness with potential of invention stimulates the dynamics of the mezzanine and arguably replicates a subtle narrative of the midlife phase too. Here the artist is wondering what comes next from a platform of what has already become, the zone of the *authentic fake* (Eco, 1998) via a state of mind rather than a bespoke physicality or the desire to experience *a* reality while dreaming. This is arguably a postmodern or poststructuralist approach and I am aware that this postulation does not sit entirely easily with the foundational theory of late modernism. However, a work that broadly explores intertextuality (despite its contested definitions, see: Allen, 2011) adopts the interdisciplinary freedom to reconnoitre experience without the burden of deductive challenges. This potentially 'undisciplined space in the interstices between disciplines' (Moran, 2010: 14) assists in both reflecting the creative uncertainties of the mezzanine zone, assists in situating analysis of the zone in sociological and cultural contexts as well as compounding the thematic metaphor of midlife. The mezzanine is a state of suspension, where rules matter not one iota.

The mezzanine remains a zone but does not — and cannot — exist in vacuum; it is a phase of a creative process with a history and a *future effect*. The artists all engage in the suspended state of the creative arc, but they acknowledge its temporality. Midlife — real life — exists outside of the zone and they are not, necessarily, seeking to *stop* time or to abandon the wisdom of time. It follows that the mezzanine is affected by structural things and, whatever the beauty of the 'moment' might be, all things that come forth from the creative phase are somehow laden in a pre-existing history, biography or ideology and experienced across such defining matters in correlation with Raymond Williams and his idea of *structure of feeling* (Williams, [1958] 2017; 1961). The effect can be understood by considering the editing phase that follows the creative pique of the mezzanine. Terry Eagleton, discussing Marxist *literary criticism*, considered the tension of *context and form* via Hegelian compromise of meaning (Eagleton, [1976] 2002: 20) via superstructural manipulation and influence of ideology in *reproducing* form. Form is negotiated — a result of compromise — within the super-structural (interpretative) oeuvre (Eagleton, [1976] 2002: 21; Jameson, 1971), resulting in a lazy determinism. What is needed is a cultural response, understanding paradigmatic shifts and how time and transformations of societal norms and values can be applied and reapplied to our understanding of cultural forms and the content of literature, art and music. This is something of a 'democratisiation' of art, a response by people and further determines structure of feeling. The mezzanine is arguably the moment where the artist gets as *close as they can* to a 'value free' aesthetic (Wolff, 1983) before the work is re-immersed into the oeuvre of the everyday, analysed and massaged and 'made good' by a combination of externally situated considerations. While form is affected by superstructure, the dynamics of the mezzanine clarify the meanings applied, via analysis, to the responses of the artists themselves while approaching and experiencing the aperture of real life and creative-artistic 'disorder'.

Earlier in the book I noted the value of the contemporary shift towards recognition of autoethnography as an esteemed tool of analysis in social research. It is valuable in understanding creativity because creative selves are often complex, reactive, reflexive and subjective, acting on skilled impulses and the harnessing of fantasy. The technique appeared in Dominic's story quite prominently, and as reflexive, self-reflective and discursive traits in all of the artists, but does the auto-ethnographic process exist and flourish *inside or outside of the mezzanine*? This is a crucial question; the outside influence must penetrate for the auto-ethnographic 'system' to be induced, but the external must be utilised in the internal mechanism of the mezzanine whereby the only place for the echoes of memory and emotion to thrive is inside the place where the memories and emotions have free reign. Thus, the late modern dichotomy of individualisation and the associative freedom from ties and the sought-chaos of the mezzanine itself to the creative individual is impossible to state on one hand, while distinct and observable on the other. The predictability and blandness of the everyday must be set aside for the mezzanine to permit freedom of thought and action; the mundane is challenged inside the mezzanine by the drawing on the echoes of trauma, experience, joy and fantasy. This is a fantasy — a 'positive' fantasy — where everything exists at once to be utilised and ordered and exploited while, in the outside world (the flanks) the 'negative fantasy' is experienced (namely, where interpretation is governed by the strictures of the system, mores, values and necessity). The artists make sense of their freedom inside the bubble of the creative self: the space, the *opportunity*, the *possibilities of anything*. Positive fantasy — the freedom to confront your deeper, ontological insecurities — is 'dangerous' outside of the mezzanine (and they know this), that is why negative fantasy is ostensibly 'safety' in the real world. This is in complete reverse to the late modern anxiety of the lack of safety nets, the credentialisation of the biography, the dog-eat-dog, risky *real life*; this is a place where, as Lyotard would have it, the consciousness is protected from doubt about the 'realness' of things, where familiarity is fortified and perpetuity is prized (Lyotard, 1992: 5–6). This segues with Grossberg's reading of structure of feeling; positive fantasy being the embodiment of the ontological anarchy of the 'now', whereas negative fantasy is the mode of thinking and acting when dealing with ordinary things or, as Steve Fuller would suggest, the understanding of 'what one does not do but could have done' (Fuller, 2005: 29). To further crystallise, negative fantasy is the embodiment of *regret*. While such regret might be an omnipresent threat to the individual in midlife, positive fantasy is the confrontation of the anxiety of regret, the antithesis of stagnation and the embodiment of the 'anything is possible' sense that dominates the mezzanine, but it is a two-way process. The artist can make a 'pact' with the anarchy and unpredictability that he or she seeks inside the mezzanine, but the mezzanine can also be a place of risk and insecurity *to* the artist *because* of its anarchy. This is the risk, an *individualised* risk, of the creative state; identity is 'played' as part of a wider risk stratagem that involves *gambling* with a sense of the secure and reliable *now* via the seeking of insecurity, excitement and fulfilment of creative aims. 'Identity' is therefore considered a *place* where the creative self essentially separates from a space of possibilities, being simultaneously considerate of the requirements of the outside world (making a living, paying the bills, being commercial, doing what the publisher wants and so on) while a symmetrical 'self' exists inside the mezzanine. Thus, *inside* the mezzanine it is not exactly 'fantasy' that is experienced, but *reality offering a chance to use fantasy as the place where ideas exist and are enacted with immunity from judgement* and as a place without boundaries, at the same time allowing the individual to make gentle mockery of the productive, reproducing ideology of capitalism while relating instead to the perceived freedom of a life full of choice and without ties. The maintenance and development of the *identity* of the individual, however, is permanently attached to either or both, pulling in two directions, mindful of reality and fantasy and being equally insecure about the validity of either.

While the mezzanine is a 'place' that cannot be *defined* exclusively by spatiality, it is *influenced* by time and space and – put broadly – psychology. The 'fantasy' may well be a state of ontological exposure or an evocation of the episteme, but it is also owing a little to the broad vagaries of 'psychoanalysis'. While there is a subtly detectable psychoanalytic feel to the mezzanine (Freud, [1915] 1991) via the poetic/hermeneutic feel and the instinctive action of creation (i.e. in the moment), sublimation is not exclusively representative of the authors' subduing of desire or trauma and so on. I do not detect the articulation of neuroses – the artists are all aware, to a greater or lesser degree, of their own *reasons for creating* and are also aware of the processes and routines that *feed into* the time of creation; their ideologies, their biographies and moods all act as responsive, reflexive initiators of artistic object, leaving only a small space for the uniquely subliminal to perform constructive function in the shaping of the art. To be sure, there is something of the Lacanian essence of the 'whole subject' in play here – hence, the artist is self-aware as well as aware of abstraction, empiricism and the overall distinction between ego and discourse (Lacan, [1977] 2002). However, the synthesis of such players in the creation of art is deemed as affective and is something that, by definition, is incremental and occasionally explosive when enacted with synchronicity. The 'affect' principle applied to art, therefore, can be considered as both synchronic and diachronic much in the same way that Formalists see the defining of 'literariness' as a process of displacement springing from a fragmented and volatile history that results in some kind of temporal dominance of a genre or school and so on (Jauss, 1982: 17). The defining of 'art' can be drawn from a discursive history, applied in the moment as self-defined and can be retracted from the public domain – if only temporarily – and considered a deeply individual statement, or something of a 'reflection' of the creator. Affective theory is abounded in psychology/psycho-analysis and associated with literary critique, occasionally focussing on the auto-ethnographic reflection (Freeman, 2015) of the writer and his or her biography, exploring a deeper domain of (real) experiences that may be distant and blurry to the writer and often associated with 'trauma' (Clough, 2007), occasionally interpretative, but detectable in the text (Craps, 2013). The theory is useful to understand the *echoes* of influence, not from the existing paragons of the art establishment but via the biography (Clough et al., 2007; Wynn, 2007), memory and the sense that it is a digestion of experience, reading, fantasy and so on that combines to produce an affect in the creator. Auto-ethnography can provide the tools for constructing a framework of understanding of the field (Bochner & Ellis, 2016; Denzin, 2013) and the self and combining such subjectivity with ana-lysis of the *other*, but it is the experience *of* the other that takes precedence in this instance.

Art and music and literature, however, *can* also be affective to those who make it; it can be in the eye (and ear) of the beholder who is also the creator. Thus, affect theory can be considered in many guises; music is explored by many as a psychotherapeutic facility that asserts a framework for understanding the way we feel and think, anchoring emotions into memory and sensuality via sound (Williamson, 2014), further connecting music to the greater appreciation of the mechanisms of neurology (Sacks, [2007] 2011) and such affectations can be transformative for the creative identity (Coleman, 2013), utilising the approach of Wright-Mills (1959) on the link of biography and history in our sociological interpretation of the generation of meaning in art and, in this case, the creator's own art. The mezzanine is also a place where affect is dragged in, processed and transmogrified into a force that exists beyond the moments of aura, creation, maintenance and editing of work. I posit that there is a real sense that the moment of feeling, the ontological present, suspension of the outside and the harnessing of positive fantasy is a 'place' where art is *awareness*, thus insisting that the artists *know what they are doing and why they are doing it*, how their lives and phases of life *affect* their actions but still maintaining that the iso-lated dynamic of art that makes most sense is the *possibility* of novelty, not the *ideology* of novelty, of life or of commerce. Ideology, experience and commerce are secondary effects of the process; the primary effect is ontological, naked and anarchic.

The art *does* take on a 'life of its own' and the artists all speak of their anxiety of separation, of losing the power over their art as they 'let go' of it to a public, a critique or a private buyer. The art, in essence, *performs*. To consider the word 'performativity' is to relate to an idea connected predominantly to literature (and, in various forms, to linguistics, see: Matthews, 2003; Trudgill, [1974] 2000) centring on the notion that words can trigger reactions in the audience via some kind of uttered intentionality (Austin, [1962] 1976) thus creating both a reflective absorption as well as an active effect *in* the reader that can be transferred to external actors (Loxley, 2007: 2). Therefore, performativity has a potentially transformative role in how we construct our realities and our communications as well as the development of our language. It is, as Jonathan Culler would say, 'the extent to which language performs actions rather than merely reporting on them' (Culler, 2011: 96). There is a *persuasive* element that can only be 'activated' via *speech*, the 'utterance', in this case, being the intentionality (Culler, [1975] 2002: 127), an 'I will do' that can only be *inferred* through art; it is a promise that cannot be spoken, just suggested subliminally. However, the identity of the beholder must, in many cases, draw the 'reader' to the art itself (taste, experience and so on), which does half the job for the creator and the abstract work of art (the song, the painting, the novel). It is then that the performativity of the text is *between* text and reader/interpreter – with the exception of music, which has the more common element of performance that has the power to accentuate any missing elements.

Performativity, when applied to text, can see the identity (even the *personality*) of the author and the reader transferred to the external world. This can be applied not only to literature but to fine art and music. Authorial routine and the dynamics of midlife and matured identity is best understood as a social process despite the isolation in which art is often created. 'Performativity' can also be applied to *performance*. This mutation of the word is referring to existing art that is being 'performed', performative in the same way that the process of internalising and externalising literature was explained previously. Art is created and exhibited in different ways, but is ultimately performed, it is just by *whom* and *where the performance becomes unified*. The writer requires the work to be 'performed' by the audience (i.e. in their heads or, alternatively in the case of drama, by actors), whereas the musicians are required to perform their own music as a communicative art form (Read, [1931] 2017). It is clear, even at this stage, that the idea of the communication of art is dependent on an art world – it is just whether the art world is conjoined, social, active and participant-led or separated, individuated and anonymous. This lends itself to Judith Butler's (1990) argument that – in this case – *gender* is performative via action, intent and ultimately developmental via such behaviours. Art, like gender, is also technically abstract, in that it has an intentionality both by its creator and its consumer to change something. In the mezzanine it is 'genderless' but is given its meaning after the creation has taken place like a 'contract' that is subliminally agreed by creator and consumer. The art is a new stimulus each time one engages with it, shifting the beholders identity conscientiously and with consent – it is our identities that are shaped, *inter alia*, by art and the artist and, in many ways, we quite enjoy the directives. The artist/creator and the consumers' identities liminally merge in the moment of artistic communication. The mezzanine is the place where the artist *creates* and is distinct from the idea of a *transmission of ideology* that occurs outside of the mezzanine, in an unreconstructed *future* and, while the artist may not have an audience in mind when creating, he or she *is* the audience for those moments of purest novelty. The principles of performativity are therefore at play, contributing to the explosiveness of the mezzanine, adding to the 'turmoil' and the 'chaos', self-reflective, almost narcissistic, but always *constructive*. The mezzanine, when considered artistically, is therefore in-between diachronic universality and synchronic reflexivity, closer to the latter in terms of pure inventiveness but indebted to the former via the educational, experiential-cultural and phenomenological incrementalism of the individual. In providing a crucial poetic and hermeneutic platform (Wolff, 1975), the mezzanine 'joins together' historical and contemporary, immediate experience and facilitates the structure of inventiveness (or 'feeling'), providing a crucial bonding as well as an imperative time-space dimension for the invention of novelty.

The creative process is a cornucopia of thoughts, actions, ideas, decisions, tensions and breakthroughs and a place where things are synthesised – but 'synthesis' perhaps suggests an *orderly* process, where the *synthesis itself* is the *desired end-product*. There remains a great deal of chance involved; things have to be 'just right' for the process to yield significant novelty. While Robin earlier stated that art is, in effect, a way of organising (or 'arranging') things and that each variation is, in itself *novel*, there remains a nagging doubt about whether *any* arrangement can be *the* arrangement. Thus, the playfulness of the mezzanine is where the real work gets done. This is where intertextuality (Allen, 2011) of all art is communed with effect. Take an occasionally cited example in music where a chance view of a passport frontispiece resulted in an album title, mutated and punning, but drawn from an establishment artefact. This story suggests that there is the issue of an intertextual tension that exists at the centre of all creative processes – the anxiety of influence (Bloom, 1973) is superseded by a potentially unconscious connectivity with the wider oeuvre of art and literature and sound and lyrics where, in this case, the 'satanic majesties' of The Rolling Stones' 1967 album title *could* have been – according to the accepted folklore and biographical narratives of rock 'n' roll history – Mick Jagger looking at his passport (Davis, 2002: 224; Norman, 2001: 290) and considering the wordplay while subconsciously referencing the Joe Hynes' explanation of the *satanic majesty's* racing colours in Joyce's *Ulysses* (2000 [1922]: 429). One 'satanic majesty' is lost 'into' the other and then the other, disrupting the artistic genealogy of the observation-joke, situating the meaning in different subcultural contexts (Irish pubs and British colonialism all the way through to counterculture of the 1960s, acid and antagonism towards the Establishment and authority therein) and being reinterpreted in the present day by fans or musicians who may, themselves, be accused (arguably, unfairly) of being 'derivative'. This example also illustrates how the narrative (in this case an intertextual reference to 'satanic majesties') is malleable, flexibly re-interpreted (without plagiarism) and re-embedded into a new opus. It is, in effect, the place where Julia Kristeva observes, 'utterances [...] intersect and neutralise one another' (Kristeva, 1980: 36). Kristeva, however, while alluding to the traverse essence of the intertextual, also illustrated the transference from one sign to another – ostensibly couching the intertextual as a place where 'one signifying practice is transposed into another' (McAffee, 2004: 26). This gives the understanding of midlife art and practice greater dimension: it is, in effect, the interrelated moment of *dis-unification*, the moment where all competing signifiers within the art form are 'fighting' for their order, their place in the 'code' of the art and essentially seeking to be made sense of. The artist effectively plays with the influences he or she holds via transposing the styles, form, colour, borders and the semantics of space, time and history, thus creating the effervescent element of hesitant incredulity in both the creator and the observer in either written language, visual or performed art. Texts, in whatever form, have no *uniformity of meaning* — they are open to manipulation and reinterpretation at all times, driven by hooks of contention — pretty much what Kristeva calls an 'ideologeme' (Kristeva, 1980: 36—38) that can redirect the reader, viewer or listener towards questioning elements of style and effect. The Ruins illustrate this with their multitude of influences, ordering their subconscious transposed sound into something new, vibrant and flexible, reordered and re-experienced from week to week and, arguably in similar formula, the writers and the artists draw on their education, experiences and travels to embed a sense of flexibility into the work. The artist and the observer can then experience a novelty on each visitation to the work. In midlife, the signifiers may be more expertly and elegantly placed, reflecting the virtue of experiencing the simple passage of time (and the *utility* of time) and the time drawn *upon* for the likelihood of such influences and narratives being disbursed into a wider contextualisation of cultural artefacts, associative semantics and the understanding of the practical processes of creativity.

This practice illustrates that the mezzanine is not uniquely a time-space 'thing'; it is a status, a phase and — in this instance — a 'point' where the art 'gets done' while not wholly submitting to a manifestation of totality. In other words, art is not *just* done 'in the moment', it is also 'perfected' via editing, restarting and through some significant adjustments leading to a sense that *planning* might not get 'done' while the mezzanine is active, but arguably *follows* as an 'add on' of semantic value, significance and as a leitmotif of authenticity. For example, when discussing the 'novel inside a painting', in this instance Delacroix's *Liberty Leading the People*, Italo Calvino not only alludes to the time-honoured sense that *every picture tells a story*, but also to the detected trace of an 'art world' (Becker, [1982] 2008), an anxiety of influence (Bloom, 1973), occasional hints of 'hybridity' (Bhabha, 1995) *and* a (quasi-scientific) supervention of novelty (Eliot, 1919; Kermode, 1975) along with the suggestion that there must, by definition, also be an application of *time* to the *development* of a painting. Instead of understanding a work of art that depicts an event as being painted 'on the spur of the moment', Calvino asserts that, in fact,

> the history of the work is one of a laborious composition, full of hesitations and about-turns, working out detail by detail, the artist placing side by side elements that were heterogeneous, some of them motifs from existing paintings [...] a repertoire of quotations from other works in museums, a kind of compendium of figurative culture (Calvino, 2013: 53).

Therefore, not only does art get inspired by other things, it is clearly a process, a culmination and a discursive method that may or may not be assembled by one person (i.e. it can be a 'group' too) but is in debt to many. However, what augments this idea is the fact that art *develops* over time, with considerations; there is a requirement to step back from the flow of the everyday to take stock of something, percolate it into a knowable form and develop the narrative of the art work itself. Thus, the mezzanine can regain importance and function as a space for such *development* – a place where the past and the future are suspended for a creative present, even if it is to *adjust and alter* an existing artefact.

This, of course, sounds like I am 'having it both ways'. The mezzanine is established as a place where the structure of feeling (Williams, 1961) is most keenly felt; it is an ontological playground (Grossberg, 2012), a place where positive fantasy can break all perceived boundaries and facilitate play with the tools of abstraction and result in being that space where the 'line' (as Ingold, 2013, would have it) can go anywhere, ostensibly uncontrolled by the conscious artist but arguably later tamed. However, that said, the mezzanine is also a function of skill, knowledge and the place where elite capital (Bourdieu, [1984] 2010) is exercised very consciously. Again, it is not a *physical* place (though physicality is perceived as a recording or light-filled artists' studio or writing garret, etc.) but an intellectual stillness, scholarly equilibrium or platform of reflective judgement that defines the art as art. Thus, the mezzanine is a crucial – and defended – place of self-efficacy, self-respect and self-authentication bound up in a process that leads to legitimation of an artistic identity. The mezzanine says that you 'have arrived'.

The mezzanine is a subjective experience that can (but not necessarily *must*) lead to objectification of the process – in other words, the artistic routine can lead to communication with readers of texts (listeners, observers/admirers or literal readers of novels and so on). The novelist Rachel Cusk made a telling observation when she said that the 'fundamental anonymity' in writing itself is penetrated by the requirement of 'the fact that each reader came to your book a stranger who had to be persuaded to stay' (Cusk, [2016] 2017: 114). This implies (albeit via fictional narrative) that the mezzanine *is* separate from the reading/affect/reception process and that it can only be verified by the in-between state of the artefact – in this case, a novel – in that it appears to be the role of the creator to 'invite in' to the anteroom of post-creation the *external verifier of value* and, thus, convince others of the value of the creative *process* by proxy. This situates the mezzanine as both the process and the outcome, the symbiotic process of method and result that is only 'made real' by an external in-between zone of verification. To 'leave' is to de-legitimise the process publically, consigning the mezzanine to the status of continual private experimentation. It is therefore possible to 'reposition' the mezzanine back into the realms of its original context – namely as a place of resistance. While I have been keen to elaborate on the conglomerate character of the 'thing' that is the mezzanine, it is still simply an in-between state that is utilised and exploited as a combining point of chaos and creativity that acts as a resistance to midlife conformity, banal and routine as it may be perceived. It is also a place where structure of feeling is 'experienced' ontologically and where the 'episteme' is utilised to experience influential dissonance and, therefore, expectant originality in the creation of things. As Foucault puts it, 'one is trying to reveal between positivities, knowledge, epistemological figures, and sciences, a whole set of differences, relations, gaps, shifts, independences, autonomies, and the way in which they articulate their own historicities on one another' (Foucault, [1969] 1972: 191). The mezzanine is a chance to gather and to challenge as well as to enjoy and create.

9.6.   Conclusion: Midlife Creativity and Identity

Throughout this book I have positioned the actions and considerations of a set of ten artists as being simultaneously conscious and subconscious pursuits of the creation of novelty. I have further situated their routines as being indicative of a curious fusion of late modern individualisation (i.e. centring on the self, on identity maintenance and proliferation of 'capital') and the will to communicate with significant others (band colleagues, audiences, readers, buyers and so on), detecting an intrinsic sociality of art as well as a highly individuated process (routine) of achieving art. This late modern oeuvre is further summarised by Zygmunt Bauman as a series of shifts from the taken-for-granted structures of an 'old' society (or lived reality) and towards a sequence of changes that shift from certainty to desire (Bauman, 2000: 92). This idea can envelop *community* (perhaps *togetherness*) and our nostalgic view − despite having *experienced* it − of what it *was* and our desire to seek it out once more (despite being isolated, individual and competitive) as a form of what Julia Kristeva calls a 'primal shelter', replacing rebellion with a desire to retreat to conformity from disarray or to assured lifestyle from fragmentations and the quelling of late modern anxiety (Bauman, 2000: 213−214). If anything, the primal shelter is a community that is drenched in uncertainty, excitement and anarchy. The banal 'shelter' of midlife − however experienced via the intrinsic uncertainties of the late modern age − is a boring, predictable, coherent, and compliant stage of life and one that can be effectively resisted through creative work. To be sure, liquid modernity is still effective in delivering anxiety that flows from our fluxional identities; it is an anxiety that exemplifies the fear of not being 'up to date' or qualified enough or in-step with trends or the shifting requirements of occupations or sociality (Bauman, 2005: 2−9). This anxiety is arguably experienced in tandem with the shift towards the reflexive individualisation witnessed in modern life throughout the globe, laden in risk (Beck, 1999) and challenging to our basic − arguably subconscious − requirement for ontological security (Giddens, 1991) and consequent social order. Such fragmentation of life and identity is essentially about risky autonomy and uniqueness, a 'biographical centrism' influenced by shifting patterns of employability, permanently revising mores, shifting values and the incessant flow of the social in the domains of public life and online. This entrenched sense of the command of the mechanisms of a maintained and developing individuality is paradoxical because, according to Bauman, we need *others* to assist us in our defining of autonomy (Bauman, 2005: 19) and, while the creation of works of art can be seen as both inherently individual and 'structurally' social, on the impact on identity and the role of identity in the creation of art itself Bauman cites Foucault in saying that *identity is created and not given* and *art is created and not bestowed* (Bauman, 2008: 54). It is this laying down of the sacrosanct nature of identity – the empowering dynamics of the self and the response to the society around us and the system in which we operate – that reigns here. It suggests that people are still capable of utilising their own power to resist ideology (a penetration of hegemony, after all) but it still feels like a negotiated status, as though we are still having to ask permission to deviate despite being convinced of our own autonomy via the 'choices' of the liquid modern economy. I have therefore argued that music, art and literature as created 'things' *are*, in many ways, a negotiated outcome – however, such negotiation tends to be with the *self* and how one sees oneself and how one wants oneself to be at a time of life, rather than a negotiated compromise with the zeitgeist of the everyday.

Late modernism, while distinctively autonomous, status-driven, reflexive and insecure and seeking to fly free of the restrictions of Marxism and the base-superstructural discourse of ideology and culture, nevertheless is flimsy and transient by definition, seeing identity still created and maintained but now founded on transience, the abstract and the disposable (Bauman, 2008: 55). The late modern identity is transforming in time, transformative in nature and dependent on conferral of legitimacy by others; we are responsible for ourselves, to ourselves and unable to extricate ourselves from risks, dazzled by tantalising promises of consumption and the belief that happiness somehow resides in the apparel of status, skills and the various criteria of popularity. Consequently, Bauman states that the *state* of happiness is replaced by the tantalising *pursuit* of happiness (ibid.: 29) and, perhaps, via creativity the individual is able to command the greatest power, and greatest self-control, over destiny. Creativity is happiness on the creator's terms.

In this study I have sought to segue the understanding of the late modern 'biographically centric' individual, seeking distinction and self-legitimacy via art and performance with the sense of a personal legitimacy in midlife and to investigate what happiness feels like to an individual in this stage of the life course. While the ideas of late modernism are intrinsically connected to the active, reactive and reflexive forces of economy, politics and 'life politics' (Bauman, 1999; Giddens, 1994), I have also sought to understand individual states of self-worth refracted via age and situation. Late modernity is arguably concerned with our processes of, and our *search for*, legitimacy in the morass of constant flux, insecurity of meaning and value. How an idea of 'culture' emerges from the diversification and *fragmentation* of social relations, institutions and economy is also moot. The respondents have all illustrated here that culture is complex but it is also ordinary. Creativity is ordinary, but it is also treasured. It is, in essence, an escape from insecurity *via* insecurity on *one's own terms*. Art is therefore transformational in effect and in construction.

Via the ideas of Williams and Bourdieu, this project has arguably its best foundation in understanding *intention*, lifting out the structurally hegemonic essence of midlife by finding a space for 'lawless' and ideologically-free thinking and action. As Henri Lefebvre argues, it is 'practical-sensuous [that] shows us what praxis is [...] [t]he unity of the sensuous and the intellectual, of nature and

culture [that] confronts us everywhere [...] the immediate discloses the media-
tions it involves' (Lefebvre, 1968: 38–39). Action begets sensuality and sensuality itself is immediate and discernible. The in-between moments of the
mezzanine are consequently sensuous and immediate, framing a crucial parox-
ysm in the overall dialectic of creativity. While acknowledging a strong influence
of the Marxist tradition of understanding the creation and *appreciation* of art as
ideologically framed in time, I have only been concerned with the former
dynamic – namely how the artists bring their biographies into the act of *making*.
Their identities are reflexively shifting in time, drawing on their life experiences
and contemplating their situations in the contemporary (hence midlife creativity
and identity); the role of reception (and perceived value of significant others –
namely an audience if not friends and family) is for another study. What has
concerned me here is the descriptions of creativity and how I can make a sociological sense out of the value placed upon it by those who, ultimately, *do* it.
There has remained, throughout the continuing discourse on the meaning of the
sociology of art, a holistic vision of 'art' as a product situated in communicative
discourse as opposed to 'art' being simply a process of creation. The definition
of art is that is must be *considered* art and, of course, such considerations are discursive, ideological, subjective and, it follows, subject to change. To put it
plainly, art is also, despite the best intentions of materialist approach, something
that we tend to *look at* rather than something we *do*. However, art can be constructed freedom to, and for, the *self* (Marcuse, 1969), offering escape from the
structures that inherently *define* it and offering the creator the chance to identify
with such freedom. Art can be distanced from social relations if it is considered
as art in the moment of creation and product in the moment of release, separating aesthetics (and the need to consider aesthetics) and considering art as playful
and resistant (see Marcuse, [1978] 1979). It is all about where the art *comes
from*, deep inside the imaginations of the creator and where that imagination
itself is 'situated'.

The artists who have their time to explain their craft, their lives, their methods and their seemingly effervescent hopes have all, in truth, been undertaking a
simple balancing act – *simple* because the separation of the creative self from
the everyday self is an easy thing to do for these people. The chores and banality
of the everyday is easily divided from the excitement of the mezzanine, a place
where they can locate the structures of feeling, utilise the capital, commune with
the habitus and recognise and contribute to the field of their own cultural pro-
ductions. The artists are capable of penetrating the dominant ideology – the
hegemony – of everyday life and are expert at turning the impression of late
modernism on its head, differentiating the ideology from the lived reality. They
perceive fragmentation of the everyday as separated from the holism of the
everyday routine, turning instead to the unpredictability of the mezzanine as
their own sought-after anxiety of sorts. The everyday becomes the cohesive,
communal and routine and the mezzanine becomes the individualised, anarchic
and exciting place; anxiety is freedom.

Midlife creativity and identity is couched at once in the individualised world
of unpredictability and anxiety (and seen as a good thing) and in the

commonality of the wider culture, the sociality of togetherness and the sense of destiny that all of the artists retain. This destiny is understood as satiation in music, the open playfulness of sound and montage and the belief in the immediacy of the moment. The midlife identity is accredited, incrementally built and fortified by the sheer urge to commune, write, record and perform. The Ruins are driven by five individual manifestos of freedom, escape and self-legitimacy and their strength is found in the continued quest to *contribute*. Creativity and identity are nurtured and nourished in the artists' studios via a belief in the sheer possibility of the unknown. There is the will to assemble, the desire to explore, the excitement of novelty and the resistance of retreat, also revealed and revered in the routines and imaginative bursts of the writers, working in their own versions of solitude, alone with thoughts and a keyboard, pencil and paper and gradually focussing narrative. At the start of this book I asked where it was that art came from; I suggested that art was a personally transforming *activity* as well as a transforming painting, novel or sound. I have posited that art is *life* to these people and that, in passing, life is something that exists separately from art itself. Thus, midlife creativity and identity is best understood as a process of phasing life experience *into* haptic, visual and imaginative abilities and allowing those capacities to transform the sense of self. These people are all able to summon the will to tempt originality from the instinct of the moment, to draw on their emotion, their histories, their intuitive habitus and feeling and their desire to remain vitalised, relevant and virtuoso. Thus, midlife creativity *and* identity are framed by a collective desire to *do*; this is a time in life where many people may coast, considering the comfort of midlife, the achievements gained and the predictability of daily routine as a welcome stability in an otherwise anxious, unpredictable world. The creative energies of the artistic people featured here are considered best *experienced* rather than *observed*, cherished as a process or a routine and culminating in explosive episodes of output, resistant to the core and bursting with sophistication.

Afterword: Monday Afternoon and the Millennium

When teaching the method and value of the ethnographic approach to students I will often comment on the strange, but enlightening, effect towards the close of Paul Willis's *Learning to Labour* (1977). After a leisurely, erudite and edifying insight into the lives of 'the lads' and their schooling, Willis turns his attention half-way through the study to an analysis of the data, picking up speed and vigour as he progresses. Towards the end of the analysis it seems — as I say to the students — like this massive intensity has taken on a *volume*, a loudness of impact if you like, somehow *musical* in its fervidity, and then, suddenly, there is a pause, a diminishing echo and then a silence. In this intermission, however brief, there is an intense calm, a moment where the sheer impact of the debate is *in order*, perfect in many ways. Then Willis speaks to the reader again, using the metaphor of *morning*, a beginning, a step out into the unknown; Monday morning, he says, and the *millennium*. This, in effect, is the *beginning of the now* and, as he concludes, Monday morning need not always be a *repeat* of the previous Monday morning.

It is apparent that the people who have been at the centre of this study are entering into their own *afternoons* of their 'millenniums' and they, like Willis's 'lads' heading into uncertain futures, need not experience a reproduction of the banal, the expected and the routine. This is where it is feasible to look back as well as forwards, to contemplate a future that is informed well by its past and be comfortable with this *midlife* state. At the cessation of fieldwork, it is necessary to leave the people that one has studied behind to carry on as they were before meeting them, acknowledging that their own trajectories continue to develop beyond the brief window of connectivity that one has with them, occasionally 'visible from a distance' through websites, Facebook posts, gigs, CDs or exhibitions, or completely invisible to the researcher as they close the door to their studios, writing rooms or rehearsal spaces in order to claim back the uniqueness of their mezzanines. To The Ruins the quest for aura and authenticity as men in midlife continues, in the studio every Thursday and *at work* most days, working simultaneously for security in life and the insecurity of the sheer release that the musical muse offers, occasionally on-stage and mostly in the construction of reproduced sound. The band works for individual satiation that can be best achieved together, creating another step forwards for their musical genre while feeling unrestrained by the requirement to conform to such musical and stylistic field. It is a freedom that cannot be bought, despite the economic capital of midlife that enables their largely unhindered communion, the freedom itself comes in the cacophony of novelty where the invention of sound is the goal and the flexibility of rehearsal is the joy of anticipation. For Peter and Robin and Dominic the days continue to conform to the unpredictability of 'where the line might go', placing the ink, paint, charcoal or chisel onto canvas, wood, lino or paper, setting the presses, shaping the clay into a myriad of ceramic form and knowing, *knowing*, that the outcome is like something of a new and unimagined form, a new artistic life and, for the record, an innovative and invigorating sense of progress in tandem with the predictability of normal life. The thrill is in the initially dichotomous *expectancy* and the *unknown*; this is what gives the afternoon such an alluring brightness, a sense that anything can happen and that anything can be creative but also that invention can be illuminating, fascinating and confounding. Like life itself, art gives form to the unknown as vividly as the senses. To Katherine and Annette, it is about the opportunity to ostensibly think beyond boundaries, of controlling and harnessing the anarchy of the imagination, of making a scene in private to invite an unseen public into, to explain, guide and enlighten, entertain and enthral. This is a skill and a liberation; the building of a scene, the clarification of narratives and the consequent liberty to shape, re-shape and manipulate scenes, people, voice, language and form. Writing is a vocation, a natural state of being and work, about life, about nature and things, people and circumstances. Writing is about harnessing that 'unknown existence' and weaving together dynamics of life, drawing on experience, ambitions, dreams and failure, sensual and emotional, private and public all at once.

These processes are not, of course, uniquely held, experienced and exploited by people in midlife, but the narrative that emerges throughout this study is that midlife is something of a platform from which the creative self can begin to seize control, be exploited as a force of self-representation, of self-efficacy and of giving the future a sense of worth. It has emotional, psychological and sociological impact, giving energy to the articulation of life narratives, stabilising a sense of self and what one can become and, of course, it can be communicative, representative, ideological and provocative (sometimes all at the same time). As the artists enter the long afternoon of life, looking forward with anticipation, not focussing on self-maintenance but, instead, on self-expression and further contribution to the wider rhythms of life, it has been possible to understand that creativity, in its many forms when harnessed and cherished, provides an intensity and meaning to the actions of those who are experiencing the potential insipidness of midlife, further infusing the excitement of sheer possibility into a life that becomes simply, by definition, less ordinary.

Bibliography

Abercrombie, N., Hill, S. and Turner, B. S. (1980). *The Dominant Ideology Thesis.* London: HarperCollins.

Adams, R. G. and Allen, G. (Eds.). (1998). *Placing Friendship in Context.* Cambridge: Cambridge University Press.

Adorno, T. (1991). *The Culture Industry: Selected Essays on Mass Culture.* London: Routledge.

Ahier, J., Beck, J. and Moore, R. (2003). *Graduate Citizens? Issues of Citizenship and higher education.* London: RoutledgeFalmer.

Ahmed, S. (2014). *The Cultural Politics of Emotion*, 2nd. Ed. Edinburgh: Edinburgh University Press.

Albrecht, M. C., Barnett, J. H. and Griff, M. (Eds.). (1970). *The Sociology of Art and Literature: A Reader.* London: Duckworth.

Alexander, V. D. (2003). *Sociology of the Arts: Exploring Fine and Popular Forms.* Oxford: Blackwell.

Alexander, V. D. and Bowler, A. E. (2014). Introduction. *Poetics, 43* (2014), pp. 1–19.

Alexander, V. D. and Rueschemeyer, M. (2005). *Art and the State: The Visual Arts in Comparative Perspective.* Basingstoke: Palgrave Macmillan.

Allen, G. (2011). *Intertextuality.* London: Routledge.

Alvarez, A. (2005). *The Writer's Voice.* London: Bloomsbury.

Alvarez, A. (2013). *Pondlife: A Swimmer's Journal.* London: Bloomsbury.

Ambrose, E. (2014). *Midlife Cabernet: Life, Love and Laughter after Fifty.* Eagle, ID: Mill Park.

Andrews, G. J. and Phillips, D. R. (Eds.). (2005). *Ageing and Place: Perspectives, Policy and Practice.* London: Routledge.

Andrews, G., Kingsbury, P. and Kearns, R. (Eds.). (2014). *Soundscapes of Wellbeing in Popular Music.* Farnham: Ashgate.

Arber, S. (1993). 'The Research Process' in Gilbert, N. (Ed.), *Researching Social Life.* London: Sage.

Archer, M. S. (2003). *Structure, Agency and the Internal Conversation.* Cambridge: Cambridge University Press.

Archer, M. S. (2007). *Making our Way through the World: Human Reflexivity and Social Mobility.* Cambridge: Cambridge University Press.

Archer, M. S. (2012). *The Reflexive Imperative in Late Modernity.* Cambridge: Cambridge University Press.

Arnold, D. (2004). *Art History: A Very Short Introduction.* Oxford: Oxford University Press.

Arnold, M. ([1865/1888] 1964). *Essays in Criticism: First and Second Series.* London: J.M. Dent and Sons/Everyman.

Arnold, M. ([1869] 2006). *Culture and Anarchy*. ed. J. Garnett, Oxford: Oxford University Press.

Arnot, M. (2007). 'Freedom's Children: A Gender Perspective on the Education of the Learner-Citizen'. *International Review of Education*, *52*(1), pp. 67–87.

Ashcroft, B., Griffiths, G. and Tiffin, H. (Eds.). (1995). *The Postcolonial Studies Reader*. London: Routledge.

Atkinson, P. (2006). *Everyday Arias: An Operatic Ethnography*. Lanham, MD/ Oxford: AltaMira Press.

Atwood, M. ([2003] 2015). *On Writers and Writing*. London: Virago.

Auslander, P. (2008). *Liveness: Performance in a Mediatized Culture* (2nd Ed.). London: Routledge.

Austen, S. and Ong, R. (2010). 'The Employment Transitions of Mid-life Women: Health and Care Effects'. *Ageing and Society*, *30* (2), pp. 207–227.

Austin, J. L. ([1962] 1976). *How to Do Things with Words*. Oxford: Oxford University Press.

Bachelard, G. ([1964] 2014). *The Poetics of Space*. New York, NY: Penguin.

Bainbridge, D. (2012). *Middle Age: A Natural History*. London: Portobello.

Back, L., Bennett, A., Edles, L. D. et al. (2012). *Cultural Sociology: An Introduction*. Oxford: Wiley-Blackwell.

Bakhtin, M. (1982). *The Dialogic Imagination: Four Essays*. Austin, TX: University of Texas Press.

Barker, F., Coombes, J., Hulme, P. et al. (Eds.). (1978). *1848: The Sociology of Literature*. Colchester: University of Essex Press.

Barnes, K. (1988). 'Top 40 Radio: A Fragment of the Imagination' in Frith, Simon, (Ed.), *Facing The Music*. New York: Pantheon.

Barthes, R. (1977). *Image, Music, Text*, transl. Stephen Heath, London: Fontana.

Barthes, R. (2000). *Camera Lucida: Reflections on Photography*, transl. Richard Howard, London: Vintage.

Barthes, R. ([1957/1972] 2000). *Mythologies*, transl. Annette Lavers, London: Vintage.

Barthes, R. ([1953] 2010a). *Writing Degree Zero and Elements of Semiology*, transl. Annette Lavers and Siân Reynolds, London: Vintage.

Barthes, R. ([1953] 2010b). *Writing Degree Zero*, transl. Annette Lavers and Siân Reynolds, London: Vintage.

Barthes, R. ([1964] 2010). *Elements of Semiology*, transl. Annette Lavers and Siân Reynolds, London: Vintage.

Baron, S., Finn, D., Grant, N. et al. (1981). *Unpopular Education: Schooling and Social Democracy in England since 1944*, London: Hutchinson/CCCS.

Bate, J. (2010). *English Literature: A Very Short Introduction*. Oxford: Oxford University Press.

Baudrillard, J. (1994). *Simulacra and Simulation*, transl. Sheila Faria Fraser, Ann Arbor: University of Michigan Press.

Bauman, Z. (1999). *In Search of Politics*. Cambridge: Polity.

Bauman, Z. (2000). *Liquid Modernity*. Cambridge: Polity.

Bauman, Z. (2001). *Community: Seeking Safety in an Insecure World*. Cambridge: Polity.

Bauman, Z. (2002). *Society Under Siege*. Cambridge: Polity.

Bauman, Z. (2005). *Liquid Life*. Cambridge: Polity.

Bauman, Z. (2008). *The Art of Life*. Cambridge: Polity.

Beck, U. (1992). *Risk Society: Towards a New Modernity*, transl. Mark Ritter, London: Sage.

Beck, U. (1999). *World Risk Society*. Cambridge: Polity.

Beck, U. and Beck-Gernsheim, E. (2002). *Individualization: Institutionalized Individualism and its Social and Political Consequences*. London: Sage.

Beck, U., Giddens, A. and Lash, S. (1994). *Reflexive Modernization: Politics, Tradition and Aesthetics in the Modern Social Order*. Cambridge: Polity.

Becker, H. (1963). *Outsiders: Studies in the Sociology of Deviance*. New York, NY: Free Press.

Becker, H. (1971). *Sociological Work: Method and Substance*. London: Allen Lane.

Becker, H. ([1982] 2008). *Art Worlds*, 25th Anniversary Edition. Berkeley and Los Angeles, CA: University of California Press.

Beer, D. (2014). *PunkSociology*. Basingstoke: Palgrave Pivot.

Benjamin, W. ([1923] 2008). *The Work of Art in the Age of Mechanical Reproduction*. London: Penguin.

Bennett, A. (2005). *The Author*. Abingdon: Routledge.

Bennett, A. (2000). *Popular Music and Youth Culture: Music, Identity and Place*. Basingstoke: Macmillan.

Bennett, A. (2001). *Cultures of Popular Music*. Buckingham: Open University Press.

Bennett, A. (2005). *Culture and Everyday Life*. London: Sage.

Bennett, A. (2006). 'Punk's Not Dead: The Continuing Significance of Punk Rock for an Older Generation of Fans'. *Sociology*, *40*(1), pp. 219–235.

Bennett, A. (2013). *Music, Style and Aging: Growing Old Disgracefully?* Philadelphia, PA: Temple University Press.

Bennett, A. and Hodkinson, P. (Eds.). (2012). *Ageing and Youth Cultures: Music, Style and Identity*. London: Berg.

Bennett, A. and Kahn-Harris, K. (Eds.). (2004). *After Subculture: Critical Studies in Contemporary Youth Culture*. Basingstoke: Palgrave Macmillan.

Bennett, A., and Peterson, R. A. (2004). *Music Scenes: Local, Translocal, and Virtual*. Nashville, TN: Vanderbilt University Press.

Bennett, H. S. ([1980] 2017). *On Becoming a Rock Musician*. New York, NY: Columbia University Press.

Bennett, T. (1986). 'The Politics of the "Popular" and Popular Culture', in Bennett, T., Mercer, C. and Woolacott, J. (Eds.), *Popular Culture and Social Relations*. Milton Keynes: Open University Press.

Bennett, T., Mercer, C. and Woolacott, J. (1986). (Eds.). *Popular Culture and Social Relations*. Milton Keynes: Open University Press.

Bennett, T., Savage, M., Silva, E. et al. (2009). *Class, Culture, Distinction*. Abingdon; Routledge.

Berger, J. (1972). *Ways of Seeing*. London: BBC/Penguin.

Berger, J. ([1980] 2009). *About Looking*. London: Bloomsbury.

Berger, J. (2016). *Confabulations*. London: Penguin.

Berger, P. L. and Luckmann, T. (1966). *The Social Construction of Reality: A Treatise in the Sociology of Knowledge*. London: Penguin.

Bernard, M., Rickett, M., Amigoni, D. et al. (2015). 'Ages and Stages: The Place of Theatre in the Lives of Older People'. *Ageing and Society*, *35*(6), pp. 1119–1145.

Bernstein, B. ([1971] 2009). *Class, Codes and Control: Volume 1 — Theoretical Studies Towards a Sociology of Language*. Abingdon: Routledge.

Betts, R. F. and Bly, L. (2013). *A History of Popular Culture: More of Everything, Faster and Brighter*, 2nd Ed. London: Routledge.

Bhabha, H. K. (1995). 'Cultural Diversity and Cultural Differences'. in Ashcroft, B., Griffiths, G. and Tiffin, H. (Eds.), *The Postcolonial Studies Reader*. London: Routledge.

Blake, A. (2007). *Popular Music: The Age of Multimedia*. London: Middlesex University Press.

Blaikie, A. (1999). *Ageing and Popular Culture*. Cambridge: Cambridge University Press.

Blau, J. R. (Eds.). (1989). *Art and Society: Readings in the Sociology of the Arts*. New York, NY: State University of New York Press.

Blom, D. and Encarnacao, J. (2012). 'Student-Chosen Criteria for Peer-Assessment of Tertiary Rock Groups in Rehearsal and Performance: What's Important?'. *British Journal of Music Education*, 29(1), pp. 25–43.

Bloom, H. (1973). *The Anxiety of Influence: A Theory of Poetry*. Oxford: Oxford University Press.

Bochner, A. P. and Ellis, C. (2016). *Evocative Autoethnography: Writing Lives and Telling Stories*. London: Routledge.

Bohm, D. (1998). *On Creativity* (Ed. L. Nichol). London: Routledge.

Bonefeld, W. and Holloway, J. (1992). *Post-Fordism and Social Form: A Marxist Debate on the Post-Fordist State*. Basingstoke: Palgrave Macmillan.

Bordoni, C. (2016). *Interregnum: Beyond Liquid Modernity*, transl. Wendy Doherty, Bielefeld: Transcript Verlag.

Bottomore, T. ([1984] 2002). *The Frankfurt School and its Critics*. London: Routledge.

Bourdieu, P. (1977). *Outline of a Theory of Practice*, transl. Richard Nice, Cambridge: Cambridge University Press.

Bourdieu, P. ([1984] 2010). *Distinction: A Social Critique of the Judgement of Taste*, transl. Richard Nice, London: Routledge.

Bourdieu, P. (1990). *The Logic of Practice*, transl. Richard Nice, Cambridge: Polity.

Bourdieu, P. (1992). *Les Règles de L'Art*. Paris: Seuil.

Bourdieu, P. (1993). *The Field of Cultural Production: Essays on Art and Literature*. (Ed. R. Johnson), Cambridge: Polity.

Bourdieu, P. ([1994] 1998). *Practical Reason: On the Theory of Action*. Cambridge: Polity.

Bourdieu, P. (1996). *The Rules of Art: Genesis and Structure of the Literary Field*, transl. Susan Emanuel, Cambridge: Polity.

Bourdieu, P. and Passeron, J.-C. ([1970] 1977). *Reproduction in Education, Society and Culture*, transl. Richard Nice, London: Sage.

Bourdieu, P. and Wacquant, L. ([1992] 2002). *An Invitation to Reflexive Sociology*. Cambridge: Polity.

Bronner, S. E. (2011). *Critical Theory: A Very Short Introduction*. Oxford: Oxford University Press.

Brook, P. ([1968] 2008). *The Empty Space*. London: Penguin.

Brown, P. (1987). *Schooling Ordinary Kids: Inequality, Unemployment and the New Vocationalism*. London: Tavistock.

Burnard, P. (2006). 'Reflecting on the Creativity Agenda in Education'. *Cambridge Journal of Education*, *36*(3). pp. 313–318.

Burke, C. (2016). *Culture, Capitals and Graduate Futures: Degrees of Class*. Abingdon: Routledge.

Burns, E. and Burns, T. (Eds.). (1973). *Sociology of Literature and Drama*. Harmondswoth: Penguin.

Burrows, R. and Loader, B. (Eds.). (1994). *Towards a Post-Fordist Welfare State?* London: Routledge.

Butler, J. (1990). *Gender Trouble: Feminism and the Subversion of Identity*. London: Routledge.

Byun, C. H. C. (2016). *The Economics of the Popular Music Industry*. Basingstoke: Palgrave Macmillan.

Callahan, R. and Stack, T. (2007). 'Creativity in Advertising, Fiction and Ethnography' in Hallam, E. and Ingold, T. (Eds.), *Creativity and Cultural Improvisation*. Oxford: Berg.

Calvino, I. (2013). *Collection of Sand*, transl. Martin McLaughlin, London: Penguin.

Campbell, M. S. and Martin, R. (Eds.). (2006). *Artistic Citizenship: A Public Voice for the Arts*. London: Routledge.

Chambers, I. (1985). *Urban Rhythms: Pop Music and Popular Culture*. Basingstoke: Macmillan.

Chaney, D. (1993). *Fictions of Collective Life: Public Drama in Late Modern Culture*. London: Routledge.

Chaney, D. (1994). *The Cultural Turn*. London: Routledge.

Chaney, D. (1996). *Lifestyles*. London: Routledge.

Christian, H. (1987). 'Convention Among Semi-Professional Jazz Musicians', in Levine-White, A. (Ed.), *Lost in Music: Culture Style and the Music Event* (pp. 220–240). London: Routledge.

Clarke, C., Critcher, C., & Johnson, R. (Eds.). (1979). *Working class culture: Studies in history and theory*. London: Hutchinson/CCCS.

Clough, P. T. (2007). 'Introduction', in Clough, P. T. and Halley, J. (Eds.), *The Affective Turn: Theorizing The Social* (pp. 1–33). Durham: Duke University Press.

Clough, P. T. and Halley, J. (Eds.). (2007). *The Affective Turn: Theorizing The Social*. Durham: Duke University Press.

Coates, K. and Silburn, R. ([1962] 1973). *Poverty: The Forgotten Englishmen*, 2nd Ed. Harmondsworth: Pelican.

Coffey, A. (1999). *The Ethnographic Self: Fieldwork and the Representation of Identity*. London: Sage.

Cohen, S. (1991). *Rock Culture in Liverpool*. Oxford: Oxford University Press.

Colebrook, C. (2002). *Gilles Deleuze*. London: Routledge.

Coleman, R. (2013). *Transforming Images: Screens, Affect, Futures*. London: Routledge.

Corrigan, P. (1979). *Schooling The Smash Street Kids*. London: Macmillan.

Cottington, D. (2005). *Modern Art: A Very Short Introduction*. Oxford: Oxford University Press.

Craps, S. (2013). *Postcolonial Witnessing: Trauma Out of Bounds*. Basingstoke: Palgrave Macmillan.

Creighton, J. V. (1985). *Margaret Drabble*. London: Methuen.

Crespi, F. ([1989] 1992). *Social Action and Power*. Oxford: Blackwell.
Crossley, N. (2015). *Networks of Sound, Style and Subversion: The Punk and Post-Punk Worlds of Manchester, London, Liverpool and Sheffield, 1975-80*. Manchester: Manchester University Press.
Crossley, N. and Bottero, W. (2015). 'Music Worlds and Internal Goods: The Role of Convention'. *Cultural Sociology*, 9(1), pp. 38–55.
Crystal, B. (2007). *Shakespeare on Toast: Getting A Taste for The Bard*. Cambridge: Icon.
Culler, J. ([1975] 2002). *Structuralist Poetics: Structuralism, Linguistics and the Study of Literature*. London: Routledge.
Culler, J. (2011). *Literary Theory: A Very Short Introduction*. Oxford: Oxford University Press.
Cumming, N. (2000). *The Sonic Self: Musical Subjectivity and Signification*. Bloomington and Indianapolis: Indiana University Press.
Cummings, A. S. (2013). *Democracy of Sound: Music Piracy and the Remaking of American Copyright in the Twentieth Century*. Oxford: Oxford University Press.
Cusk, R. ([2001] 2008). *A Life's Work: On Becoming a Mother*. London: Faber and Faber.
Cusk, R. ([2016] 2017). *Transit*. London: Vintage.
Dauvignaud, J. (1972). *The Sociology of Art*, transl. Timothy Wilson, London: Paladin.
Davis, M. (Ed.). ([2013] 2016). *Liquid Sociology: Metaphor in Zygmunt Bauman's Analysis of Modernity*. London: Routledge.
Davis, S. (2002). *Old Gods Almost Dead: The 40-year Odyssey of the Rolling Stones*. London: Aurum.
de Certeau, M. (1984). *The Practice of Everyday Life*, transl. Steven Rendall, London: University of California Press.
de Saussure, F. (2013). *Course in General Linguistics*, ed. and transl. Roy Harris, London: Bloomsbury.
Degnen, C. (2007). 'Back to the Future: Temporality, Narrative and the Ageing Self', in Hallam, E. and Ingold, T. (Eds.), *Creativity and Cultural Improvisation* (pp. 223–235). Oxford: Berg.
Delanty, G. (2003). *Community*. London: Routledge.
Deleuze, G. (1990). *The Logic of Sense*, transl. Mark Lester, ed. Constantin V. Boundas, New York, NY: Columbia University Press.
Demjén, Z. (2015). *Sylvia Plath and the Language of Affective States: Written Discourse and the Experience of Depression*. London: Bloomsbury.
DeNora, T. (2000). *Music in Everyday Life*. Cambridge: Cambridge University Press.
DeNora, T. (2003). *After Adorno: Rethinking Music Sociology*. Cambridge: Cambridge University Press.
Denzin, N. K. (2013). *Interpretive Autoethnography*. London: Sage.
Derrida, J. (1988). *Limited Inc.*, (Eds. G. Graff, S. Weber and J. Mehlman). Evanston, IL: Northwestern University Press.
Derrida, J. ([1978] 2001). *Writing and Difference*, transl. A. Bass, London: Routledge.
Dewey, J. (2009). *Art as Experience*. New York, NY: Perigee Books.

Dilthey, W. (1996). *Hermeneutics and the Study of History: Selected Works, Vol IV*, (Eds. R. A. Makkreel and F. Rodi). Princeton/Chichester: Princeton University Press.

Dix, H. R. (2013). *After Raymond Williams: Cultural Materialism and the Break-Up of Britain*. Cardiff: University of Wales Press.

Draaisma, D. (2004). *Why Life Speeds Up As You Get Older: How Memory Shapes Our Past*. Cambridge: Cambridge University Press.

Drabble, M. (1980) *The Middle Ground*. London: Weidenfeld and Nicolson.

Duffett (2013). *Understanding Fandom: An Introduction to the Study of Media Fan Culture*. London: Bloomsbury.

Eagleton, T. ([1976] 2002). *Marxism and Literary Criticism*. London: Routledge.

Eagleton, T. ([1983] 2008). *Literary Theory: An Introduction*, Anniversary Ed. Oxford: Blackwell.

Eagleton, T. (2013). *How to Read Literature*. New Haven, CT: Yale University Press.

Eagleton, T. (2016). *Culture*. New Haven, CT: Yale University Press.

Eco, U. ([1979] 1981). *The Role of the Reader: Explorations in the Semiotics of Texts*. London: Hutchinson.

Eco, U. (1998). *Faith in Fakes: Travels in Hyperreality*. London: Vintage.

Eco, U. ([2002/2004 transl.] 2005). *On Literature*, transl. Martin McLaughlin, London: Secker and Warburg.

Edgell, S. (1993). *Class*. London: Routledge.

Eliot, T. S. (1919). 'Tradition and the Individual Talent', in Kermode, F. (Ed.), *Selected Prose of T.S. Eliot* (pp. 37-44). London: Faber and Faber.

Ellis, C. (2003). *The Ethnographic I: A Methodological Novel About Autoethnography*. Walnut Creek: Altamira Press.

Evans, J. (2014). 'Painting Therapeutic Landscapes with Sound: *On Land* by Brian Eno' in: Andrews, G., Kingsbury, P. and Kearns, R. (Eds.), *Soundscapes of Wellbeing in Popular Music* (pp. 173−187). Farnham: Ashgate.

Fanthome, C. (2008). 'Articulating Authenticity Through Artifice: The Contemporary Relevance of Tracey Emin's Confessional Art'. *Social Semiotics*, (*18*)2, pp. 223−236.

Fassler, J. (2017). *Light the Dark: Writers on Creativity, Inspiration, and the Artistic Process*. New York, NY: Penguin.

Faulks, K. (2000). *Citizenship*. London: Routledge.

Featherstone, M. (1991). *Consumer Culture and Postmodernism*. London: Sage.

Feldman, D., Csikszentmihalyi, M., Gardner, H. (1994*)*. *Changing the World. A Framework for the Study of Creativity*. Westport, CT: Praeger.

Finnegan, R. ([1989] 2007). *The Hidden Musicians: Music-Making in an English Town*, 2nd Ed. Middletown, CN: Wesleyan University Press.

Flaubert, G. ([1857] 2003). *Madame Bovary: Provincial Lives*, transl. Geoffrey Wall, London: Penguin.

Flew, T. (2012). *Creative Industries: Culture and Policy*. London: Sage.

Fornäs, J., Lindberg, U. and Sernhede, O. (1995). *In Garageland: Rock, Youth and Modernity*. London: Routledge.

Foster, A. W., & Blau, J. R. (Eds.). (1989). *Art and society: Readings in the Sociology of the Arts*. New York, NY: State University of New York Press.

Fowler, B. (1997). *Pierre Bourdieu and Cultural Theory: Critical Investigations*. London: Sage.

Freeland, C. ([2001] 2003). *Art Theory: A Very Short Introduction*. Oxford: Oxford University Press.

Freeman, J. (2015). *Remaking Memory: Autoethnography, Memoir and the Ethics of Self*. Faringdon: Libri.

Freud, S. ([1915] 1991). *Introductory Lectures on Psychoanalysis (The Penguin Freud Library, Vol. 1)*. London: Penguin.

Frith, S. (1984). *The Sociology of Youth*. Ormskirk: Causeway Press.

Frith, S. (1987). 'Why Do Songs Have Words?' in Levine-White, A. (Ed.), *Lost in Music: Culture, Style and the Music Event* (pp. 77–106). London: Routledge.

Frith, S. (Ed.). (1990). *Facing The Music: Essays on Pop, Rock and Culture*. London: Mandarin.

Frith, S., Goodwin, A. and Grossberg, L. (Eds.). (1993). *Sound and Vision: The Music Video Reader*. London: Routledge.

Frosh, S., Phoenix, A. and Pattman, R. (2002). *Young Masculinities: Understanding Boys in Contemporary Society*. Basingstoke: Palgrave.

Frow, J. (2015). *Genre*, 2nd Ed. Abingdon: Routledge.

Foucault, M. ([1969] 1972). *The Archaeology of Knowledge*, transl. A.M. Sheridan Smith, London: Routledge.

Foucault, M. ([1977] 1980). *Language, Counter-Memory, Practice: Selected Essays and Interviews*, (Ed. Donald F. Bouchard), transl. Donald F. Bouchard and Sherry Simon, New York, NY: Cornell University Press.

Foucault, M. ([1977] 1980). 'What is an Author?' in *Language, Counter-Memory, Practice: Selected Essays and Interviews* (pp. 113–138) (Ed. Donald F. Bouchard), transl. Donald F. Bouchard and Sherry Simon. New York, NY: Cornell University Press.

Fuller, S. (2005). *The Intellectual*. Cambridge: Icon.

Furlong, A. and Cartmel, F. (1997). *Young People and Social Change: Individualization and Risk in Late Modernity*. Buckingham: Open University Press.

Geertz, C. (1973). *The Interpretation of Cultures*. New York, NY: Basic Books.

Geldof, K. and Martin, A. (1997). 'Authority, Reading, Reflexivity: Pierre Bourdieu and the Aesthetic Judgement of Kant'. *Diacritics*, *27*(1), Spring 1997, pp. 20–43.

Genette, G. (1983). *Narrative Discourse: An Essay in Method*, transl. Jane E. Lewin, Ithaca: Cornell University Press.

Giddens, A. (1976). *New Rules of Sociological Method*. London: Hutchinson.

Giddens, A. (1984). *The Constitution of Society: Outline of the Theory of Structuration*. Cambridge: Polity.

Giddens, A. (1990). *The Consequences of Modernity*. Cambridge: Polity.

Giddens, A. (1991). *Modernity and Self-Identity: Self and Society in the Late Modern Age*. Cambridge: Polity.

Giddens, A. (1994). *Beyond Left and Right: The Future of Radical Politics*. Cambridge: Polity.

Giddens, A. (1996). *In Defence of Sociology: Essays, Interpretations and Rejoinders*. Cambridge: Polity.

Giddens, A. (1999). *Runaway World: How Globalisation is Reshaping our Lives*. London: Profile Books.

Gilbert, N. (Ed.). (1993). *Researching Social Life*. London: Sage.

Gilot, F. and Lake, C. ([1964] 1990). *Life with Picasso*. London: Virago.

Glaser, B. G. and Strauss, A. L. ([1967] 1999). *The Discovery of Grounded Theory: Strategies for Qualitative Research*, 2nd Ed. London: Aldine Transaction.

Glendinning, S. (2011). *Derrida: A Very Short Introduction*. Oxford: Oxford University Press.

Glynn, M. A. (2002). 'Chord and Discord: Organizational Crisis, Institutional Shifts, and the Musical Canon of the Symphony'. *Poetics*, *30*(1–2), pp. 63–85.

Goffman, E. (1959). *The Presentation of Self in Everyday Life*. London: Penguin.

Goffman, E. (1963). *Stigma: Notes on the Management of Spoiled Identity*. London: Penguin.

Gompertz, W. ([2012] 2016). *What Are You Looking At? 150 Years of Modern Art in the Blink of an Eye*. London: Penguin.

Gompertz, W. (2017). 'Foreword', in Read, H. (Ed.), *The Meaning of Art*. London: Faber and Faber.

Gramsci, A. (1971). *Selections from the Prison Notebooks of Antonio Gramsci*. New York, NY: International Publishers.

Green, B. (2016). 'I Always Remember that Moment: Peak Music Experiences as Epiphanies'. *Sociology*, *50*(2), pp. 333–348.

Grenfell, M. and Hardy, C. (2007). *Art Rules: Pierre Bourdieu and the Visual Arts*. Oxford: Berg.

Grossberg, L. (1992). *We Gotta Get Out of this Place: Popular Conservatism and Postmodern Culture*. New York, NY: Routledge.

Grossberg, L. (2012). 'Raymond Williams and the Absent Modernity', in Seidl, M., Horak, R. and Grossberg, L. (Eds.). *About Raymond Williams*. Abingdon: Routledge.

Hall, J. (1979). *The Sociology of Literature*. London: Longman.

Hall, S. (1980). 'Cultural Studies and the Centre', in Hall, S., Hobson, D., Lowe, A. and Willis, P. (Eds.), *Culture, Media, Language: Working Papers in Cultural Studies, 1972–79*. London: Hutchinson/CCCS.

Hall, S. and Jefferson, T. (Eds.). (1976). *Resistance Through Rituals: Youth Subcultures in Post-War Britain*. London: Routledge.

Hall, S., Critcher, C., Jefferson, T. et al. (1978). *Policing the Crisis: Mugging, the State and Law and Order*. London: Macmillan.

Hall, S., Hobson, D., Lowe, A. and Willis, P. (Eds.). (1980). *Culture, Media, Language: Working Papers in Cultural Studies, 1972–79*. London: Hutchinson/CCCS.

Hallam, E. and Ingold, T. (Eds.). (2007). *Creativity and Cultural Improvisation*. Oxford: Berg.

Halliday, S. (2013). *Sonic Modernity: Representing Sound in Literature, Culture and the Arts*. Edinburgh: Edinburgh University Press.

Hamilton, C. ([2009] 2014). *Middle Age*. Abingdon: Routledge.

Hammersley, M. and Atkinson, P. (1995). Ethnography: Principles in Practice, 2nd Ed., in Hanquinet, Laurie and Savage, Mike, (Eds.), *The Routledge International Handbook of the Sociology of Art and Culture*. London: Routledge.

Hanquinet, L., & Savage, M. (Eds.). (2016). *The Routledge International Handbook of Sociology of Art and Culture*. London: Routledge.

Harris, A. (2011). *Virginia Woolf*. London: Thames & Hudson.

Harris, D. (1992). *From Class Structure to the Politics of Pleasure: The Effects of Gramscianism on Cultural Studies.* London: Routledge.

Harrison, J. and Ryan, J. (2010). 'Musical Taste and Ageing'. *Ageing and Society, 30*(4), pp. 649–669.

Hauser, A. ([1974] 1982). *The Sociology of Art*, transl. Kenneth. J. Norcott, London: Routledge.

Hawkes, T. ([1977] 2003). *Structuralism and Semiotics*, 2nd Ed. Abingdon: Routledge.

Hebdige, D. (1979). *Subculture: The Meaning of Style.* London: Routledge.

Henry, i. P. (2001). *The Politics of Leisure Policy*, 2nd Ed. Basingstoke: Palgrave.

Hepworth, M. and Featherstone, M. (1982). *Surviving Middle Age.* Oxford: Basil Blackwell.

Hesmondhalgh, D. (2013). *Why Music Matters.* Chichester: Wiley-Blackwell.

Hesmondhalgh, D. and Baker, S. (2011). *Creative Labour: Media Work in Three Cultural Industries.* London: Routledge.

Hetherington, K. (1998). *Expressions of Identity: Space, Performance, Politics.* London: Sage.

Hey, V. (1997). *The Company She Keeps: An Ethnography of Girls' Friendship.* Buckingham: Open University Press.

Higgins, J. (1999). *Raymond Williams: Literature, Marxism and Cultural Materialism.* Abingdon: Routledge.

High, C., Kelly, A. H., and Mair, J. (Eds.). (2012). *The Anthropology of Ignorance: An Ethnographic Approach.* Basingstoke: Palgrave.

Highmore, B. (2011). *Ordinary Lives: Studies in the Everyday.* Abingdon: Routledge.

Hills, M. (2002). *Fan Cultures.* Abingdon: Routledge.

Hobbs, D. (1988). *Doing The Business: Entrepreneurship, the Working Class, and Detectives in the East End of London.* Oxford: Oxford University Press.

Hobbs, D. (1995). *Bad Business: Professional Crime in Modern Britain.* Oxford: Oxford University Press.

Hobbs, D., Hadfield, P., Lister, S. and Winlow, S. (2003). *Bouncers: Violence and Governance in the Night-Time Economy.* Oxford: Oxford University Press.

Hoggart, R. ([1957] 2009). *The Uses of Literacy.* London: Penguin.

Holton, R. J. and Turner, B. A. ([1989] 2011). *Max Weber on Economy and Society.* Abingdon: Routledge Revivals.

Horsfall, S. T., Meij, J.-M. and Probstfield, M. D. (Eds.). ([2013] 2016). *Music Sociology: Examining the Role of Music in Social Life.* Abingdon: Routledge.

Horst, H. A. and Miller, D. (Eds.). (2012). *Digital Anthropology.* London: Berg.

Hsieh, C. (2011). Money and happiness: Does age make a difference? *Ageing & Society, 31*(8), 1289–1306.

Hughes, J. (2011). *"Affective Worlds": Writing, Feeling & Nineteenth-Century Literature.* Brighton: Sussex Academic Press.

Inglis, D. and Hughson, J. (Eds.). (2005). *The Sociology of Art: Ways of Seeing.* Basingstoke: Palgrave Macmillan.

Ingold, T. ([2007] 2016). *Lines: A Brief History.* London: Routledge Classics.

Ingold, T. (2013). *Making: Anthropology, Archaeology, Art and Architecture.* London: Routledge.

Iser, W. (1974). *The Implied Reader: Patterns of Communication in Prose Fiction from Bunyan to Beckett.* Baltimore, MD: Johns Hopkins University Press.

Iser, W. (1978). *The Act of Reading*. Baltimore, MD: Johns Hopkins University Press.

Jabri, V. (2002). 'The Self in Woman as Subject of Art and Politics'. *International Feminist Journal of Politics*, *4*(1), pp. 122–128.

Jameson, F. (1971). *Marxism and Form*. Princeton, NJ: Princeton University Press.

Jameson, F. ([1981] 2002). *The Political Unconscious*. Abingdon: Routledge.

Jauss, H. R. (1982). *Towards an Aesthetic of Reception*, transl. Timothy Bahti, Minneapolis, MN: University of Minnesota Press.

Jenkins, R. (1983). *Lads, Citizens and Ordinary Kids: Working-Class Youth Life-Styles in Belfast*. London: Routledge and Kegan Paul.

Jenkins, R. (1996). *Social Identity*. London: Routledge.

Jockers, M. L. and Mimno, D. (2013). 'Significant Themes in 19th Century Literature'. *Poetics*, *41*(2013), pp. 750–769.

Johnson, G. A. (2005). *Renaissance Art: A Very Short Introduction*. Oxford: Oxford University Press.

Jones, P. ([2004] 2006). *Raymond Williams's Sociology of Culture: A Critical Reconstruction*. Basingstoke: Palgrave Macmillan.

Joyce, J. ([1922] 2000). *Ulysses*. London: Penguin.

Karlsen, S. (2010). 'Boom Town Music Education and the Need for Authenticity – Informal Learning Put into Practice in Swedish Post-Compulsory Music Education'. *British Journal of Music Education*, *27*(1), pp. 35–46.

Katz, J. (1999*)*. *How Emotions Work*. London: University of Chicago Press.

Kaufman, S. (1986). *The Ageless Self: Sources of Meaning in Late Life*. Madison, WI: University of Wisconsin Press.

Kermode, F. (1975) (Ed.), *Selected Prose of T.S. Eliot*. London: Faber and Faber.

King, S. ([2000] 2012). *On Writing: A Memoir of the Craft*. London: Hodder.

King, N. and Horrocks, C. (2010). *Interviews in Qualitative Research*. London: Sage.

Kingsbury, H. (1988). *Music, Talent and Performance: A Conservatory Cultural System*. Philadelphia, PA: Temple University Press.

Khodyakov, D. (2014). 'Getting in Tune: A Qualitative Analysis of Guest Conductor-Musicians Relationships in Symphony Orchestras'. *Poetics*, *44* (2014), pp. 64–83.

Komp, K. and Johansson, S. (Eds.). (2015). *Population Ageing from a Lifecourse Perspective: Critical and International Approaches*. Bristol: Policy Press.

Koppman, S. (2014). 'Making Art Work: Creative Assessment as Boundary Work'. *Poetics*, *46* (2014), pp. 1–21.

Kristeva, J. (1980). *Desire In Language: A Semiotic Approach to Literature and Art*, (Ed.) Leon S. Roudiez, transl. Thomas Gora, Alice Jardine and Leon. S. Roudiez, New York, NY: Columbia University Press.

Lacan, J. ([1977] 2002). *Écrits: A Selection*. New York, NY: W.W. Norton.

Laing, D. (1978). *The Marxist Theory of Art: An Introductory Survey*. Brighton: The Harvester Press.

Laing, D. ([1985] 2015). *One-Chord Wonders: Power and Meaning in Punk Rock*. Oakland, CA: PM Press.

Laning, E. (1971). *The Act of Drawing*. Newton Abbot: David and Charles.

Laurenson, D. (Ed.). (1978). *The Sociology of Literature: Applied Studies (Monograph 26)*. Keele: University of Keele Press.

Laurenson, D. and Swingewood, A. (1971). *The Sociology of Literature*. London: MacGibbon and Kee.

Lawler, S. (2014). *Identity: Sociological Perspectives*, 2nd Ed., Cambridge: Polity.

Leavis, F. R. ([1948] 2008). *The Great Tradition: George Eliot, Henry James, Joseph Conrad*. London: Faber and Faber.

Leavis, F. R. ([1952] 2008). *The Common Pursuit*. London: Faber and Faber.

Leavis, F. R. ([1962] 2013). *The Two Cultures? The Significance of C.P. Snow*. Cambridge: Cambridge University Press.

Leavis, F. R. and Thompson, D. (1933). *Culture and Environment: The Training of Critical Awareness*. London: Chatto & Windus.

Lee, H. (1996). *Virginia Woolf*. London: Chatto & Windus.

Lee, L. (1959). *Cider With Rosie*. London: Penguin.

Lefebvre, H. (1968). *The Sociology of Marx*, transl. Guterman, Norbert. London: Allen Lane/The Penguin Press.

Lena, J. C. and Lindemann, D. J. (2014). 'Who is an Artist? New Data for an Old Question'. *Poetics*, *43* (2014), pp. 73–85.

Lévi-Strauss, C. (1966). *The Savage Mind*. Chicago: University of Chicago Press.

Levine-White, A. (1987). (Ed.), *Lost in Music: Culture, Style and the Music Event*. London: Routledge.

Lewis, L. A. (1992). *The Adoring Audience: Fan Culture and Popular Media*. London: Routledge.

Lloyd, R. (2010). *Neo-Bohemia: Art and Commerce in the Postindustrial City*. New York, NY: Routledge.

Lloyd, R. (2016). 'Institutionalizing Neo-Bohemia'. In Hanquinet, L. and Savage, M. (Eds.), *The Routledge International Handbook of Sociology of Art and Culture* (pp. 455–470). London: Routledge.

Lodge, D. (1977). *The Modes of Modern Writing: Metaphor, Metonymy, and the Typology of Modern Literature*. London: Edward Arnold.

Lodge, D. ([1966] 2001). *Language of Fiction*. Abingdon: Routledge Classics.

Lodge, D. ([1992] 2011a). *The Art of Fiction*. London: Vintage.

Lodge, D. ([1996] 2011b). *The Practice of Writing*. London: Vintage.

Loxley, J. (2007). *Performativity*. Abingdon: Routledge.

Lukács, G. ([1968] 1971). *History and Class Consciousness: Studies in Marxist Dialectics*, transl. Rodney Livingstone, Cambridge MA: The MIT Press.

Lukács, G. ([1971] 2006). *The Theory of the Novel: A Historico-Philosophical Essay on the Forms of Great Epic Literature*, transl. Anna Bostock, London: The Merlin Press.

Lyotard, J.-F. (1992). *The Postmodern Explained: Correspondence 1982–1985*, transl. Don Barry, Bernadette Maher, Julian Pefanis, Virginia Spate and Morgan Thomas, Minneapolis, MN: University of Minnesota Press.

Mac an Ghaill, M. (1988). *Young, Gifted and Black: Student-Teacher Relations in the Schooling of Black Youth*. Milton Keynes: Open University Press.

Mac an Ghaill, M. (1994). *The Making of Men: Masculinities, Sexualities and Schooling*. Buckingham: Open University Press.

Macherey, P. ([1978] 2006). *A Theory of Literary Production*, transl. Geoffrey Wall, London: Routledge.

Mann, S. (2016). *The Research Interview: Reflective Practice and Reflexivity in Research Processes*. Basingstoke: Palgrave Macmillan.

Manning, P. (1982). 'Analytic Induction', in Smith, Robert and Manning, Peter K. (Eds.), *Qualitative Methods (Vol III of Handbook of Social Science Methods)* (pp. 273–302). Cambridge: Ballinger.

Marcuse, H. (1969). *Eros and Civilisation*. London: Sphere.

Marcuse, H. ([1978] 1979). *The Aesthetic Dimension*. London: Macmillan.

Marr, J. (2016). *Set the Boy Free: The Autobiography*. London: Century.

Martin, R. (2006). 'Artistic Citizenship: Introduction', in: Campbell, Mary Schmidt and Martin, Randy, (Eds.) *Artistic Citizenship: A Public Voice for the Arts*. London: Routledge.

Matthews, P. H. (2003). *Linguistics: A Very Short Introduction*. Oxford: Oxford University Press.

May, T. (1997). *Social Research: Issues, Methods and Process*, 2nd Ed. Buckingham: Open University Press.

May, V. (Ed.). (2011). *The Sociology of Personal Life*. Basingstoke: Palgrave Macmillan.

May, T. and Perry, B. (2017). *Reflexivity: The Essential Guide*. London: Sage.

McAffee, N. (2004). *Julia Kristeva*. Abingdon: Routledge.

McDonald, N. (2001). *The Graffiti Subculture: Youth, Masculinity and Identity in London and New York*. Basingstoke: Palgrave Macmillan.

McGuigan, J. (1992). *Cultural Populism*. London: Routledge.

McRobbie, A. (2000*). Feminism and Youth Culture*, 2nd Ed. Basingstoke: Macmillan.

McRobbie, A. and Garber, J. (1976). 'Girls and Subcultures: An Exploration', in Hall, Stuart and Jefferson, Tony, (Eds.), Resistance Through Rituals: Youth Subcultures in Post-War Britain. London: Routledge.

Melly, G. (1970). *Revolt into Style: The Pop Arts*. London: Faber and Faber.

Merleau-Ponty, M. (1964). *The Primacy of Perception*. Evanston: Northwestern University Press.

Miles, P. (2004). *Educational Transitions and Late-Modern Anxiety: The Impact of Credentialism and Individualisation on Working Class Youth*, unpublished PhD thesis, University of Cambridge.

Miller, D. (2011). *Tales from Facebook*. Cambridge: Polity.

Miller, D. (2008). *The Comfort of Things*. Cambridge: Polity.

Milner, A. (2005). *Literature, Culture and Society*, 2nd Ed. Abingdon: Routledge.

Moran, J. (2005). *Reading the Everyday*. Abingdon: Routledge.

Moran, J. (2010). *Interdisciplinarity*, 2nd Ed. London: Routledge.

Muggleton, D. (2000). *Inside Subculture: The Postmodern Meaning of Style*. Oxford: Berg.

Negus, K. (1996). *Popular Music Theory: An Introduction*. Cambridge: Polity.

Newman, A., Goulding, A. and Whitehead, C. (2013). 'How Cultural Capital, Habitus and Class Influence the Responses of Older Adults to the Field of Contemporary Visual Art'. *Poetics*, 41 (2013), pp. 456–480.

Norman, P. (2001). *The Stones*. London: Sidgwick and Jackson.

Orwell, G. (1970). *The Collected Essays, Journalism and Letters of George Orwell (Vol. 1)*, (Ed. S. Orwell and I. Angus). London: Penguin.

Orwell, G. (1970b). 'Why I Write', in Orwell, George and I. Angus (Eds.), *The Collected Essays, Journalism and Letters of George Orwell* (Vol. 1). London: Penguin.

Pahl, R. (2000). *On Friendship*. Cambridge: Polity.

Pakulski, J. and Waters, M. (1996). *The Death of Class*. London: Sage.

Parker, H. J. (1974). *View From The Boys: A Sociology of Down-Town Adolescents*. London: David and Charles.

Parkin, F. (2002). *Max Weber* (revised edition). London: Routledge.

Patrick, J. ([1973] 2013). *A Glasgow Gang Observed*, 3rd Ed. Glasgow: Neil Wilson Publishing.

Pink, S. ([2009] 2015). *Doing Sensory Ethnography*, 2nd Ed. London: Sage.

Pink, S. (2012). *Situating Everyday Life: Practices and Places*. London: Sage.

Pink, S. (2013). *Doing Visual Ethnography*, 3rd Ed. London: Sage.

Pink, S., Horst, H., Posthill, J. et al. (2016). *Digital Ethnography: Principles and Practice*. London: Sage.

Pinkney, T. ([1989] 2007). 'Editors Introduction: Modernism and Cultural Theory', in Williams, Raymond (Ed.), *Politics of Modernism: Against the New Conformists*. London: Verso.

Pinkney, T. (1991). *Raymond Williams*. Bridgend: Seren Press.

Plato (1994). *Republic*, transl. Robin Waterfield, Oxford: Oxford University Press.

Plath, S. ([1977] 1979). *Johnny Panic and the Bible of Dreams*. London: Faber and Faber.

Plath, S. (1981). *Collected Poems*. London: Faber and Faber.

Pollock, G. ([1988] 2003). *Vision and Difference: Feminism, Femininity and Histories of Art*. London: Routledge.

Porter, R. and Tomaselli, S. (Eds.). (1989). *The Dialectics of Friendship*. London: Routledge.

Potolsky, M. (2006). *Mimesis*. Abingdon: Routledge.

Pye, P. (2017) *Sound and Modernity in the Literature of London, 1880–1918*. London: Palgrave Macmillan.

Racz, I. (2014). *Art and the Home: Comfort, Alienation and the Everyday*. London: I.B. Tauris.

Ramus, C. (1926). *Outwitting Middle Age*. USA: The Century Co.

Read, H. ([1931] 2017]). *The Meaning of Art*. London: Faber and Faber.

Read, H. (1956). *Art and Society*, 3rd Ed. London: Faber and Faber.

Reid, L. (1969). *Meaning in the Arts*. London: George Allen and Unwin.

Renfrew, A. (2015). *Mikhail Bakhtin*. Abingdon: Routledge.

Reuter, M. E. (2015). *Creativity – A Sociological Approach*. Basingstoke: Palgrave Macmillan.

Richards, I. A. (1970). *Poetry and Sciences*. New York, NY: W.W. Norton.

Roberts, K. (1970). *Leisure*. London: Longman.

Rogaly, B. and Taylor, B. (2009). *Moving Histories of Class and Community: Identity, Place and Belonging in Contemporary England*. Basingstoke: Palgrave Macmillan.

Rojek, C. (1995). *Decentring Leisure: Rethinking Leisure Theory*. London: Sage.

Rojek, C. (2001). *Celebrity*. London: Reaktion.

Routh, J. and Wolff, J. (1977). *The Sociology of Literature: Theoretical Approaches (Monograph 25)*. Keele: University of Keele Press.

Royle, N. (2003). *Jacques Derrida*. London: Routledge.

Sacks, O. ([2007] 2011). *Musicophilia: Tales of Music and the Brain*. London: Picador.

Sanden, P. (2013). *Liveness in Modern Music: Musicians, Technology, and the Perception of Performance*. London: Routledge.

Sanders, J. (2015). *Adaption and Appropriation*, 2nd Ed. London: Routledge.

Savage, M. (2001). *Class Analysis and Social Transformation*. Buckingham: Open University Press.

Savage, M. (2010). *Identities and Social Change in Britain since 1940: The Politics of Method*. Oxford: Oxford University Press.

Savage, M., Cunningham, N., & Devine, F. et al. (2015). *Social class in the 21st century*. London: Pelican.

Schneider, A. and Wright, C., 'Between Art and Anthropology', in Schneider, Arnd and Wright, Christopher (Eds.), *Between Art and Anthropology: Contemporary Ethnographic Practice*. Oxford: Berg.

Schneider, A. and Wright, C. (Eds.). (2010). *Between Art and Anthropology: Contemporary Ethnographic Practice*. Oxford: Berg.

Scholette, G. (2011). *Dark Matter: Art and Politics in the Age of Enterprise Culture*. London: Pluto Press.

Schücking, L. L. ([1944] 1966). *The Sociology of Literary Taste*. London: Routledge and Kegan Paul.

Searle, J. (1979). *Expression and Meaning: Studies in the Theory of Speech Acts*. Cambridge: Cambridge University Press.

Seidl, M., Horak, R. and Grossberg, L. (Eds.). (2010). *About Raymond Williams*. Abingdon: Routledge.

Setiya, K. (2017). *Midlife: A Philosophical Guide*. Princeton, NJ: Princeton University Press.

Shelby Jr., H. (2011 [1966]). *Last Exit to Brooklyn*. London: Penguin.

Shepherd, S. and Wallis, M. (2004). *Drama/Theatre/Performance*. London: Routledge.

Shuker, R. (2008). *Understanding Popular Music Culture*, 3rd Ed. Abingdon: Routledge.

Silva, E. (2008). 'Cultural Capital and Visual Art in the Contemporary UK'. *Cultural Trends, 17*(4), pp. 267–287.

Silver, H. and Silver, P. (1997). *Students: Changing Roles, Changing Lives*. Buckingham: SRHE and Open University Press.

Skeggs, B. (1997). *Formations of Class and Gender: Becoming Respectable*. London: Sage.

Skeggs, B. (2004). *Class, Self, Culture*. Abingdon: Routledge.

Small, C. (1987). 'Performance as Ritual: Sketch for an Enquiry in to the True Nature of a Symphony Concert', in Levine-White, A., (Ed.), Lost in Music: Culture, Style and the Music Event (pp. 6–33). London: Routledge.

Smith, R. and Manning, P. K. (Eds.). (1982). *Qualitative Methods (Vol III of Handbook of Social Science Methods)*. Cambridge: Ballinger.

Spradley, J. P. (1979). *The Ethnographic Interview*. New York, NY: Hold, Rinehart and Winston.

Stallabrass, J. ([2004] 2006). *Contemporary Art: A Very Short Introduction*. Oxford: Oxford University Press.

Stebbins, S., Robert, A. (1989). 'Music Among Friends: The Social Networks of Amateur Musicians' in Foster, Arnold W. and Blau, Judith R., (Eds.), *Art and*

Society: Readings in the Sociology of the Arts (pp. 227–242). New York: State University of New York Press.

Sternberg, R. J. and Lubart, T. I. (1999a). *Handbook of Creativity.* Cambridge: Cambridge University Press.

Sternberg, R. J. and Lubart, T. I. (1999b). 'The Concept of Creativity: Prospects and Paradigms', in Sternberg, R. J. and Lubart, T. I. (Eds.), *Handbook of Creativity.* Cambridge: Cambridge University Press.

Storer, R. (2009). *F. R. Leavis.* London: Routledge.

Storr, A. (1972). *The Dynamics of Creation.* London: Penguin.

Swingewood, A. (1986). *Sociological Poetics and Aesthetic Theory.* Basingstoke: Macmillan.

Swingewood, A. (1998). *Cultural Theory and the Problem of Modernity.* Basingstoke: Macmillan.

Swinnen, A. (2018). '"Writing to Make Ageing New": Dutch Poets' Understandings of the Late-Life Creativity'. *Ageing and Society*, 38(3), pp. 543–567.

Tanner, J. (Ed.). (2003). *The Sociology of Art: A Reader.* Abingdon: Routledge.

Thompson, J. B. (1990). *Ideology and Modern Culture: Critical Social Theory in the Era of Mass Communication.* Stanford, CA: Stanford University Press.

Thornton, S. (2008*).* *Seven Days in the Art World.* London: Granta.

Tomars, A. S. (1940). *Introduction to the Sociology of Art.* Mexico City: Columbia University.

Touraine, A. (2000). *Can We Live Together? Equality and Difference*, transl. David Macey, Cambridge: Polity.

Tröndle, M., Kirchberg, V. and Tschacher, W. (2014). 'Is This Art? Study on Visitors Judgement of Contemporary Art'. *Cultural Sociology*, 8(3), pp. 310–332.

Trollope, A. ([1883] 2016). *An Autobiography and Other Writings*, (Ed. N. Shrimpton). Oxford: Oxford University Press.

Trudgill, P. ([1974] 2000). *Sociolinguistics: An Introduction to Language and Society*, 4th Ed. London: Penguin.

Truzzi, M. (Ed.). (1974). *Verstehen: Subjective Understanding in the Social Sciences.* Reading MA: Addison-Wesley.

Turkle, S. (2017). *Alone Together: Why We Expect More from Technology and Less from Each Other*, 3rd Ed. New York: Basic Books.

Tusa, J. (2003). *On Creativity: Interviews Exploring the Process.* London: Methuen.

Twigg, J. (2012). 'Adjusting the Cut: Fashion, the Body and Age on the UK High Street'. *Ageing and Society*, 32(6), pp.1030–1054.

Van Dijk, Y. (2014). Amateurs Online: Creativity in a Community'. *Poetics, 43* (2014) pp. 86–101.

Van Maanen, J. (2011). *Tales of the Field: On Writing Ethnography*, 2nd Ed. Chicago and London: University of Chicago Press.

Vincent, J. (2008). *An Alternative Derby.* Morrisville, NC: Lulu.com.

Walkerdine, V., Lucey, H. and Melody, J. (2001). *Growing Up Girl: Psychosocial Explorations of Gender and Class.* Basingstoke: Palgrave.

Waters, M. (2001). *Globalization*, 2nd Ed. London: Routledge.

Waugh, P. (1984) *Metafiction: The Theory and Practice of Self-Conscious Fiction.* London: Routledge.

Weber, M. ([1968] 2013). *Economy and Society Vols. 1&2*, Edited by G. Roth and C. Wittich. Berkeley, CA: University of California Press.

Westerlund, H. (2006). 'Garage Rock Bands: A Future Model for Developing Musical Expertise?'. *International Journal of Music Education*, *24*(2), pp.119–125.

Whitworth, M. H. (2005). *Virginia Woolf*. Oxford: Oxford University Press.

Williams, R. ([1954] 1991). *Drama in Performance*. Milton Keynes: Open University Press.

Williams ([1958] 1989). 'Culture is Ordinary' in Williams, (Ed.), *Resources of Hope*. London: Verso.

Williams, R. ([1958] 2017). *Culture and Society*. London: Vintage.

Williams, R. (1961). *The Long Revolution*. Harmondsworth: Pelican.

Williams, R. (1970). *The English Novel: From Dickens to Lawrence*. London: Chatto & Windus.

Williams, R. ([1973] 2015). *The Country and the City*. London: Vintage.

Williams, R. ([1974] 2003). *Television*. London: Routledge.

Williams, R. ([1976] 2014). *Keywords: A Vocabulary of Culture and Society*. London: Fourth Estate.

Williams, R. (1977). *Marxism and Literature*. Oxford: Oxford University Press.

Williams, R. ([1979] 2015). *Politics and Letters: Interviews with New Left Review*. London: Verso.

Williams, R. ([1980] 2005). *Culture and Materialism*. London: Verso.

Williams, R. (1981). *Culture*. London: Fontana.

Williams, R. ([1989] 2007). *Politics of Modernism: Against the New Conformists*. London: Verso.

Williams, R. (1989). *Resources of Hope*. London: Verso.

Williams, S. J. (2001). *Emotion and Social Theory: Corporeal Reflections on the (Ir) Rational*. London: Sage.

Williamson, H. (2004). *The Milltown Boys Revisited*. Oxford: Berg.

Williamson, V. (2014). *You Are the Music: How Music Reveals What It Means to Be Human*. London: Icon.

Willis, P. (1977). *Learning toLabour: How Working Class Kids Get Working Class Jobs*. Farnborough: Saxon House.

Willis, P. (1978). *Profane Culture*. London: Routledge.

Willis, P. (1990). *Common Culture*. Buckingham: Open University Press.

Willis, P. (2000). *The Ethnographic Imagination*. Cambridge: Polity.

Willis, P. (2005). 'Invisible Aesthetics and the Social Work of Commodity Culture' in: Inglis, David and Hughson, John, (Eds.), *The Sociology of Art: Ways of Seeing* (pp. 73–86). Basingstoke: Palgrave Macmillan.

Willis, I. (2018). *Reception*. London: Routledge.

Willmott, P. ([1966] 1969). *Adolescent Boys of East London*. Harmondsworth: Pelican.

Wilson, R. and Dutton, R. (Eds.). (1992). *New Historicism and Renaissance Drama*. Harlow/London: Longman.

Wilson, S. (1995). *Cultural Materialism: Theory and Practice*. Oxford: Blackwell.

Witkin, R. W. (2005). 'A 'New' Paradigm for a Sociology of Aesthetics', in Inglis, David and Hughson, John, (Eds.), *The Sociology of Art: Ways of Seeing* (pp. 57–72). Basingstoke: Palgrave Macmillan.

Wolff, J. (1975). *Hermeneutic Philosophy and the Sociology of Art: An Approach to some of the Epistemological Problems of the Sociology of Knowledge and the Sociology of Art and Literature*. London: Routledge & Kegan Paul.

Wolff, J. (1983). *Aesthetics and the Sociology of Art*. London: George Allen & Unwin.

Wolff, J. (1993). *The Social Production of Art*, 2nd Ed. Basingstoke: Macmillan.

Woolf, V. (1989). *The Letters of Virginia Woolf: Volume Three, 1923–1928*, (Ed. N. Nicolson and J. Trautmann). London: Harvest.

Woolf, V. ([1925] 2011). *A Room of One's Own*. London: Penguin.

Wright-Mills, C. (1959). *The Sociological Imagination*. Harmondsworth: Pelican.

Wynn, J. R. (2007). 'Haunting Orpheus: Problems of Space and Time in the Desert', in Clough, Patricia Ticineto and Halley, Jean (Eds.), *The Affective Turn: Theorizing The Social* (pp. 209-230). Durham: Duke University Press.

Young, E. ([1759] 2013). *Conjectures on Original Composition*. Miami FL: Hard Press.

Young, M. and Willmott, P. ([1957] 1962). *Family and Kinship in East London*. Harmondsworth: Pelican.

Index

www.ingramcontent.com/pod-product-compliance
Lightning Source LLC
Chambersburg PA
CBHW052005270326
41929CB00015B/2797